D0342271

SCARED
SELFLESS

SCARED SELFLESS

MY JOURNEY FROM
ABUSE AND MADNESS TO
SURVIVING AND THRIVING

Michelle Stevens, PhD

G. P. Putnam's Sons
New York

G. P. PUTNAM'S SONS
Publishers Since 1838
An imprint of Penguin Random House LLC
375 Hudson Street
New York, New York 10014

Library of Congress Cataloging-in-Publication Data
Names: Stevens, Michelle (Psychologist), author.
Title: Scared selfless : my journey from abuse and madness to surviving and
thriving / Michelle Stevens, Ph.D.
Description: New York : G.P. Putnam's Sons, [2017] | Includes bibliographical
references. Identifiers: LCCN 2016041381 (print) |
LCCN 2016043819 (ebook) | ISBN 9780399173387 (print) |
ISBN 9780698185562 (EBook)
Subjects: LCSH: Stevens, Michelle (Psychologist) | Stevens, Michelle
(Psychologist)—Childhood and youth. | Adult child sexual abuse
victims—United States—Biography. | Sexually abused children—United
States—Biography. | Child sexual abuse—United States—Case studies. |
Mental illness—United States—Case studies. | Healing—United
States—Case studies. | Women psychologists—United States—Biography. |
BISAC: BIOGRAPHY & AUTOBIOGRAPHY / Personal Memoirs. |
SELF-HELP / Abuse.
| FAMILY & RELATIONSHIPS / Abuse / Child Abuse.
Classification: LCC HV6570.2 .S74 2017 (print) | LCC HV6570.2 (ebook) |
DDC 362.76092 [B]—dc23
LC record available at https://lccn.loc.gov/2016041381

Printed in the United States of America
1   3   5   7   9   10   8   6   4   2

Book design by Meighan Cavanaugh

This book is dedicated to

Mikey, Chris, Steve, and Leah,

who taught me that

love is the best medicine

CONTENTS

AUTHOR'S NOTE

What I present here is the true story of my life. While I have changed names and identifying information to protect the anonymity of a few people and places, I have otherwise chosen to relay events exactly as they occurred. Because I was a victim of horrific physical and sexual abuse, some of these events are quite disturbing. Despite this, I decided to include them because I feel it is the right of every victim of violence to tell their truth.

For those of us who are able, I feel it is a responsibility.

Child abuse, domestic violence, sexual assault, hate crimes, war crimes, genocide, and all other forms of interpersonal violence flourish in a culture of silence and shame. In order to stop abusers, those who have been abused must be encouraged to speak out. The rest of us must be willing to bear witness—even if the truths we hear are sometimes shocking, grotesque, and frightening.

Some of the events from my childhood that are depicted in this book may be hard to witness. But the only way to truly appreciate how far any victim has come is to know what they've had to overcome. I've overcome both abuse and the mental illness it created. But my reward for many hard years of hard work is a happy Hollywood ending.

It's been a hell of a journey—one I chose to share here in the hope that I can inspire others to persevere.

It pays to stick it out through the hard parts. I promise.

Everything can be taken from a man but one thing: the last of the human freedoms—to choose one's attitude in any given set of circumstances, to choose one's own way.

—Viktor Frankl, *Man's Search for Meaning*

Miracle on Geary Street

We almost didn't make it. There was traffic on the 5 all the way from LA. By the time I got into the building, I could see that people were already in their gowns. I found mine and threw it on, taking care with the peculiar-looking cap, known as a tam, that is the pride and humiliation of all doctorates.

I took my place in line just as the class marched into the auditorium. After a series of predictably boring speeches, the dean started calling out names. We had to sit through a couple of hundred master's degrees before they even started on the PhDs. There were about fifty of us in our medieval hats. Knowing my last name starts with *S*, I wished I'd hidden a snack in my fancy robe. Better yet, a scotch.

Finally, they got to our row. I watched with anticipation as each graduate stood up and stepped forward. By the 239th time, I knew the drill: name gets called out, graduate walks up, diploma and handshake from the provost while the dean inelegantly shoves the hood over the poor graduate's head. Once the person's hair is thoroughly messed up, a fast *click-click* from the school photographer. Then it's get off the podium; they're already calling the next name.

So, when the lady next to me got called up, I readied myself for the mad dash. But as she left the stage, there was an unexpected lull. The provost turned away from the microphone as the president walked to it. I panicked. What the hell was going on? *Oh, God,* I thought. *I must have screwed up my credits.* Suddenly, I was regretting the seven-hour drive to San Francisco when I wasn't even going to graduate.

"Every year," the president said, "the faculty chooses one graduate to receive the award for the dissertation of distinction. This year's award goes to an ambitious project that simultaneously tells the story of a girl whose life is taken over by a skilled, determined, and extremely cruel pedophile, while presenting an anthropological, sociological study of the pedophile and sadomasochism subcultures in the western world. It is the bravest piece of academic writing I have ever read. It was written by Michelle Stevens."

The auditorium erupted into applause. People who knew me hurrahed. The president stepped back from the microphone and shot me a smile. It vaguely occurred to me that I was supposed to go up there. Pushed forward by my classmates, I reluctantly walked to the stage. Along the way, it was moving to see all the people who had supported me. My wife, Chris. Our little boy, Mikey. My best friend, Steve. My whole dissertation committee was there, plus a slew of supportive professors. It was miraculous, really, that moment.

Miraculous that I was even alive.

_____

See, up until that point, I'd led a very dangerous life. First, as a result of heinous child abuse. Later, as a result of the severe mental illness that stemmed from it. Just six years prior to graduation, I'd been confined to a mental hospital because one of my alternate personalities kept trolling for sadistic men who aimed to hurt me. Another was continuously suicidal and had made quite a few attempts.

While at that hospital, which specializes in treating people who have suffered severe psychological trauma, I was told by a seasoned therapist that my prognosis was not very good. I was diagnosed with dissociative identity disorder, more commonly referred to as multiple personality disorder, which is one of the worst psychiatric diagnoses a person can get. All around me were patients who had lost everything due to the disease. Their jobs. Their spouses. Their kids. I was told I would never be able to lead a normal, functional life. I was told I was a lost cause.

So to say it was a miracle to be standing on the podium that night in front of the faculty and student body is not an overstatement. And to be lauded for my dissertation, well, that was a miracle too. See, the topic of the dissertation was my fucked-up life. Not the usual academic fare, I know. But as the survivor of a child-sex ring, I wanted to shed light on pedophiles. I needed to explain why they do what they do and how it affects their young victims.

I had noticed that we, as a society, are fed a steady stream of news stories about abductions, fallen clergy, and child pornography. But despite all the TV ratings and magazine sales these stories garner, we seem to know very little about sexual abuse or why it occurs. Thus, every time a big story breaks—Elizabeth Smart, Catholic priests, Jaycee Dugard, Jerry Sandusky, the Cleveland kidnappings—we are left with the same questions:

How could it happen?

How could it happen in that neighborhood?

Why didn't they try to escape?

Why didn't they tell anyone?

Why didn't anybody notice?

How could it go on for so long?

Why didn't anybody do anything?

On a deeper level, I could see that these stories trouble us. They make us worry about our personal safety and the safety of our children. We wonder:

How do I know who to trust?

How can I protect myself and the ones I love?

I knew I had answers to these questions. I had answers to all of them. I had answers because I survived more than six years of rape and torture at the hands of countless predators—men who, due to their nefarious activities, are notoriously difficult to find and study. During those years, I had a front-row seat to the operations of a career pedophile. I watched him pull off his dirty deeds, watched him molest lots of typical kids from middle-class families. I also watched a considerable number of his pervert friends. As a voyeur, I learned a lot about sexual predators—how they think, how they choose their prey, how they keep their conquests quiet. Furthermore, as a survivor, I knew what it was like to suffer abuse—what it does to a person's spirit, to their psyche. I knew because I'd been there; I'd lived it.

So I wrote down all I knew. Then I read books and studies and interviews to learn more. After eight years of research, I had a hell of a lot of information on predators and victims and society's response to them, and I was ready to share it with the world.

I was even ready to share the details of my own abuse and healing.

But I was nervous.

How would people react?

As I WALKED onto the stage and stared out at the sea of faces, I suddenly flashed back on a story from my History of Psych class. Once upon a time, another therapist stood behind a podium and talked openly about child sexual abuse. Things didn't turn out so good for him.

The year was 1896, and the therapist was a fellow by the name of Sigmund Freud. Freud was working with patients who suffered from hysteria, a catchall diagnosis for a dizzying array of symptoms in women, including insomnia, irritability, and sexual desire (or lack thereof). Freud saw more serious cases of hysteria—cases involving women with hallucinations, unexplained paralysis, and radical personality changes with amnesia for certain events. Searching for the cause of his patients' symptoms, Freud made a monumental discovery: He realized his patients were screwed up because they'd suffered "one or more occurrences of premature sexual experience, occurrences which belong to the earliest years of childhood."

Basically, Freud had figured out that his patients were victims of childhood sexual abuse and that such abuse causes long-term psychological damage. Excited by his findings, the good doctor decided to share them with colleagues in a lecture. Unfortunately, his cronies didn't react well to the news. Hysteria, after all, was a widespread diagnosis.

If Freud was right, it meant thousands of little girls were being molested all over Vienna. Rather than accept this unpleasant reality, the boys' club expressed extreme skepticism. They figured Freud must have inadvertently implanted false memories of abuse into his suggestible patients. Bowing to societal pressure (and perhaps his own discomfort with the reality of widespread abuse), Freud recanted. He decided, instead, that his patients' horrific memories of child sexual abuse were just wishful fantasies.

Thanks to Herr Freud, for the next eight decades, if a woman went to therapy and reported her memories of child sexual abuse, she was told the memories weren't real, just wishful thinking. Yeah, that's right: She only *wished* she'd been raped as a kid! This ridiculousness was so thoroughly accepted that a 1975 psychiatry textbook still claimed that the incidence of father-daughter incest was just one in a million.

While I'd love to believe I'm one in a million, nowadays we know that, far from being rare, child sexual abuse is actually all too common. Up to 40 percent of all women and 13 percent of all men in the United States were sexually abused in childhood. Internationally, some regions report that up to 50 percent of female children and 60 percent of male children are sexually abused. This means everyone reading these words was either a victim of abuse or has a close personal relationship with someone who was. Sadly, child sexual abuse is one of the few life experiences that the entire world population shares in common.

Knowing this, you'd think the sexual abuse of children would be an ordinary topic of conversation, as commonplace a subject as work or the weather. But, of course, it's not. For, unlike the weather, sex is a rather taboo subject. And sex with a child? Well, that just makes us cringe. We're so uncomfortable with the topic that we've banned it from polite conversation. As psychiatrist Judith Herman says, "Certain violations of the social compact are too terrible to utter aloud: this is the meaning of the word *unspeakable*."

THE PROBLEM IS: If we don't speak to each other about child sexual abuse, how can we ever hope to make things better? If we want to protect children, thwart perpetrators, and help adult victims, we need to talk openly and honestly about the problem.

That's why, when my name was called on graduation night, I made the decision to walk to the stage, stand behind the podium, and share my personal story of abuse and healing.

It's the same story I tell here—the story of an eight-year-old girl who is forced to become a sex slave.

I was raped and tortured and prostituted to countless men. I was used in child pornography. As a result of this abuse, I grew mentally disturbed and was in danger of a wasted existence. But I made a decision not to give in to despair. I vowed that, no matter what, I was going to fight for a good, decent, normal life. The journey to that good life wasn't easy. It was fraught with pain and self-doubt and self-loathing. But I persevered and eventually found the help and love I needed to be happy.

In time, I went back to school to become a psychologist. I wanted to help people who suffer like I did. I've now had the honor of working with hundreds of survivors of childhood abuse. And no matter how crazy they seem, I never, ever tell them they're a lost cause.

BUT THAT'S GETTING ahead of things. Let me take you back to the beginning.

PART I

ABUSE

When fear rules, obedience is the only survival choice.

—Toni Morrison, *God Help the Child*

Stalin's Chicken

I t all started because of a doll. Not for me, mind you, though I was eight and still played with them. But this doll was special. "A genuine replication of an antique bisque," my mother said. She found it in an antiques store at the flea market. The price tag: three hundred dollars.

Even by today's standards, three hundred bucks for a doll is outrageous. But this was 1976, and my mother was a twenty-eight-year-old with a minimum-wage job and a kid to feed. We were living in a one-bedroom apartment where utilities were frequently turned off for lack of payment. So, obviously, my mother had no business buying some three-hundred-dollar doll.

But no one ever accused my mom of being sensible.

A layaway plan was set up. The old woman behind the counter took a deposit, put the doll in a paper bag, and tossed it under a table. Every few weeks, my mother would drag me back to the store and hand the lady a few more bucks toward the doll's ransom. Frankly, at eight years old, I didn't think much about any of this. The flea market was just one more place to go on a Saturday. Run around. Kick stones. Eat hot dogs. And the dusty store that my mother frequented was especially interesting, filled with dolls, electric trains, baseball cards. It seemed fun.

Little did I know I was being stalked.

There was a man at the store, a fifth-grade teacher who owned the place as a side business. Gary Lundquist had a penchant for toys and games and all the other fun stuff of childhood. And, right after he laid eyes on me, he also claimed to have a penchant for my mom.

The two started dating. It seemed like a whirlwind. Within a few weeks, things had gotten so serious that Gary suggested to my mom that I start spending time with him. Alone. He said he wanted us to have our own special relationship. A sleepover was planned for a long weekend. My mom dropped me off at Gary's place and drove away, promising to pick me up in three days.

The first thing I noticed about Gary's house was how large it was. Standing alone on a big plot of grassy land, it was definitely the fanciest house I'd ever entered. It had three bedrooms, an office, and a full basement. It even had a fireplace in the living room—the first I'd ever seen. As an adult, I now realize that this was just a middle-class home, probably no more than 1,800 square feet. But since I came from an impoverished background, it seemed like a mansion to me.

The décor, however, was curious. A stuffed deer head hung over the fireplace, and a Confederate flag covered the dining-room wall. Neon beer signs cast gloomy light in the hallway. On every surface in the house, there was some kind of baseball card or bottle cap or military memento. And there was lots and lots of political memorabilia, particularly pictures of President Carter's young daughter, Amy.

Walking into the den, I noticed a wall of bookcases lined with photo albums. Lots of them. "What're those?" I asked.

"Take a look," he said, moving past me. At six feet two, he easily plucked a few albums off the top shelf. He plopped them on the coffee table then plopped himself on the couch. He patted the cushion next to him, beckoning me over. Once I was seated, he opened the first book. There on the page were pictures. Pictures of children. Maybe thirty of them. Their hair all nicely combed, they were staring at the camera and smiling in that dorky way kids smile for their school portrait.

On the next page, there was one big photo of a class. The same thirty kids all dressed nicely and standing on risers. Next to them stood Gary. The print on the bottom said, MR. LUNDQUIST's 5TH GRADE CLASS—1969.

Gary explained that he was a schoolteacher and had been one for more than ten years. This particular photo was of a class early in his career, when he still taught in Kansas. He talked about going to college in Kansas and how the co-eds there were frigid bitches. Of course, being eight years old, I had no idea what he was talking about. Clueless. Like those kids on the page. Page after page. First, the official school shots. Then the official class shots. Then Polaroids—candids of just certain kids. "The special ones," he said.

They were laughing or hugging one another or goofing around the way kids do. Just normal pictures. But so many of them. The kids in his classes, the kids in his drama club, the kids in the gifted and talented group he mentored after school. Neighbor kids. Kids he hired to work with him on weekends. Kids who traveled with him in the summer. Kids he took in for a while when their parents couldn't care for them. Hundreds and hundreds and hundreds of kids.

But not one of his own, he said.

He wanted one all his own.

So I guess that's why I was there. To audition. In the few weeks that he'd been dating my mom, Gary had already made it clear he was willing to play a major role in my life. This was a relief to my mom, who'd given up hope of meeting a guy willing to take on responsibility for her illegitimate daughter. And what a guy! Educated. Solid job. Respectable house. Successful small business. For my mother—a young woman from an impoverished family with no education, no job skills, no future—Gary was a serious catch.

AFTER A FEW more photo albums, Gary announced that it was time for bed. I got my nightgown and went into the bathroom to change. When I came out, I found Gary in a bedroom at the end of the hall. It was sparse, with a simple twin bed. Gary had already turned down the sheets, so I crawled in and pulled up the covers. Gary suddenly looked sad.

"You know," he said. "I'm very unhappy. For years, I've had to live in this big house all by myself. I've been so lonely. But now you can be my daughter!" He stated it brightly, as if it were that simple. But I wasn't so sure. I barely knew this man. And for all of his attempts to ingratiate himself, I really didn't think I liked him. The idea of having a father, of living in a real house, of having my own bedroom certainly appealed to me. But there was something about Gary that seemed phony. Scary even.

"Let me see your nightgown," he suddenly exclaimed, as he

yanked off my covers. This made me excited, because I was wearing my absolute favorite: a long-sleeved pink flannel with ruffles at the bottom and a pretty lady on the front. She was holding flowers and wearing a bonnet. Santa gave it to me for Christmas.

"Wow, that is so pretty," he cooed, picking up on my obvious pride. "Would you like a picture of yourself in that pretty nightgown?"

I nodded.

He left the room for a second then came back with a Polaroid camera. He positioned himself at the foot of the bed and proceeded to pull down the remaining covers before aiming his lens. I asked him to wait a minute so I could smooth out my nightgown. I wanted to be sure he had a good view of the lady on the front. Then he snapped the shot. Two times. One for him, and one for me. I still have mine. It shows a petite girl with long brown hair and bangs lying flat on a bed, engulfed in a sea of baby-pink ruffles. She has milky white skin and thin pink lips set in a shy smile. Her big strikingly blue eyes are open wide, staring straight into the camera. There is an innocence to this small child, a trusting vulnerability that pains me today.

Still, it is a picture I cherish, for it's the last one where I ever looked directly at a camera with those bright untroubled eyes. A strange sort of gift, the first of many profound gifts I would receive from the man who would also shatter my life. A treasure, really. I mean, how many people can say they know exactly how they looked at the last moment of their childhood?

LATER THAT NIGHT. A basement. I am naked and locked in a cage.

I can no longer remember how I got there.

There are a lot of things I can't remember about my life.

This is probably a good time to stop and explain that I suffer from amnesia. I've had it since I was a kid. Everyone with multiple personalities has memory loss for the traumas we sustained in childhood. I, for instance, had completely forgotten that I'd been raped and tortured as a little girl. I didn't recover those memories—the memories I'm about to share—until I was an adult.

The idea that someone can forget something as important as being raped—or can develop more than one personality—is hard for many people to fathom. As a result, there are some who say recovered memories and multiple personalities aren't real. Of course, those people didn't have to live through the torture I endured. If they did, I bet they'd understand why my mind worked so hard to forget.

There's a saying: Never judge someone until you've walked a mile in their shoes. Yet we live in a society where victims of violence are condemned all the time. Battered wives are dubbed "weak" when they can't leave their husbands. Rape victims are criticized for the way they dressed. Even innocent children get criticized for failing to flee their kidnappers!

For the most part, this happens because people make judgments based on what they know. But what bystanders know about a crime is usually very limited. Think about it. Most perpetrators don't abuse their victims in the middle of a mall. Unless they're total idiots, they do their beating and raping and threatening in private. This keeps the rest of us from knowing what really goes on.

That's why others are often skeptical of victims and their strange symptoms like amnesia, recovered memories, and multiple personalities—because they have no idea what terrifying things had to happen to create such disorders. The only way bystanders can ever know what victims go through is if victims share. But victims rarely talk about their shameful ordeals, creating a vacuum of information that leads to a lot of misunderstanding, insensitivity, and ignorance.

One of my goals is to clear up the misunderstandings. But, in order to do this, I'm going to have to share details about the abuse I suffered in childhood. I realize it may be hard to read. However, if people want to understand a victim's complicated responses to violence, they have to walk in the victim's shoes. They have to *experience* violence—at least on the page.

And so I will tell my story exactly as I remember it. Sometimes those memories are as lucid and colorful as a Hollywood movie. Other times they are as dark, murky, and disjointed as the pages of a fading photo album. Whether the bits are vivid or foggy, they've all been pieced back together over the years to become a single, true story. It is the story of my enslavement, and it begins in a basement.

A COLD, DARK BASEMENT with a cement floor and cinder-block walls. It seems huge. From where I sit, the shadows go on forever.

I am naked and locked in a cage: three feet by three feet probably. Just big enough to sit up with my legs stretched out or lie down in a fetal position. It's made of thin metal bars with a metal tray on the floor. A tiny padlock secures the clasp on the door. It's a dog cage. The kind they use to crate puppies. At eight years old, I don't know that yet, though. We can't have a puppy in our one-bedroom apartment. The closest thing I've ever had to a pet is the gerbil my mom bought at Woolworth's. It lives in a glass cage in our living room and bites me every time I try to touch it.

I want to be home now with my gerbil and my Snoopy pillow and my Raggedy Ann. I want to lie on the carpet in the bedroom and watch *Sesame Street* on my little black-and-white TV. I want my mom to warm up frozen fish sticks and Tater Tots, then sit with me on the couch so we can both watch Archie Bunker.

I'm hungry.

When was the last time I ate anything?

What day is it?

When is Mommy coming back?

A sudden noise.

The front door opening? Mommy's here! Relief. Only for a moment.

Then I hear the heavy thud of male feet. He's back. My tummy hurts. I have to pee.

As his feet move across the floor above me, I become paralyzed. My breathing shallows. My arms and legs go weak. I have lost all control of my body, but my mind is sharp and focused. All attention is fixed on the sound of the feet. Every step—farther, closer—is life. Maybe death.

This is terror. Absolute terror. The kind most people will only ever experience in their dreams. But even after the worst nightmare, a person can wake up. Jump out of bed. Throw open a curtain. Try to shake off the horrible feeling.

I want to shake off this feeling. This awful, awful terror. I want to forget it somehow and feel anything else. It is unbearable to be this scared. Unbearable even for a minute, much less an hour. Or a day.

Two days maybe? How long has it been now?

When is my mother coming?

What's that sound?

Men are talking.

Oh, God, there must be two of them!

The door at the top of the stairs creaks open. Gary comes down, followed by another man. I can't see him very well—he's covered in shadows—but I can already tell he's going to be mean. He's tall, like Gary, with black hair and a black moustache. He kind of looks like the villain in some old-time silent movie.

Someday, not today, I will learn that this man's name is Joe. He's a friend of Gary's who shares his interests in political history, antique collectibles, and sadistic pedophilia.

Just as the man hits the last step, Gary starts to walk toward me. They both have stern looks on their faces and neither one is talking, which only makes the whole scene feel more like a nightmare. If I have a body, a mind, a name, I'm not aware of it right now. All I know is paralysis. Of my limbs, my brain, my self. Time is standing still; every step that Gary takes toward me takes an hour. I don't feel fear, exactly. In this moment, I don't feel anything.

The black-haired man is carrying something, some kind of ropes. He stops a few feet away from the stairs and starts to hang them on the beams of the basement ceiling. Gary keeps walking all the way to my cage. He is standing over it now, peering down at me.

"It's time to start your training, Slave," he says. His voice is low and forceful, not the way it usually sounds. His face is different too. It's got no expression. Just blank. Except for the eyes. The eyes stare down with a coldness that I have never seen before. Not on anybody. The coldness, the blankness, is so inhuman, so weird, that it makes me feel confused.

Maybe Gary is just playing with me—doing that scary fake-mad act that grown-ups do just before they make a funny face and start to laugh.

"Get out of your cage, Slave," Gary says, in that same fake-forceful voice. He bends over and undoes the latch.

The door swings open a little bit.

He waits.

What's he waiting for? I'm paralyzed. None of this makes sense.

"I told you to get out of the cage, Slave. You will do as I say. You will learn to obey me!"

He bends over again, sticks an arm through the cage opening, and grabs one of my legs. He yanks hard, starts to pull me out.

I drag along helplessly. There's a metal lip on the bottom of the cage, and as my back gets wrenched over it, I am aware of cold steel scraping my skin. Everything is happening so fast. I can't really focus on anything.

Suddenly, I am being lifted up. The man with black hair has me. He and Gary tie my arms and legs to the ropes hanging from the ceiling and stuff a bandanna in my mouth. It all happens so quickly, is so strange, that I have no idea what is going on. Abruptly, the men let go of me, and the full weight of my body hangs down, tightening the ropes around my wrists, my thighs, my knees. I am hanging there, naked and gagged, with my legs spread apart.

"When you do not obey me, you will be punished," Gary says. Then he holds up some kind of stick, probably the cut-off end of a broom handle. I am scared—sure I'm about to be hit. Instead, after a long threatening pause, Gary rams it between my legs.

Pain. Shock. Panic. I have to get away. I fight. Struggle. But I am tied. Can't move. Can't run. Helpless. I try to scream. Must scream. Scream from the shock, the pain. Scream for help. For him to stop. "Stop! Stop!" I try to scream.

But I'm gagged. Gagged and bound. Helpless to run or scream or shield myself from the pain. Suddenly, a horrible taste floods my mouth. I'm vomiting.

Instinctively, I turn my head and open my jaw to let the nasty liquid escape. But my mouth is covered. My screams are drowning in vomit. I'm choking. Can't breathe. Can't breathe.

The ramming stops. Gary is at my head. Pulling at the bandanna. Fumbling to get it out of me. Groping, yanking, he shoves his fat fingers into my mouth, pulls out the crumpled wet cloth full of stench. Vomit pours out of my mouth onto my lips, my face, my neck. I keep gagging, coughing, trying to catch my breath. After a while, I am able to breathe again. I am aware of my burning throat, the putrid taste in my mouth, pain between my legs.

Gary looks at the black-haired man. His face is serious but normal. He seems like a normal person again.

"She could've choked," he says quietly.

Without further words, Gary lifts up my body while the black-haired man undoes the ropes. Gary carries me back to the cage, lowers me to the ground, and tells me to get in.

Automatically, I obey. I crawl in, lie in the fetal position, close my eyes. I am too weak to fight, to scream, to think. I just want to sleep.

OTHER THINGS HAPPEN that weekend. At one point, Gary and the man come back, open the cage, tell me to get out. It's time to start my training. I crawl out, so exhausted it doesn't even occur to me not to do what they say. As I kneel on the floor, the black-haired man puts a leather collar and leash around my neck. He hands the leash to Gary, who forces me to walk back and forth on my hands and knees. I am taught how to heel, to sit, to stay. Through all of this, I am expected to be blindly obedient. I am a slave now, I am told. No better than a dog. I must learn to obey my master.

I hate all of this, obviously. It's physically uncomfortable to crawl on the hard cement floor. Even more uncomfortable to remain motionless in a stay for long periods of time. What bugs me most, though, is not the pain or the cold or even the fear. What bugs me most is having to do things I don't want to do, things I find embarrassing. Mortifying. I don't want to be naked. I don't want to wear a dog collar. I don't want to crawl on a leash. I don't want to do any of it. I hate it. It makes me feel so mad. But I can't say anything. What I want, think, feel doesn't matter. I just have to do what they say.

Eventually, my training session ends. I am told I've done well, that I've been a good and obedient slave. For this, I will earn a reward. I will be allowed to eat. This is a relief. I'm starving. At the mention of food, my stomach instinctively growls. When the black-haired man brings over my dinner, though, I realize it is just a trick, a way to induce more shame. He places two dog bowls in front of me. One with water. The other with wet dog food. I am told to kneel over the bowls with my hands behind my back. I stay like that for a long moment. I know I am expected to eat the dog food, but the thought of it, the smell of it, makes me nauseated. I just can't will myself to put it in my mouth.

"What's the matter, Slave? Don't you like your dinner? You're going to have to learn to appreciate everything I give you. And you're gonna learn to like it. Now eat!"

The tone of Gary's voice tells me what I need to know—that

eating the wretched food will surely be less painful than what he'll do to me if I don't.

So I bow my head into the bowl, and I eat the dog food. Ignoring the smell. Ignoring the taste. Ignoring every urge in my body telling me to run away, spit it out, throw it up. I turn off my thoughts, my feelings, my senses, my body. I turn into a numb, mindless eating machine, impervious to the smell, the taste, the texture, to any of it. It is the only way to get through. The only way.

I AM ALONE AGAIN. In my cage. How long have I been here now? It's surely been a few days already. I am somewhat aware of the passage of time; I've seen the light come and go through the high windows on the other side of the basement. I haven't been counting, though. Don't know how many times the sun has come around. But it must be time for Mommy to come. Right? When is she going to come get me?

I am cold and cramped in this little cell. The dog collar is too tight. I have to pee. I've quickly come to appreciate being left alone in my cage, though. When they take me out, that's when the bad things happen. So I kind of like it in here. Like being by myself and just letting my mind go. I think about nice things like kittens and toys and ice cream and the horse I'm going to get one day. I don't have to think about being naked or hungry or tired or scared. I just pretend I'm somewhere nice and happy and safe.

The door opens. Light pours down the staircase. Gary and Joe are back. They have mean looks on their faces. I'm in trouble. Something bad is going to happen again. And just like that, I am transformed from a happy girl riding her horse to a mindless, bodiless ball of terror. I don't matter. My daydreams don't matter. All that matters is the look on Gary's face.

"I am very disappointed with you, Slave," he says. "I keep trying to train you, but you don't seem to want to learn your lessons. I don't think you appreciate how much I'm doing for you. I don't think you're grateful for all my time and attention.

"I think you need a harder approach. I think pain is the only thing that will teach you to be more obedient." He bends over and opens the cage. "Get out," he says.

Immediately, I crawl out of the cage. I have learned already that it's best to obey him and the sooner the better.

"Stand up," he says, grabbing me by the collar. Then he pushes me over to the ropes.

Oh, God! Not the ropes again. Not the stick. So much pain! Mindless terror overtakes me. Instinctively, I start to crumble and try to back away. But he is there, hoisting me up again, tying me into the sling.

"No, please, no, no," I beg. "I'll be good! I promise! I'll be good!"

"Quiet," he growls, as he holds up the stick ominously. I am petrified. Crazy, out-of-my-mind terror. I brace for the pain, but it doesn't come. Instead, he puts his hand there and starts to gently rub.

"Now, doesn't that feel nice?" he's saying.

I—I don't know what I'm supposed to think. Does it feel nice? Yes, I suppose it does. It feels much nicer than the stick and the pain.

He keeps on rubbing, but it's hard to understand. Hard to understand what's happening. I thought I would be hurt. Thought I would be tortured. But this is not bad. This doesn't hurt at all. Still, I'm confused. Can't trust it. It must be some kind of a trick. Why isn't he hurting me? Why is he rubbing me? Why has his face suddenly turned nice?

"Isn't that better?" he's saying. "Doesn't that feel good? Do you like that? You like that, don't you? Yeah, just relax. Just relax."

The next thing I know, the men are taking me down. Gary has me in his arms, and he's carrying me upstairs. Back to the same house as before it all started. Through the kitchen and the dining room, down the long hall. I'm so confused. Don't know what's going on. Don't know to be afraid or relieved. Don't know what I'm supposed to feel. Don't quite feel anything.

Before I can make any sense of things, we are in Gary's bedroom. He is pulling back the covers. Laying me in his giant green bed. He gets in after me. Pulls up the covers. Cradles me in the crook of his arm. Starts rubbing between my legs again. Gentle. Rhythmic. "There, doesn't that feel nice?"

It's warm and soft. The rhythmic rubbing, the gentle voice soothes me. I am so tired, and it is so peaceful, and in spite of everything, I start to relax. Relief washes over me. The basement is gone. I am warm now. I finally, finally feel safe.

I drift off to sleep to the lull of the rubbing. I can't help it. My body hasn't relaxed in days. It is a sudden, deep, lifeless sleep. The kind one only enjoys in childhood.

FOR AS LONG as I knew him, Gary was fond of history. He liked to regale people with tales about presidents and politicians. But his very favorite story was the one about Stalin's chicken. From the head of the dinner table, Gary would talk about Stalin and his quest for power. How Stalin stood up in front of his Cabinet one day, and said,

"Do you want to know how to control the people?" Then a door was opened, and a chicken was brought in. Stalin put it on the table in front of him and, one by one, plucked out every feather. For the chicken, the pain was unbearable, and the bird fought mightily to get away. Yet, when Stalin was all done, the frightened, vulnerable chicken refused to leave his side.

It took me thirty years to understand that I was the chicken.

The Pied Piper

Over the past forty years, there's been a lot of interest in child molesters. As a result, pedophiles are probably the most researched group of sexual deviants. But despite a plethora of studies, articles, and books, there is little consensus on what makes these guys tick. A big part of the problem is finding subjects. How exactly does one meet a wide range of child molesters to study when the nature of their actions makes them want to hide? Historically, the favorite place to find such subjects is prisons, but this presents an obvious bias. Are child molesters as dumb, disordered, and low functioning as some studies suggest? Or is this only true of those who are incompetent enough to get caught?

Further complicating things is the fact that criminals, well, lie. So any information gleaned from a forensic population is bound to be iffy. According to criminologist Dr. Dennis Stevens, author of *Inside the Mind of Sexual Offenders*, child molesters are particularly tight-lipped because, in prison, men who rape children are notoriously targeted by other inmates. As a result, child molesters tend to keep mum about their offenses. And when they do talk, they frequently omit or fabricate pertinent information—unless they know their lies will be detected. Case in point: When pedophile inmates were asked to disclose the number of children they had victimized, they revealed four to six times more victims if they knew their answers would be verified by a polygraph test.

Knowing that pedophiles blatantly lie is important, because those lies have created some powerful myths. For instance, most people assume that child molesters were themselves molested as children. This popular assumption comes from research studies that claim between 28 and 93 percent of pedophiles suffered childhood sexual abuse (versus 15 percent for random control groups). But those studies relied solely on the criminals' own accounts. When pedophiles were asked the same question knowing they'd be monitored by a polygraph, only half as many said they'd been molested as kids.

So why do pedophiles lie—even to researchers who keep their identities confidential? Because they're obsessed with their own PR; they want to present socially acceptable justifications for their crimes. By casting themselves as abused abusers, they manage to make the rest of us feel a little sorry for them. We can suddenly fathom why they want to have sex with children, something that is utterly incomprehensible otherwise.

Playing the victim has worked quite well for pedophiles. Many researchers have described them as sad, lonely, immature men who lack the self-confidence to woo adult women and instead look to children for love and affection. But pedophiles may not be the misguided romantics they portray themselves to be. So who are they?

What do we know about them? First, we know that almost all are male (although some studies suggest the number of female perpetrators could be higher than people assume). Second, we know that the vast majority are heterosexual; one study found the ratio of straight to gay pedophiles was 11:1. Third, we know that child molesters come from all races and socioeconomic groups, with no particular group grossly overrepresented compared to the general population.

People tend to assume that most molesters are strangers to their victims. One of parents' worst fears, in fact, is that their kids will be abducted by a stranger. That fear, though, is irrational. It's far more likely that a child will be struck by lightning. What parents should fear are acquaintance molesters, because acquaintances are the biggest culprits of child sexual abuse. But that gets sticky, as these people are our teachers, Cub Scout leaders, friends, neighbors. They're Catholic priests and Jerry Sandusky. They're everywhere our children are. And they look and act just like us.

Acquaintances perpetrate 60 percent of all child sexual abuses. (Family members contribute another 30 percent; strangers, 10 percent.) The average acquaintance molester victimizes 50 to 150 children before he is ever arrested, *if* he is ever arrested. Even after incarceration and/or treatment, an acquaintance molester's chance of reoffending is between 52 and 77 percent.

Most acquaintance molesters are preferential pedophiles, meaning they are obsessed with having sex with kids. Since puberty, the typical acquaintance molester has fantasized about children, masturbated to images of them, and collected child pornography. They feel the compulsion to molest the way a serial killer feels the compulsion to murder. They are true predators who are always, always hunting for the next victim. As a result, the typical acquaintance molester chooses his home, spouse, career, hobbies, his entire life based on the singular goal of gaining access to children. In short, for the acquaintance molester, having sex with children is a lifelong professional pursuit.

GARY LUNDQUIST was a professional acquaintance molester. While I don't know his entire history, I do know that he had been pursuing sex with kids for many, many years before we met. He'd already been teaching, working with kids for at least eleven years. During that time, he'd concocted a lot of ways to gain access to children. Besides his normal teaching job, which kept him surrounded by twenty kids for seven hours a day, he also ran a gifted and talented program and a drama club after school. These extracurricular activities added another ten to fifteen hours a week to his teaching duties, and they provided Gary with another thirty to forty kids to stalk.

Once Gary spotted a child he desired, the next goal was to spend more time with her through the guise of tutoring or extra rehearsals. (Gary almost always chose females.) He had to get to know the kid better, find out if she was an easy mark. This generally meant that she had to be smart and outgoing, not just because these were the qualities Gary found attractive, but because such children displayed a natural curiosity and need for attention that Gary could use to entice and manipulate them. Being an easy mark also meant that the kid had to come from some kind of difficult home situation—for example, the parents were embroiled in a messy divorce, the father was already out of the picture entirely, the parents were neglectful of the child due to work schedules or a family crisis. It was imperative that children be from this kind of broken home. First, because kids from unhappy homes are particularly needy for attention and willing to do just about anything to keep an interested adult in their lives. Second, because overwrought parents are usually desperate for child care and are far more likely to hand their kids over to someone else.

When a family was in crisis, that's when "Mr. L." stepped in. He was purported to be a great guy who loved kids and was always willing to lend a helping hand. If a kid needed transportation or couldn't afford school supplies, Mr. L. was the go-to guy. He would give the kid money, give her a ride home, even stop at the candy store to buy treats for the poor child. If the girl was really lucky, she would become one of Mr. Lundquist's extra-special kids—the kind who got to work for Mr. L. at his antiques store on the weekends. Even more exciting, she might get the honor of traveling with Mr. Lundquist to an antiques show in a faraway town. These antiques shows, where Gary sold his wares all summer, were usually held out of state and lasted five days at a stretch, necessitating at least four nights in a motel. If Gary especially liked a girl, he would offer to hire her as his worker for the event. This meant a nine- or ten-year-old would get the special treat of staying in a motel room with him for a whole week. Just the two of them. No parents allowed.

Over the years, I watched the same scenario play out again and again with lonely kids from troubled families: Nina, the foster child whose biological mother had abandoned her; Katie, the ignored middle child whose parents always worked; Marcy, the timid girl who would do anything to avoid her authoritarian father; Dick, whose little sister had recently died. It was always the same MO with Gary. First, he'd identify a kid from a family in crisis. Next, he'd befriend the kid, offering attention, admiration, and a shoulder to cry on. Later, he'd befriend the family, offering tutoring, transportation, child care, sometimes even financial support. To these parents, Gary's brand of reliable, convenient, economical baby-sitting was invaluable. A godsend, really. I mean, who wouldn't want a credentialed teacher to tutor, mentor, and watch one's child free of charge? Apparently, a lot of parents desired such a service, because Gary was always, always surrounded by kids. At school, at home, in stores, in restaurants, wherever he went he brought children along. Kids followed him around so loyally, in fact, that people in town jokingly referred to him as the "Pied Piper."

Little did they realize it was no joke.

Gary Lundquist was in the business of stealing childhoods.

And the townspeople happily enabled him.

ACQUAINTANCE MOLESTERS, in general, do not abduct children. They don't need to. Parents are usually all too willing to hand over their kids, never realizing that the nice man they are entrusting their babies to isn't really nice at all. Children rarely tell their parents what the nice man does to them behind closed doors. And even in the odd event that a child does disclose the abuse to her parents, it's common for the parents to dismiss the allegation. As a result, acquaintance molesters often break the law repeatedly, without detection, for thirty years or more. On the rare occasion when an acquaintance molester is publicly accused of sexual relations with a child, those around him—his family, friends, neighbors, colleagues—usually don't believe it. They rally to his defense, claiming he is a fine upstanding kind of guy. This is exactly what happened with the Catholic priests, Michael Jackson, and Jerry Sandusky.

How can parents, friends, colleagues, an entire community be so easily fooled? The answer is simple. Acquaintance molesters are master manipulators, capable of conning not only children and parents, but also nearly everyone they meet. Considering the fact that the average child molester starts abusing in his early teens, one must remember that he has had many, many years to perfect his skills of deception. Most acquaintance molesters effectively fool others by leading a double life. They get married, become stalwart members of the community, and seek out professions or volunteer opportunities where they can, ostensibly, help children (e.g., teachers, camp counselors, pediatricians, youth ministers, coaches, foster parents).

Because child molesters are so prone to helping professions and volunteerism, they are often seen as the nice guys in the neighborhood. When one of these nice guys is accused of sexually molesting a child, is it any wonder that the people who know him have trouble believing it? He has been their beloved neighbor, coach, teacher, priest, uncle, husband for years. He seems so helpful and altruistic. How could he suddenly turn around and do something so horrible?

What people don't understand and can't accept is that he didn't just suddenly, in some weak moment, turn around and molest a child. This is something he's been doing (or at least fantasizing about) for years. People see him as the dedicated coach/teacher/priest/uncle who inexplicably may have molested a child. In reality, what he is dedicated to is molesting children. The role of coach/teacher/priest/uncle is just his cover, his means of accessing victims.

This kind of deception is very hard for most people to accept. It means that someone close to them—someone they like and trust and maybe even love—has been conning them since day one. This is simply impossible for most to believe, because people are highly confident in their ability to detect a lie. But they are wrong. Studies have consistently shown that no one, including judges, police officers, and psychiatrists, can spot a liar more than 50 percent of the time. That means even the professionals can't do better than chance. Yet the typical layperson is positive he or she would be able to spot a practiced con man.

Parents' false sense of confidence regarding their ability to judge others is one of the main reasons child molesters are able to victimize so many children for so many years without detection.

Child molesters are notorious for exploiting parents' trust; most revel in it. They are so skilled, in fact, that many parents who have been duped will go to their graves believing that their "friend" was trustworthy. If their children disclose abuse or law enforcement contacts them after other victims come forward, they may have some doubts. Still, anecdotal stories suggest that many parents dismiss the allegations or, if that is not possible because of irrefutable evidence, find a way to minimize the painful, inconvenient truth.

THAT'S WHAT HAPPENED to me when I tried to tell my mother about Gary Lundquist. Just a few days after she picked me up from the weekend in his basement, she dropped the bombshell: We would be moving into Gary's house. Effective immediately.

Needless to say, I was distraught. I panicked and yelled, "No! I won't go!" I doubt I gave her the details of what Gary had done to me. At eight years old, I had no words for such an experience. But I made it exceedingly clear that I hated Gary, feared Gary, and absolutely, positively never wanted to see him again. I cried. I shook. I screamed. I was hysterical with terror and dread.

When my mother tried to leave the room, I wrapped my arms around her legs in a death grip. I was desperate to make her understand. As she dragged me into the hallway, I pleaded frantically, "Don't move in with him! Don't move in with him! I hate him! I don't want to go! Don't make me go! Please!"

Despite my impassioned protest, my mother dismissed the scene as child's play. "I don't know why you're carrying on like this," she chided. "Gary said you two had a really good time together."

My mother had known this man for less than two months. She had known me—a good-natured and easygoing kid by all accounts—since the day I was born. Still, when witnessing my fervent disdain for this near stranger, her immediate reaction was to dismiss it. "He's a nice man," she assured me. "A teacher. You know, you should give him a chance. He really likes you a lot."

When her attempts to persuade me failed, she moved on to accusations. "Aw, you just don't want me to be with anyone," she said. "You're just jealous. You just want me all to yourself."

Looking back, the timing was astoundingly suspicious. Their first date was in early spring. By the middle of May, my mother was packing boxes. The move to Gary's necessitated that I change schools. But it was less than six weeks till the end of the semester. Stranger still was the fact that Gary's house was not located in the school district where he taught; it wasn't even in the same state. Since he was adamant that I attend his elementary school, this meant he would need to sell his current house in Pennsylvania and purchase a new (and far more expensive) home in New Jersey. Such transactions take time, of course, and generally happen over the summer. But instead of simply waiting to enroll me in his district at the start of the new school year, Gary petitioned the school board to enroll me as an out-of-state student immediately. For this favor, he agreed to pay the public school a sizeable tuition.

What kind of teacher demands that a third grader change schools a few weeks before the end of the semester? What kind of man agrees to buy a more expensive house and pay school tuition for a child he has known for less than two months? What was so urgent that Gary couldn't wait a mere six weeks to cohabitate? What, exactly, was the big rush?

The big rush was that Gary Lundquist, professional acquaintance molester, had grown bored with simply seducing other people's children. He was looking for some new sexual thrills, hoping to play out some deeper, darker sexual fantasies. Long before we met, he had come up with a sinister plan. He had already worked out the whole scheme, visualized the perfect scenario. He just needed to find the right victim. And as soon as he met me, he wanted to get started. But first, he needed to secure physical control of me. It was the only way he could move forward with his wicked plot.

IT'S NOT UNCOMMON for a sexual predator to raise the stakes as the years go by. Exhibitionists may gradually feel the need to make physical contact with their victims. Child molesters might go from touching breasts and genitals to penetration. This escalation is fueled by sexual fantasies. An offender may masturbate to specific images and scenarios for years before he gains the confidence to act out his fantasy in real life. Once the fantasy becomes reality, though, it loses its oomph. The sexual predator must then find a new, more depraved scenario to get aroused. In this way, sexual perversion is much like drug addiction. One must constantly up the ante to get the same high.

Gary, already molesting for years, had turned up the dial quite a bit on his perversions. By the time we met, he had developed a thing for sadomasochism, like a third of all pedophiles, and he liked the really hard-core stuff. I don't know how he got into it or how long he'd fantasized about it, but Gary was obsessed with S/M. He fed this obsession through stories in books and images in magazines. He collected all sorts of S/M paraphernalia and delighted in dirty movies. Inspired by all these sources, Gary had developed his own S/M fantasy—one he was determined to fulfill.

Gary's dream was to get himself a sex slave. Freaky, I know. But to an S/M enthusiast, the sex slave is literally half of the equation. The slave/master duo usually involves two consenting adults. Some masters, though, are not content with Craigslist hookups and safe words. Some men are real sadists, and they want real slaves to cater to their perverted whims.

Gary Lundquist yearned for a *real* slave, one he could completely control. That's what sadism is: a need to dominate. At its most rudimentary, domination can be achieved by brute force—tying people up, torturing them, degrading their bodies in various ways. That's all fun stuff for the basic sadist, but for a guy like Gary, who considered himself a man of superior IQ, physical coercion got boring. He needed a bigger challenge. So he decided he would not only dominate his slave but also get her to willingly want to submit.

What I'm talking about here is brainwashing. Robbing someone of their free will is a time-honored tradition and, sadly, not that difficult. But it does require a lot of time and privacy. For an acquaintance molester, the desire for a sex slave gets a bit tricky. I mean, how does one torture other people's children and get away with it? What if the whip leaves marks? Gary came up with an easy solution; he decided to procure his very own kid.

My mother was the perfect target. Young, uneducated, poor. Working full time at a dead-end job, she necessarily left me to fend for myself since she couldn't afford child care. From the start, Gary portrayed himself as her savior. He offered her a house to live in, a bit of financial security, and a built-in babysitter. Is it any wonder that she jumped at the chance to move in with the guy? Any wonder that she ignored the frantic warnings of her eight-year-old daughter?

RIGHT FROM THE START, Gary began to enact his plans for me. That first weekend in the basement was the beginning of his explicitly planned brainwashing campaign. To those unfamiliar with the concept of brainwashing, this probably sounds pretty strange. But in the world of hard-core sadists, tips on how to brainwash victims are openly shared through books, magazines, Internet articles, and chat rooms. Even without prior knowledge, any run-of-the-mill bully seems to inherently understand that a mix of violence, terror, degradation, and occasional small kindnesses is all that's required to rob someone of their free will.

Gary certainly knew the techniques.

And he couldn't wait to try them out.

On me.

Story of M

Tap, tap.
 Huh? What's that?
Tap, tap.
A noise. Noise. Coming from somewhere.
Tap, tap. Bang! "Shit," in a low whisper.
Is that a man's voice? God, what's happening?
I was asleep. Dead to the world. But now, even from the deepest slumber, any little noise puts me on high alert.
Tap, tap. "Shell! Shell, wake up!"
I scan around searching for clues, searching for danger, but I see nothing. The room is pitch-black. I don't even know where I am. It takes a few seconds to remember I'm in Gary's house. We just moved in today. Now I'm in my new room. The room at the end of the hall where he took the pictures before. Except the twin bed is gone now. Replaced with the full-size canopied bed I used to share with my

mother. The white princess-style furniture we shared is in the room too. It's all mine now. My mother now shares her dresser, her closet, her bed with Gary Lundquist. I'm supposed to be happy about all this. I'm supposed to feel that living in a house, having my own room, sleeping in my own bed is a dream come true. It is, I guess. For my mother anyway.

Tap, tap. "Shell! Shelley-Bell!"

The voice is louder now. And familiar. A woman. My aunt Laura! I fumble across the bed to the window and open my Snoopy curtains. There she is. Her face is right up next to the glass.

"Open the front door, Shell," she whispers. "Hurry up."

Stumbling out of my room into the hallway, I assume it must be late because the house is completely dark. Very quietly, I open the door to the room across from mine. Gary's room. He and my mother are lying under the big green bedspread, their bodies dimly visible under the glow of a neon beer sign hanging over the bed. I gently rouse my mother, whispering, "Laura's here."

MY MOM COMES FROM a big family; she's one of thirteen kids. From the moment I was born, I was surrounded by aunts and uncles and an endless stream of cousins. They all converged at my grammy's house in Maryland—a modest two-bedroom place with no running water, just an outhouse in the backyard. There was no dining room, either. Everybody ate in an unfinished basement. All the kids slept in the attic. When my mother was little, they averaged several to a bed. By the time I came along, though, most of Grammy's kids were already out of the house. Just a few of the youngest remained, one of whom was Laura.

To a middle-class outsider, I guess my mother's family would be called white trash. But to me, the Brechbills were a fun, close, loving bunch. Every single one of them, save my mother, lived within a few miles of Grammy's house. Some of them even lived on the same street. My grandparents' house was a constant hub of activity with relatives coming in or out to visit, eat, or drop off their kids. Most of my cousins got dropped off for an afternoon or a weekend, but my mother often left me there for months at a time.

I didn't mind. I loved living with Grammy. She was a gentle, soft-spoken woman who showered me with maternal attention and the very best kind of unconditional love. Every morning, she would make me pancakes. Then I'd follow her around while she cleaned and tended her lavish flower beds. In the afternoons, when my teenage aunts got home from school, playtime would begin. The girls would tell me stories, play games, or take me on long walks. Laura was like a sister to me. She was my mom's best friend too.

On the night she was tapping on my window, Laura had just rented a new apartment. The timing of my mother's move was fortunate; it meant Laura could take Mom's old couches. So Laura had rented a U-Haul and driven three hundred miles to pick the furniture up. It was night when she finally arrived, but that was no big deal. Laura was expected. What's more, she was family. Mom thought nothing of it.

But Gary didn't see it that way. He marched into the living room just as Mom was letting Laura in and pointed a gun at her. "What the fuck do you think you're doing?" he boomed. "Who the hell do you think you are, showing up like this? Waking us up in the middle of the night? What kind of a lowlife are you? How dare you come into my house?"

My aunt was shocked and terribly shaken. She looked helplessly to my mother, who looked helplessly back. Laura tried to explain herself, defend herself, but Gary would have none of it. He berated her with insults—"stupid . . . retard . . . lowlife . . . redneck . . ." Offended, my aunt left quickly, vowing never to come back.

At the time, I didn't understand the implications of the blowup. It was only later, in adulthood, that I realized Gary's seemingly impulsive rant was probably well planned. He knew Laura was coming; he also knew she was my closest relative and my mother's confidante. Gary couldn't do whatever he wanted to me if Laura was snooping around. And so, with a few well-placed insults and a handgun, he distanced a potential threat.

IN DOING SO, Gary was enacting step one of the brainwashing playbook: isolation. In order to abuse, a perpetrator must first isolate his victim. During rape, the offender attacks his prey in an isolated area—a car, a motel room, a deserted park. Kidnap victims and political prisoners are locked in secret cells far from the eyes of would-be rescuers. While domestic abusers rarely hide their wives and kids, they must also find a way to keep them from potential do-gooders—coworkers, teachers, relatives, friends. They do this by systematically severing all of their victims' close relationships. That's why Gary iced out Aunt Laura.

Isolation serves the predator's needs for privacy and secrecy. It also helps him monopolize his victims' perceptions, limiting what they hear, see, and, ultimately, know—which is brainwashing step two. Monopolization of perception is key because once a perpetrator controls the flow of information he can create a false reality based on self-serving lies. Dictators do this to their subjects with propaganda. Cult leaders use dogma. Abusive husbands spew misogynistic rants.

Children are naturally dependent on their caregivers. So, in attempting to isolate and monopolize me, Gary had a head start. Nonetheless, he pulled out all the stops. Just two days after he sent my favorite aunt packing, he packed me into his Pacer and set off for the school where he worked, the school I would now attend. When we arrived, yellow buses and kids were already crowding the parking lot. Classes were about to start, but I wasn't registered yet. So Gary hurried me into the school's office.

The place was bustling with activity. Teachers getting their mail. Parents dropping off forms. Gary stood impatiently at the counter, tapping his foot and checking his watch as he glared at the busy secretaries.

"Yes, Mr. Lundquist, how can I help you?" said the lady behind the counter.

"I need to register my daughter."

"Oh . . . ," she said, with surprise, glancing past him to look at me. "Oh . . ."

She scurried over to a file cabinet and returned with some papers. "First name?" she asked.

"Michelle." He spelled it.

"Last name?" she asked.

"Lundquist."

Lundquist? Had I heard right? Lundquist was not my name. My last name was Brechbill. Like my aunts. Like my grammy. When had they changed my name?

The truth is: They hadn't. My mother and Gary were not married. He hadn't adopted me or gone through any court. No one had spoken to me about changing my name. I doubt my mother even knew Gary was going to do it. She wasn't using his name, after all. How could she? She had no legal standing to do so. Nor did I—a fact that would make it difficult for me to get a Social Security number and all other legal documents in future years.

So why did he do it? Why did Gary suddenly give me his last name? I think it was because he had to put his brand on me. His mark. He had to demonstrate his omnipotence—another essential step in brainwashing—and what demonstrates omnipotence more than the power to change someone's name? Slave owners have always known this, so have patriarchal societies. It's a symbolic way to rob the disempowered of their identities.

S/M culture revels in this sort of authoritarian display. It's no surprise, then, that S/M masters routinely give their slaves new names. In some cases, infantilizing terms of endearment like Baby, Kitten, and Bunny are used. On the other end of the spectrum are names meant to degrade and humiliate, such as Bitch, Whore, Slut, or simply an initial—a practice famously portrayed in the book *Story of O*. Somewhere in the middle, there are mildly derogatory slave names that sound endearing but still belittle the recipient, like Trinket and Pet.

Gary gave me such a slave name about two weeks after our first meeting. During his first visit to my mother's apartment, he jokingly referred to me as a "mooch" because, as with any child, I was financially dependent. Afterward, Gary only ever referred to me by the name Mooch or The Mooch. He used it so exclusively that, within weeks, his family, kids at school, teachers, even my own mother began to refer to me that way. Soon there was no one in my life who called me Michelle. Most people didn't even know it was my name.

Since birth, I had been Michelle Brechbill. Daughter of Judy. Granddaughter of Evelyn and Glenn. Now, with the flick of a pen, I was Mooch Lundquist, daughter of Gary, new student at his out-of-state school. In 1976 no one seemed to question any of this. No one seemed to care that my school records displayed a different name or that Gary was not my legal guardian. We weren't even related. Were Gary's coworkers oblivious to the discrepancies? Did they buy his sudden and bizarre announcement of a daughter? Or did they notice that things seemed a bit off and chose to look the other way? My guess is they *did* notice; they *did* think it was odd. But social norms dictate that we do not insert ourselves into other people's personal lives, particularly coworkers or other casual acquaintances. Being polite means keeping one's mouth shut.

And so I, the newly minted Mooch Lundquist, became a third grader at Delaware Township School. My classroom was on the first floor of the elementary building—just a staircase away from Gary. Every day at three p.m., as soon as the bell rang, I was expected to climb those stairs and report to Gary's desk. Inevitably, a few of his favored ten-year-old students would still be hanging around—joking with him, sitting on his lap, climbing under his desk to escape his tickling hands.

Some days Gary would oversee an afterschool activity. The gifted and talented club was invitation only—Gary's invitation, that is. Gary considered himself to be a genius, so he felt it was his right and duty to identify other geniuses and exalt their superiority too. Trouble was: Gary had no real training or authority to be administering IQ tests. He didn't use the validated tests that I, or any other psychologist, would use. Instead, he gave kids a short multiple-choice test, the Mickey Mouse kind sold in bookstores. Then, based on his findings, he labeled certain kids—the kids he liked and wanted to spend more time with—as "gifted."

I was gifted, according to Gary. This was a real convenience, as he demanded I join his, and only his, after-school clubs. He signed me up for his drama club too and encouraged me to sing in the school talent contest. On the night of the show, various kids performed their acts, and the winner was chosen based on audience response. Gary was among the judges who awarded me first prize. After that, I was given the lead in all the school plays that he directed.

Have I mentioned that Gary could be shameless?

To the other parents, I suppose it seemed that Gary was harmlessly lauding his new daughter. In a certain way, he was. Not because he actually thought I was gifted or talented. I doubt he really thought much about me. Gary was a narcissist, and narcissists view their families as extensions of themselves, as trophies. Gary believed he was superior, so it was imperative that the world see his daughter as superior too.

BEHIND CLOSED DOORS it was a different story. Gary treated me with a dizzying blend of overinvolvement, neglect, overindulgence, and cruelty. With Svengali-like skill, he quickly took over every aspect of my life, dictating what I wore, to whom I talked, even what toys I used. The enforcement of trivial demands is another classic brainwashing technique.

So was the way he strove to monopolize my time—an easy accomplishment since my mother left for work before I awoke and didn't return until evening. During the school year, this meant Gary had me all to himself for an hour each morning and at least three hours every afternoon. Once summer came, he had me all day, every day, all to himself.

Summer was the time when Gary could really play out his S/M fantasies and treat me like a full-time sex slave. This meant being subjected to daily "training sessions"—intense periods when I was explicitly instructed on how to behave and think like a slave. Much like a dog must be trained to sit, to stay, to heel, practitioners of sadomasochism believe a sex slave must be trained in how to speak, sit, serve. In short, like a dog, she must be taught total obedience.

Slave training is a rather formal activity. The slave is usually taken to a special room, known as the dungeon, where she is alternately instructed, commanded, humiliated, degraded, praised, and punished. Often, training sessions will also include bondage, stress positions, sexual violations (both from people and objects), and torture. Gary's dungeon was in the basement. Because he had to avoid my mother's prying eyes, though, he could not leave it permanently set up like other S/M enthusiasts. Instead, he left a series of nails and hooks attached to the ceiling beams, which could quickly and easily hold a harness, a rope, or some other type of bondage device. While much of Gary's paraphernalia had to be kept hidden, I could tell he also had some fun in displaying a few tools of his trade. The dog cage, for instance, was left in plain sight—folded up in a cluttered corner where it appeared to be waiting for the next garage sale. He also kept a wooden paddle hanging on the wall of his home office, which he jokingly told guests was for "errant children." Little did they realize it was no joke. Nor did most people realize that he kept a set of metal handcuffs in his desk drawer, right next to a stun gun and his handgun.

I can't remember being threatened with the gun—although it

may have happened. (Due to amnesia, as well as the normal forgetfulness of memory, there are many details about my abuse I can't recall. I know this because, over the years, eyewitnesses have told stories about my abuse that I cannot personally remember.) I do, however, remember Gary threatening me with the stun gun repeatedly. He even used it on me once. Once was all it took. For after experiencing the excruciating, utterly indescribable pain it inflicted, I never, ever wanted to experience it again. What that little black box could do was so awful that afterward even the sight of it would trigger a panic attack. It was Gary's most effective device for controlling my behavior, as I would do anything, *anything*, to avoid its wrath.

Slave training, though, is not just about controlling behavior through threats, pain, and fear. It is far more insidious than that. It's about controlling someone's mind and spirit by manipulating her thoughts, emotions, and self-image. It's not enough for a slave to simply obey her master. She must come to believe that she wants to obey. She must become so enmeshed in the psyche of her master that she eventually gains the ability to anticipate his needs before he verbalizes them.

Before a slave can fully tend to the needs of her master, though, she must first learn to ignore her own. I believe this is a fundamental purpose of slave training: to habituate the slave to ignoring her own physical and emotional needs. One way to accomplish this is through the use of stress positions. When people think of stress positions, they probably envision the naked men with underwear on their heads who were forced to contort themselves at Abu Ghraib. These positions, which can look as simple as kneeling or as complicated as Twister, are actually torture techniques that were banned by the Geneva Convention. They can cause excruciating pain by putting a lot of weight on a small area of the body. Redubbed as "slave positions," they are also an integral part of S/M and are used to teach submission, patience, and helplessness.

During slave-training sessions, I was instructed in how to assume several different positions, mostly of a sexual nature. The slave position I remember most vividly, though, was not really used for sex. Instead, it was a position I was required to assume while waiting for another command—a wait that sometimes lasted for hours. In this position, I had to kneel with my legs spread slightly past shoulder width while my body remained extremely erect. At first, this seems like an easy position to assume. Very quickly, though, my knees would begin to hurt from the hardness of the floor, and all the while, they would be trying to slide outward into a split. This meant I had to constantly tense my thighs in order to avoid falling. Having to keep my eight-year-old's body erect meant I was continuously working my back and shoulder muscles. The sum of all this effort equaled muscles that were constantly tense, with no hope of relaxation. This was fairly easy to do for two minutes, maybe five. But after that, the pain really started.

First, my knees would begin to hurt from the weight of my body. The pain started off as a pesky ache but very quickly started shooting through my legs. Meanwhile, my thigh and back muscles began to shake from overuse. It took every bit of mental and physical effort just to steady them. At that point, all I wanted to do was relax my body. My muscles screamed for it. They demanded release. I could not release them, though. For I knew that if I broke position, I would receive a far worse punishment.

This is the point of slave positions: to teach the slave how to endure the unendurable. For when the muscles tolerate the intolerable and the body must bear the unbearable, the mind begins playing tricks with itself just to find some escape. Personally, I would try to ignore the pain, pretend it wasn't there. In my mind, I would try to rise above my crushing knees, my burning thighs, the spasms in my back. And blessedly, somehow, such escape was possible. Eventually, my mind would drift away to some other place, a place of fantasy so engrossing that I was no longer aware of the basement, of the knots in my shoulders, of the passage of time. I have since come to learn that I was willing myself into a state of altered consciousness—a common coping technique when one is subjected to repeated torture.

IT WAS THE ABILITY to alter my consciousness that helped me endure more extreme training techniques—those that involved bondage, penetration with foreign objects, and extreme pain, including the use of needles and electric shock.

Why did Gary do these things to me? The obvious answer? He was a sadist, and that's what sadists do. It's their idea of fun. But in this case, it was more than that. Gary was gunning for domination, and any good tyrant knows that terror is essential for success.

Perpetrators use unimaginable violence to shock their victims into states of paralyzing fear. Literally petrified, victims lose the ability to think clearly and act in their own defense, like the proverbial deer caught in headlights. After the initial campaign of shock and awe has achieved its purpose, abusers don't have to work so hard. Occasional random acts of violence are usually enough to keep victims terrified and psychologically weakened. Feeling constantly threatened, they remain passive to avoid further punishment.

Fear fosters compliance. But torture alone doesn't breed loyalty—only contempt. Paradoxically, to brainwash someone, you have to mix the pain with comfort and perks. So, after Gary would torture me and turn me into a ball of utter despair, he would offer me hugs and solace—as he had after the first weekend in the basement. I was so grateful the abuse was over that I willingly accepted Gary's warmth and rewards. And I learned very quickly that it was to my advantage to acquiesce, to do anything to stay in Gary's good graces.

As weird as this will sound, Gary's good graces could feel quite wonderful. After all, when he wasn't hurting me, he lavished me with parental attention. On the long drives to and from school, for instance, he would initiate conversations about history, politics, and art. We ate nearly every meal together while he instructed me on things like table manners and ethnic cuisine. In those early days, he introduced me to many of my lifelong passions, including music, theater, and New York. He gave me my first typewriter and influenced my decisions to become both a writer and psychologist. He took the time to open up the world for me. He was my first and most significant mentor.

Under my mother's care, I'd been neglected and deprived. She was constantly at work, leaving me alone and lonely. Gary preyed on that loneliness. Like any skilled pedophile, he identified what I needed, and he gave it to me. He made me feel special, talented, smart.

Even sexually, staying on Gary's good side had its advantages. For once he felt I had become sufficiently trained and submissive, most of the torture tapered off. Afternoons in the basement were replaced by the bedroom. And his fervor to cause me pain was replaced with a passion to bring me pleasure. I'm not quite sure why Gary was so obsessed with my pleasure, but I suspect it made him feel powerful—like more of a man.

While I can only guess at his motives, Gary's actions are forever seared in my mind. Nearly every day at four o'clock for years, he would summon me to bed for what can only be described as a lovers' tryst. The weird part, of course, was that his "lover" was just under four feet tall and weighed less than sixty pounds.

THERE WAS ALSO the inconvenient fact that his official lover, my mother, refused to vanish. Unable to ditch her physically, he did it emotionally instead. Every evening, he locked himself in his home office. Every weekend, he went to his store. As I was expected to work for him, I followed wherever he went. Very early on, my mother began to notice this pattern, and she didn't like it. Not one bit. Being immature, she didn't handle the situation with grace. She felt excluded, which she was. So she began to yell a lot, mostly at me.

One particular Saturday morning comes to mind. We had probably been living with Gary for about six weeks. It was early morning, and I was in the bathroom getting dressed for the flea market—just as I did every weekend. But my mother wasn't happy, so she stood in the doorway, whining. "What're you gettin' dressed to go there for? Huh? You oughta be staying home with me."

Just then, Gary came into the hall. My mother cornered him. "I want Shell to stay home with me," she demanded. "She's down at that flea market with you way too much!"

Gary, as always, remained calm during my mother's onslaught. Nonchalantly, he remarked, "Why don't you let Mooch decide what she wants to do today? She's perfectly capable of choosing."

It was a brilliant retort. Machiavellian in its simplicity. With one quick remark, he had abdicated all responsibility for the situation. Instead, all blame was now placed squarely on me. At eight years old, I was being asked to choose between my mother and Gary. It was not a real decision, of course. Gary knew this. If I chose Gary, he would immediately whisk me away from my mother's ranting—and probably offer some kind of reward. But if I chose my mother, there would be no one to protect me from Gary. Crossing him would mean paying for my sins.

So I announced that I wanted to go to the flea market. I chose Gary, and my mother flew into a jealous rage. "The flea market!" she screamed. "You can't go to the flea market! I'm your mother! You're staying with me!"

But Gary was already whisking me out the door. "You asked her to choose, and she chose, Judy," he said. "Live with it."

It was with this kind of scene, played out repeatedly, that Gary was able to drive a wedge between my mother and me. He made her feel unwanted and manipulated her into believing I was to blame. In an ideal world, my mom would've been a stronger person and understood that, as a child, I was powerless and innocent. But, like many young women with low self-esteem and little earning potential, she believed she needed a man to survive. Gary played on my mother's insecurities, manipulating her into seeing me less as her daughter and more as her romantic competition. Confused into believing I was the "other woman," she made some questionable maternal choices.

I am certain that if Gary could've gotten rid of my mother entirely, he would have. He lobbied hard to adopt me, but my mother resisted. Despite being naïve in many ways, she knew that if Gary became my legal parent, he would dump her and seek full custody.

Thankfully, she never fell for the trap. Still, I'm astonished that she chose to stay with a man whose deepest desire was to kick her to the curb and steal her young daughter.

Personally, I know for a fact that Gary considered *me* his true lover. I know because he told me so. Constantly. "You are my real wife," he would say to me each morning as we drove together in the car. "You are my real wife," he would say to me each day as we worked side by side at the flea market. "You are my real wife," he would say to me each afternoon as we lay naked in the king-size bed he would share with my mother later that night.

Frankly, when he said it, I didn't quite know what to think. I knew he meant it as a compliment because he said it so often and with such pointed intensity. It was something he felt I needed to understand. But I didn't. It just didn't make sense. My eight-year-old's brain simply could not grasp that this thirty-three-year-old man saw me as his mate. I was just a little girl. He was married to my mother. (As a kid, I simply accepted this lie.) That made us a family. He was my father, and I was his child. Right?

That's how I saw it. That's how I wanted to see it. I just wanted to be normal like other kids. I just wanted to have a normal life.

So when Gary said, "I'm only with her for you. You're the one I really want," it confused me. I felt uneasy. Guilty, I guess. On some level, I knew it was very wrong. The guy was telling me to replace my own mother. This made me feel terrible. Despite her shortcomings, I loved my mother and felt a deep and innate loyalty to her. Gary, on the other hand, scared and repulsed me. The last thing I wanted to do was compete with anyone—let alone my own mother—for his affection.

———

IT'S REMARKABLE, though, how quickly a person's thoughts and feelings can become distorted when they are manipulated by a sociopath on a brainwashing campaign. Just a few months after the incident in the bathroom, I walked into the living room one morning to find my mother standing naked in front of Gary. She was posing for pictures—"before" shots for a new diet. Using his Polaroid, Gary took a few quick photos of my mother from the front, back, and side. Then he handed her the pictures and went back to his home office, taking the camera with him.

The whole exchange lasted just a few minutes. Still, as I watched the scene between them, I felt uneasy, like something wasn't quite right. Gary and my mother had been sharing an intimate moment, one that didn't involve me. It made me feel upset. Jealous. Competitive. So I marched into Gary's office and demanded he take more photos. Photos of me, that is. He enthusiastically agreed and told me to get undressed.

I took off my clothes quickly—without the hesitation and self-consciousness I usually exhibited when Gary told me to disrobe. If anything, I felt triumphant as I stood there naked in front of him. So triumphant, in fact, that I readily agreed to pose beyond the basic front-back-side pictures that my mother had modeled. So triumphant that I willingly spread my legs on Gary's suggestion so he could continue snap, snap, snapping far more pornographic shots. It was a coup to be posing for his photos. I had regained my position as his favorite subject. I had responded to the threat of my mother's supplantation, and I had won.

Never mind that I didn't love Gary—or even like him. Never mind that I had no desire to be his sexual mate. What I thought, felt, wanted had suddenly become immaterial. I was so wrapped up in Gary's version of reality—where he saw me as his soul mate, his sexual partner, his obedient slave—that I inexplicably found myself fighting to maintain the role he had assigned to me, a role I never, ever sought. Without even realizing it, I had begun to see the world as Gary saw it. What's worse, I had begun to see myself through his twisted lens.

IN THE PAST FEW DECADES, there have been multiple stories about kidnapped children who were discovered living with their captors despite having the physical ability to flee. In the 1970s, heiress Patty Hearst famously committed armed robbery alongside her abductors. Every day countless women, men, and children stay in abusive homes and keep mum about their suffering. Why do victims stay in these situations? The short answer: brainwashing.

The term *brainwash* is not currently recognized as an official psychological condition. Nonetheless, it effectively and succinctly explains why people do not flee their abusers and do not try to seek help. It's because, usually from the moment of their first meeting, the perpetrator has waged a violent campaign to gain control of his victim's body and mind.

Terrified, hurt, weakened, and cut off from anyone who can help, the victim must paradoxically turn to the only person available for all of her physical and emotional needs—the abuser. Any victim who wants to stay alive knows it's in her best interest to make nice with the sociopath in charge. Ironically, though, the victim's decision to placate the perpetrator actually binds her to him more effectively than chains ever could. This is because, in order to form a bond that can ensure her safety, the victim must seek out whatever is relatable and human in the abuser while ignoring all that is bad and monstrous. This herculean feat of pretense requires that the victim ignore her true judgments, intuitions, thoughts, and feelings.

This is the essence of brainwashing. Once a victim has made the mental leap to pretend that the monster abusing her is really a decent guy, she is primed to believe just about anything that monster says. Prisoners of war will accept the enemy's propaganda. Battered wives will believe that their husbands beat them out of love. Abducted children will accept that their parents no longer want them.

Ultimately, this is the goal of every brainwashing campaign, whether explicitly waged or not: to convince victims that they are powerless and that their only hope for salvation is the guy abusing them. In the victim's mind, the abuser becomes an all-powerful being, capable of controlling anyone and anything. The victim has no choice but to submit.

LIKE I DID.

Gary had done it. He had taken possession of my mind, body, and soul. Now, without any resistance on my part, he could command me to do every perverted, unspeakable act his twisted mind could dream up.

Tricks Are for Kids

Pedophiles and sadists are kind of like the philatelists and numismatists of the perv world because, like their stamp- and coin-collecting cousins, they pursue their hobbies with passion. Yes, pedophilia and sadism *are* cherished hobbies for these men. It usually starts out with an interest in pornography, which sexual deviants collect with fervor. But because child pornography is expensive and hard to acquire, a lot of pedophiles like to hook up with one another to trade images. Over time, these relationships can become quite beneficial. Besides porn, the guys start to swap stories, tactics, even kids. A feeling of camaraderie develops as all these guys with the same hobby form their own little club. The media call these clubs "child sex rings." Gary belonged to one of them.

Some child sex rings are purely recreational. Others are run for profit. There's big money to be made selling child pornography. There are bigger bucks still selling live children. Gary liked money, and he had a new commodity. So, soon after we met, he started selling me to other men.

To understand how this worked, it's important to explain a little more about Gary's businesses. As I've already mentioned, he owned an antiques store that was open on weekends. He also had a mail-order business he ran out of his house. In addition, when he wasn't teaching during the summers, Gary would travel around the East Coast, selling his wares in small-town shopping malls. These "mall shows," as he called them, were housed in a different mall each week. They ran from ten a.m. to nine p.m. Wednesday through Sunday. Since most of the malls were far from home, this necessitated spending four nights of each summer week in a motel.

I'm sure it was no accident that my mother, who worked a full-time job, was rarely able to join him.

Mall-show life, like carnival life, was peculiar and hard. Every Wednesday morning we would show up with a car full of merchandise, load it onto dollies, and wheel it into the middle of the mall. We would then have to unload all the merchandise onto folding tables, setting up a makeshift shop in the mall's corridor. In order to prevent theft, the booth had to be manned eleven hours a day. Most mall-show carnies traveled with their spouses, so they could trade off food and bathroom breaks. Gary needed help too. But, instead of a spouse, he brought along kids.

The mall shows, though legitimate, were much like Gary's other activities—just a clever way to molest kids. But unlike at school or in his store, this ruse provided ample time and privacy to fulfill his grander sexual fantasies. These fantasies often played out like a fucked-up Club Med commercial—the Econo Lodge becoming a romantic getaway for Gary and his current child sweetheart. After their long day at the mall, Mr. L. would treat his darling to a nighttime swim in the deserted motel pool, where they could float around in the moonlight. They would joke with each other and splash about while Gary "innocently" touched her legs, her stomach, her ass, her unformed breasts.

What he was doing, really, was lowering the girl's inhibitions. He was getting her accustomed to his touch so she would be a little less guarded when they got back to the motel room. Getting into the room with the child was, of course, the true goal of Gary's day. For it was there, alone with his conquest, that he could help her out of her wet bathing suit and into her Raggedy Ann pajamas. After that, he could summon her to bed. (There was usually only one.) Once the lights were out, he could offer to cuddle or wrestle or find some other devious way to get his hands on her.

IT MAY SEEM STRANGE that I'm speaking about Gary's motel conquests in third person. There is a reason for this: More often than not, the conquest was not me. While I was the sole kid at a few mall shows, Gary usually chose to bring two kids—one to keep and one to sell.

So, while Gary was in one motel room cuddling a student, I was usually in another motel room being raped by a total stranger. Gary had a few motives for doing this, I think. Partly, it was an S/M thing. In S/M culture the slave is seen as a possession, no different than a lamp or a cow. As such, it's the master's right to do as he wishes with the slave, including sell her, trade her, or loan her out. Giving a slave to other men for sex is considered essential training in S/M culture. It humiliates the slave, puts her in her place, and reminds her of her utter worthlessness.

In Gary's case, I suspect that money was also a serious motivator because the first time Gary gave me to another man, I actually saw the cash change hands. It was in a motel room during that first summer; Gary and I had just returned from an eleven-hour day at the mall. It was late at night, especially for an eight-year-old, and I was very tired. I couldn't wait to get back in our room and cuddle the big stuffed bear I'd brought. But when we got out of the car, instead of going to our room, I was surprised to hear that we were going to meet a man. Gary said it was a friend of his, and I'd better behave. Having already endured some of Gary's slave training, I understood what this meant. I was to do as I was commanded.

Gary led me to an unfamiliar motel door, gave me a stern look—a warning—and knocked. The door opened immediately; Gary walked in, and I followed obediently. The motel room looked exactly like ours. Same king-size bed. Same night stands. Same air conditioner sticking out of the wall. The man in the room was equally nondescript: middle-aged, medium height and weight, a moustache, kind of bald. The mood in the room, though, was anything but normal. Both men seemed very serious and stern. I had already come to recognize such gruffness as play-acting. This was the beginning of an S/M scene.

"Here she is," Gary said. "Just like I promised. Does she meet with your approval? What do you think?"

The man stared at me intensely. He eyed me up and down, even walked around me slowly to get a full look. Having been trained, I immediately understood my part in this impromptu but well-rehearsed scene: stay immobile in my position, head down, eyes cast to the floor. Do not talk. Do not make eye contact. Do not show emotion. Just submit.

"Is she pure?" the man asked, still eyeing me intensely. (This was code for being a virgin, although I didn't understand it at the time.)

"Of course! Of course! Look at her," Gary lied. "I just got her. She's brand-new."

"I want to see her," the man said.

Gary nodded, then motioned for me to take off my clothes. I understood the signal, a quick flick of his hand. Again, I had been trained; I knew what was expected of me. Still, I hesitated. I felt embarrassed.

But my feelings didn't matter to Gary, who was clearly annoyed. Impatient, he yanked up my shirt. I took it off, baring my child's torso. Then I quickly pulled down my skirt and stepped out of it.

And there I stood, absolutely rigid. Exposed. Mortified. I stared at the ground, pretending not to exist. Praying this was enough for them.

It wasn't.

"I want to see all of her," the man said.

Gary threw me a menacing glare. I knew what I had to do, but I couldn't bring myself to do it. I felt sick inside. Panicked. I wanted to run, to hide, to get away from that room and those men and the way they looked at me. But I was a well-trained slave, so I stood there motionless. I put away my feelings, my fear, my shame, my anger, my humiliation, and I pulled down my underwear.

The man looked me over, then ran his hands across my body. Shocked, I looked to Gary for help. But he just stared at me with the same cold, emotionless expression he always had during these S/M scenes. It was like he was a different person, a total stranger from the stepfather I spent my days with or even the lover who took me to bed.

"How much?" the man asked.

"Exactly what we talked about," Gary said.

The man nodded, pulled out an envelope, and handed it to Gary.

"I'll pick her up in the morning," Gary said, opening the door.

It was only at this point, with my father walking out of the room, that I realized he was going to leave me there. Terrified, I broke my position and moved toward Gary. "No!" I pleaded, grabbing on to him. He shoved me back like I was some kind of pesky dog. His face was absolutely cold. No hint of sympathy.

"No, Daddy, please, please, no!" I cried. I would've run to him again, grabbed his legs and not let go, but the strange man was holding me back. I was still struggling mightily as I watched my father leave.

AFTER THAT, I don't remember much. The man had sex with me, of course. But I don't remember it being particularly kinky or him being particularly mean. He was as gentle as a grown man can be having sex with an eight-year-old. So the next night with the next man I was a little less scared. And by the twentieth man, it had kind of become old hat.

The routine went something like this: I would spend eleven hours at the mall with Gary. Sometimes there was another kid with us, sometimes not. At nine p.m., when the mall closed, we would drive back to the motel where Gary would immediately take me to a strange man's room. Sometimes we played out the S/M inspection scene, but usually we didn't. Gary just knocked on the door, waited for it to open, and shoved me inside, promising to collect me in the morning. Frequently, the man would look familiar because he'd come to the mall earlier in the day. The men often did this; they'd show up at the booth to check out the merchandise before handing Gary a wad of cash. I was aware of these transactions, aware of being displayed for potential customers. The men never talked to me while I was at the mall, though. All the initial arrangements were made through Gary. My job was to just show up.

Once in the motel room, it was usually awkward. I would stay by the door, feeling self-conscious as the guy looked me over with a lascivious grin. Little me, standing before some grown man I didn't know. Thankfully, most of them were nice.

If that sounds weird, there's something you should know about pedophiles: They claim to love children, and they really believe their own hype. To a pedophile who's not a sadist, the idea of scaring or hurting a child is anathema. Pedophiles are looking for romance. They see sex with a child as the ultimate act of love. Who can forget Michael Jackson saying, "The most loving thing you can do is share your bed with someone"? So most of the johns who bought me spoke softly and handled me with kid gloves. When they asked me to disrobe, they were exceedingly polite. They were equally polite when they asked me to suck their penises. And they expressed great concern about my comfort as they stuffed their man-size dicks into my tiny vagina. This is the narcissistic delusion of the typical pedophile: to believe that if he ensures the child's physical comfort as he plugs her orifices he isn't really using her like a blow-up doll.

These men paid good money for me, and they expected a very full night. Needless to say, I didn't get much sleep. Maybe a few hours in the early morning, but it was hardly enough rest for a growing child. The lack of sleep often made me feel nauseated. And as the sun came up, it felt very awkward to be lying in bed with some naked man. I was never quite sure what to do with myself in the mornings.

Getting dressed meant getting out of bed and exposing my naked body. This probably sounds silly considering what we'd done the night before. Still, I never got over the embarrassment of being nude.

But I had to get out of bed. If I wasn't ready to leave when Gary came, he'd be mad. There were practical concerns too. I often had to go to the bathroom, but I didn't know quite how to manage it. Again, I didn't want to traipse across the room in my naked state, and I always felt ashamed about some strange man listening to me use the toilet. Then there was the bathing issue. Just like anyone else, a night of sex made me long for a shower. I never dared to ask for one, though. The thought of standing naked in a shower with my eyes closed made me feel too exposed when all I wanted was to disappear.

Usually, I would just quietly slink out of bed in the morning, crawl across the floor, and attempt to put on my clothes before the man in bed could see me. Then I would sit or stand in the corner of the room trying to be invisible until Gary knocked on the door. When I heard the knock, I immediately stepped outside. Gary then took me back to his motel room where I could quickly pee, shower, and change my clothes. By nine a.m., we were headed back to the mall for a long day of work.

As a concession to my sleepless nights, Gary always allowed me to set up a makeshift bed with blankets and a pillow under the tables in the booth. There, enveloped in the darkness provided by tablecloths, I would sleep on the mall's concrete floor in the middle of the day. At nine p.m., we would leave the mall and go back to the motel, to another stranger's room, to do it all over again.

This motel routine went on for about five summers. There were variations, of course. Once in a while, Gary would keep me to himself. Some nights, Gary would keep me and another child, and require that we perform sexual acts on each other as he watched. For the most part, though, my summer job was having sex with strange men in motel rooms, and I got quite used to it.

I know that's hard for most people to understand. How does a child get used to having sex with a different man every night? All I can say is: When something becomes routine—even rape—it tends to lose its shock value or meaning. Whatever fear, disgust, and shame I felt in the beginning eventually went away. Once I knew what to expect, I simply did what I had to do. I went on autopilot and shut off my feelings, my senses, even my memory in the process. That's why, if someone asked me to describe every individual man—what he looked like or said to me or did to me—I couldn't do it. Prostitution, to me, became as mundane as eating dinner. Over time, the individual episodes have all blurred together in my memory.

SOME EVENTS DO STILL stand out, though. These were the times when Gary veered from his usual MO. Most of these events happened when I was older. Twelve. Thirteen. By definition, pedophiles are interested in prepubescent children. So when I hit puberty Gary lost interest in me. Not because I'd grown breasts or gotten my period. Many pedophiles are actually attracted to a woman's body, and Gary was definitely one of them. What Gary didn't like was the attitude that came with the boobs.

Gary was on a constant quest to feed his narcissism. He always had to feel like the smartest, funniest, most special guy in the world. He needed to be adored at all times—worshipped, even. Grown women wouldn't put up with that shit.

Lonely little girls, though, bought his act. They were so desperate for attention that they'd accept anything, even their teacher's wandering hands. As the girls hit puberty and started to notice boys, they naturally grew rebellious. They wanted a say in things, but Gary-the-control-freak never permitted dissent. And why should he? When a girl hit puberty, he could just move on to the next.

Dropping a child mistress, though, is not always easy. According to former FBI agent Kenneth Lanning, the biggest problem for a child molester is not how to procure victims but how to dump the kids when they get too old. Children tend to develop deep attachments to their abusers. If a guy suddenly cuts ties with a kid, he risks a spurned lover who might seek revenge. This is where a sex ring comes in handy. The pedophile can simply pawn the child off on another member who likes older kids. If this is done with proper skill, the child victim never quite understands that they've been rejected.

For Gary, I posed a more challenging situation, as he had asked my mother and me to move in with him. At the time, I think he believed that, in me, he could finally create a sex slave who would psychologically never grow up, a partner who would never leave him. But despite his best efforts, I *did* hit puberty, and I *did* want to become my own person. I started to assert myself more and demand a say in my own life. I wanted to pick out my own clothes, choose my own activities, spend time with my own friends. While these are the normal requests of every adolescent, Gary saw even my smallest attempts at independence as major rebellion. He continued to try to control me in every conceivable way—easier to do since I was still stuck in his K–8 school. When I wanted to play flute in the school band, he insisted I play trumpet. When I wanted to take French as my foreign language, he insisted I learn Russian. When I wanted to wear the current style—blue jeans—he forbade me to own even one pair.

But despite his constant attempts, Gary could not preserve the eight-year-old version of me. And his suffocating control tactics only made me want to rebel more. The watershed moment came in seventh grade when Gary announced he'd be directing a production of *Peter Pan*. In the past, I'd been the star of his shows, so he assumed I'd play Wendy. I didn't want to do it, though. For a seventh grader, being in the elementary school play was embarrassing. So, in an act of unimaginable rebellion, I refused to be in the play. In Gary's world, this was treason, punishable by complete and utter exile.

Almost immediately, a new little girl entered the picture. Madeline was pretty and bright and had been a student of Gary's. While other kids had been around over the years, none were as omnipresent as Madeline. Suddenly, she was everywhere—at the store, working the mall shows, visiting our house. Gary gave her a gold ring much like the one he had given me years earlier to symbolize our "marriage."

I was replaced.

Just like that.

For years, I'd been told I was Gary's lover, rightful partner, and one true wife. I'd done everything he asked of me—in his bed and with other men. Now, suddenly, I was invisible. The whole thing was hurtful and terribly confusing. As naïve as it sounds, I'd actually bought into the façade that Gary was a devoted father. I thought he loved and cared about me. But once he got Madeline, I was disregarded and treated with utter contempt.

A perfect example of this involved the musical *Cats*. It was a huge hit on Broadway and I, like every little girl on the East Coast, was dying to see it. Before I became persona non grata, Gary talked about the show frequently and even bought me the cast album. He'd been the first person to introduce me to musical theater, and I'd developed a genuine passion for Broadway shows—a passion I thought I shared with my father. So, when he announced that he'd bought tickets to *Cats*, I was overjoyed. That is until he announced his intention to take Madeline, not me.

The day of the play, Gary left early to take Madeline into the city. I'm sure they toured around and had a nice dinner together; Gary could be very romantic when he was wooing a new girl. As for me, I stayed home, seething with despair and rage that my twelve-year-old brain couldn't articulate. Not that I had anyone to confide in anyway. Who could possibly understand my twisted feeling of betrayal? I sure as hell couldn't! Eventually, I went to bed. Sometime in the middle of the night—midnight? one a.m.?—I heard a bang. Then harsh light filled my room. I sleepily opened my eyes to find Gary standing over my bed, angry.

"Why didn't you clean the kitchen?" he yelled.

"W-w-what?" I asked, bewildered. I was still half-asleep.

"You didn't clean the kitchen. Get up!" he commanded. Then he grabbed me and yanked me out of the bed.

I followed him through the dark living room to the brightly lit kitchen. Sure enough, the sink was full of dishes—his dishes from earlier that day.

"Get to work," he ordered, pointing to the sink.

"Huh?" I asked, dumbfounded. I didn't understand the issue. This was not some *Better Homes and Gardens* house. We left dishes in the sink for days. "I'll do them tomorrow," I said crankily. "I'm tired. It's the middle of the night."

I turned and started back toward my bedroom.

"Do them now," he growled.

I pivoted back and, with all the sass of a typical twelve-year-old, said, "Why don't you get Madeline to do it?"

I doubt I even got the last words out before his enormous hand was coming at my head with superhuman force. It struck so hard that my whole body flew across the kitchen. I was stunned. Despite Gary's sadistic nature, he was a very controlled person. So this type of humdrum domestic violence was rare for him.

Why was he so angry with me? What had I done?

What I had done was grow up, and it really pissed him off.

Gary had wanted a child sex slave. Now he was stuck with a smack-mouth teenager and her irascible mother. He had to house us, feed us, clothe us, all the while keeping up the ridiculous front that we were some kind of a real family. Gary had never made a secret of his disdain for my mother. He belittled her constantly, even in front of other people, and they argued nonstop. Now he clearly felt disdain for me too. So why didn't he just throw us out?

While I can only speculate, I believe there were two main reasons Gary kept us around. First, my mother and I provided an excellent cover for him, making his interest in children seem far less suspicious. Second, I think Gary couldn't throw my mother out because she was an unpredictable hothead who simply knew too much.

WHEN IT COMES TO INCEST, speculation about what the mother knows or doesn't know is tricky. Historically, mothers have been vilified by social-service types who assume moms are collusive in the sexual abuse of their children—either actively encouraging the abuse or failing to prevent it. Research, though, suggests that this type of so-called mother blame is misguided. In reality, many mothers of sexually abused children genuinely don't know about the abuse until they're told, at which point they attempt to protect and support their children.

Unfortunately, my mom wasn't like that.

She knew there was abuse and did nothing to stop it. I can say this with absolute certainty because, when I was twelve years old, she found naked photos of me. Most were extremely graphic. I don't know where my mom found them. But, when she did, she became hysterical and interrogated me to learn what they were all about. Not knowing what to do, I sent her to Gary, who explained that he'd taken the pictures at my request.

Technically, this was true. I *had* asked him to take the pictures. It was right after that time I'd discovered him taking nude "before" shots of my mother for her diet. I'd asked him to take the same shots of me. Of course, I was nine at the time and didn't realize the perverse nature of my request. Nor had I requested the other shots—the ones with my legs spread wide.

Such details were lost on my mother. She was furious. At me. I realize how crazy that sounds. How could any mother find porno pics of her nine-year-old and blame her kid instead of the adult photographer? It seems indefensible, and in many ways, it is. Still, one must remember that my mother was living with a master manipulator who was far superior to her in cunning and intelligence. From the beginning, Gary created a reality where I was cast as my mother's romantic rival instead of her child. Taught to be suspicious of me, she readily accepted every lie Gary fed her.

In my mother's mind, I was to blame for the dirty photographs.

And, because I also bought into Gary's version of reality, I agreed. After all, I had initiated that particular photo session. What's more, I had posed for countless other shots, had sex with countless other men, and allowed Gary to perform countless sex acts with me. In my mind, this meant I had betrayed my mother just as much as Gary had. I was Gary's coconspirator, his partner in crime, which made me feel unbearably guilty.

It was hard to get through seventh grade dwelling on the fact that I was the most vile, perverted twelve-year-old in the world. It was equally difficult to enjoy Thanksgiving dinner with the father who pimped me out. So, psychologically, I defended against this knowledge with all my might. On a conscious level, I blocked out the ugly truth, choosing instead to believe I was a normal girl living a normal life. I didn't allow myself to think about what happened in motel rooms. Instead, I pretended to myself that I was innocent and naïve. I told myself I was a virgin just like all the other girls in middle school. This Orwellian doublethink is a typical coping mechanism employed by victims of prolonged abuse. When someone is forced to bear unbearable pain, sometimes the only option is to pretend the truth ain't so.

By the spring of 1982, when I was thirteen, I needed all my powers of denial. My beloved grammy became terminally ill, and my mother decided to move to Maryland to care for her. Indefinitely. Unfortunately, she left me at home. With Gary. But now that Gary was obsessed with Madeline, he didn't want me around. His solution was to pimp me out as often as possible, allowing him more QT with his new lover. A teenage prostitute's not worth as much as a child, though. Not unless she does kinkier tricks. So Gary started sending me out on more hard-core assignments. Dangerous stuff.

One experience that comes to mind involved what I can only describe as a sex party. It was held at a big house on Long Island—most likely the home of a management-level mobster. Gary led me to a bedroom where I changed into a simple white nightgown. Very virginal. I waited alone in the room for a long time, not sure what to expect. Eventually, two strange men came to fetch me. They led me to a set of closed doors. One of the men knocked, and the doors swung open. The men pushed me forward. They had to; I was paralyzed with fear. I was staring at a den full of men.

It was some kind of party—a birthday or stag thing—and the celebrant got first dibs. Egged on by his friends, he lifted off my nightgown in front of everyone and led me to a card table where half a dozen men were seated. The birthday boy laid me on the table, pulled down his pants, and fucked me. Even after years as a sex slave, this was surreal. I simply could not fathom a man screwing me while all his friends watched. They did not watch for long. As soon as the first guy was done, another took over. Then another. Then another. I got passed around like a joint in a college dorm room. This went on for hours while the men drank, laughed, played cards, and smoked cigars. Eventually, they all seemed to leave or pass out or fall asleep. As soon as I could, I crawled across the floor to a gigantic window, wrapped the bottom of the curtain around my body, and curled into a fetal ball. Sometime in the night, Gary finally came back. He handed me the nightgown and told me to put it on. I must have been in shock, because I couldn't will myself to move. Gary seemed to understand. He lifted me up, draped the nightgown over me, and carried me out of the room.

Another time I arrived at a sex party in the suite of a hotel. A makeshift stage was set up with about fifteen men waiting impatiently for the show. Dressed in revealing lingerie, I was expected to perform a striptease like some other girls at the party had done. Gary pushed me toward the stage, but despite the edict to be obedient, I just couldn't do it. The thought of dancing in my underwear made me too self-conscious. Again, Gary seemed to understand. He directed me into the bathroom, handed me a pill, and told me to take it. Honestly, I don't remember much after that. I know I did the striptease without feeling self-conscious, and I assume I had sex with some of the men, though I remember none of it. Considering how quickly the pill worked and how little I remember of that night, I'm guessing that Gary gave me Rohypnol, more commonly known as "roofies." They were just coming into popularity at the time.

While Gary and his friends certainly used drugs and alcohol to get me to loosen up, this was the exception rather than the norm. The sad truth is: I'd been trained to be obedient at a very young age. Gary didn't need to resort to drugs or alcohol or any type of coercion to ensure my compliance. On the contrary, in those days I usually looked like an enthusiastic participant. After so many years of abuse and prostitution, I'd learned to don a licentious persona when need be to survive. This persona was the complete opposite of the good-girl image I held of myself the rest of the time. It was also completely involuntary; my personality switched from good girl to bad girl without my conscious choice—or even my conscious knowledge. Due to doublethink, my good-girl personality was unaware that the bad girl even existed. This was an excellent coping mechanism, for it allowed me to sit through algebra on Monday mornings without pondering all the guys I'd fucked on Saturday night.

My bad-girl persona also allowed me to do things that would've made my good girl die of shame. When I was thirteen, for instance, I accompanied Gary to a hotel for a baseball-card convention. While Gary worked his booth on the convention floor, I was required to stay in the hotel room and wait for the men he sent. An endless stream of johns came knocking day and night, and like a brothel worker, I gave each man what he requested. Had I been in my normal frame of mind, this would've been unbearable. It would've felt like being raped for forty-eight hours straight. Blessedly, my bad-girl persona kicked in and convinced me that I liked having sex with countless strange men. And as the bad girl, I did like it—at least with some of them. Being grateful for my mind's ability to derive pleasure from rape may sound strange, even crazy. But when forced to live through hell, isn't it a blessed delusion to believe it's heaven?

UNFORTUNATELY, THERE WERE TIMES when things got so bad there was no hope of pretending otherwise. One incident comes to mind when I was thirteen and taken to a house where a party was in progress. Gary showed me to an empty bedroom, then opened the bag he was carrying. He pulled out a wedding dress and veil. I was told to put it on and wait for my trick. From experience, I understood that I was being hired to role-play a scene. In this case, it was a wedding-night scene, and I was to play the virgin bride. (Knowing Gary, he probably fooled the customer into believing I really *was* a virgin to get more money.) I waited for hours and, at some point, fell asleep on a window seat. When the customer finally arrived, he was noticeably drunk. He swaggered to the middle of the room and gave me a long, cold stare. I could tell from his body language that I was in trouble.

"Take off your dress," he said, slurring his speech.

I immediately complied.

"Whoo-wee!" he said, giving me the once-over. "What're you doin' here, huh? How'd you get into this?"

I stayed frozen as he pulled me in for a kiss.

Just before our lips met, though, his fist smashed into my head. The blow sent me crashing onto the floor. I was so shocked and scared that I started inching backward in a panic. I was trying to find a safe spot, I guess. But there was no safety to be found.

He was instantly on top of me, pinning me down while he slapped my face. "What're you doin', huh? Huh? You tryin' to get away? You can't get away from me. It's our weddin' night, remember?" And before I could comprehend what was happening, he was viciously raping me while he smashed the back of my head into the hard floor.

I pleaded helplessly for him to stop. That's all I remember. I think I lost consciousness.

The next thing I knew, it was the morning. Gary was there to fetch me, but I don't think he expected to find me lying on the floor naked and bruised. He pulled clothes out of a bag and helped me put them on. Then he took me to a motel room to recuperate.

SOME MAY WONDER: If I was black and blue, with a possible concussion, how did Gary keep that hidden? In this case, it was the summer, and my mother was in Maryland. So all Gary had to do was keep me out of sight until the bruises were gone. This is the only time I remember getting seriously banged up in a way that could've drawn attention to my abuse. For the most part, Gary and the other men in the ring were quite careful not to leave visible marks. Most torture was done to the genitals, which would naturally be hidden from bystanders. (Since I was still too young to date—and wouldn't have been allowed to anyway—boyfriends weren't a problem.) While I did suffer endless sprained wrists and ankles due to bondage, the ACE bandages I continuously sported were explained away as injuries from gym class. Likewise, I constantly had tiny bruises on my thighs—the result of countless men gripping their fingers into my flesh. The bruises were very small, though, no bigger than fingertips. My mother told people they were due to a vitamin C deficiency.

In truth, I got very little medical attention when I was young. I didn't have the annual checkups that normal children get. Even when my parents suspected I had a sprained ankle or strep throat, they didn't bother to take me to the doctor. I assume this was because my parents didn't want medical personnel asking too many questions. I've also come to the harsh realization that Gary simply didn't care what happened to me. I mean, what's the point in paying good money for a doctor if you don't care whether the patient lives or dies?

LOOKING BACK, I think the fact that I didn't die during my childhood is a miracle. Gary put me in so many dangerous situations with so many dangerous men that I sometimes can't fathom how I survived. Take my experiences at a place called the Revolution Motel. Gary and I stayed at the Revolution two summers in a row. The place was a dive, which wasn't unusual. Every place we ever stayed at was a dump. What was unusual about the Revolution Motel was its layout. Rather than just offering the standard rooms, the place also rented out cottages—separate structures without shared walls. This offered a unique type of privacy that Gary used to his advantage.

Our cottage, which was really just a run-down mobile home, featured two bedrooms. In the past, Gary and I had always shared a room (and usually a bed), so I thought this new arrangement was a victory—proof that my father was acknowledging my independence. Stupid me. Gary's *real* intention was to lease me out to men who wanted to fulfill their abduction fantasies. I was tied to a headboard, blindfolded, and gagged for days on end while various men played "kidnap" with me.

Once again, I get that this sounds totally fucked up. I mean, who the hell pays for a fake abductee? Believe it or not, abduction fantasies are very common, and people frequently seek out would-be abductors or abductees on Craigslist. These fantasies are so prevalent, in fact, that there are professional sex workers who specialize in this type of scene. Goddess Lady D of Wisconsin, for instance, offers a "kidnapping fantasy" special via the Internet in which she promises "24 hours of pain, discomfort, disorientation and naked humiliation" all for the low price of "only $600!" In all fairness to Goddess Lady D of Wisconsin and the posters on Craigslist, it appears that they are interested in fulfilling their abduction fantasies with consenting adults. But for the pedophile, an adult will not suffice, and the real abduction of a child can cause dire legal consequences. By offering me up as a pseudo-abducted child, Gary found a lucrative niche.

For me, the experience was terrifying. Tied to a bed without the ability to move, see, or scream, I had to wait helplessly for unknown men. Some of the johns approached the scene like it was ho-hum prostitution—"Just the acts, ma'am." Others took the whole abduction thing way too seriously—handling me roughly, calling me names, even threatening to hurt or kill me. The worst was a trio of good ol' boys who stayed for hours—drinking, brandishing weapons, and generally turning my gang rape into their own little *Clockwork Orange*. They must've been partying a little too loudly, for there was suddenly a knock at the door, followed by a woman yoo-hooing. Right away, they all hushed up. One of them clamped his hand over my mouth and dragged me into the closet. He held me there while the other two answered the door. I couldn't hear what was said, but I remember being absolutely terrified. The strange thing is: I was scared of the woman at the door. If she found me, I feared that I would be in trouble. I thought I was the one doing something wrong.

Whatever the men said to the woman, she must have been satisfied because she left. So did they. But not before tying me up, gagging me, and leaving me in the closet. Gary came back a while later. He untied me and let me go to the bathroom then gave me something to eat. This was the ritual at the Revolution Motel. Each morning and night, Gary freed me just long enough to take care of essentials. The crazy thing is: Every night when he came back and untied me, when he took off the gag and the blindfold, and gave me a hamburger, I felt immensely grateful. Even though Gary was the person locking me in the lion's den, his presence was the only thing that made me feel safe and provided relief.

COMING TO TERMS with the slave training and the sex parties and the strange men in motel rooms is all very difficult. But these memories are nothing, *nothing*, compared to my memories of Frank. Frank was a professional pornographer who lived in Manhattan. He worked out of his apartment in an uptown high-rise. Frank's place was big by New York standards, with a den, sunken living room, three bedrooms, and a spiral staircase that led to a loft. Fronting two corners like it did, the place should've been bathed in light. It was always dark, though. In adulthood, I realized this was because every single window was covered by drapes. This was practical. Frank made dirty movies. He didn't want natural light. Or prying eyes.

The first time I went to Frank's, I was nine or ten. Gary dropped me off one weekend with no explanation. I'd had enough slave training by then to understand the game. Frank was to play the master; I was to play the obedient servant. The minute I met him, though, I understood that Frank did not play games. He was a different kind of person than anyone I'd met before—or have met since. Frank was the kind of person one hopes never to meet.

Frank was probably associated with the mob. It's not the way he spoke, looked, or acted that makes me think this—although he certainly resembled the characters in a Martin Scorsese film. Instead, my hunch is based on knowledge of the pornography business circa 1977.

Before the era of free love, pornography was banned by censorship laws. As a result, porn could only be acquired on the black market, a market dominated by organized crime. In the 1960s, the Supreme Court ruled that porn was protected by the First Amendment. Now legal, the pornography business exploded, with adult bookstores, movie theaters, and peep shows providing an ever-increasing variety of product for horny customers. By the early 1970s, pornography had become so profitable for the mob that it was netting an income of approximately $250 million a year—a sum that would be considerably higher today if adjusted for inflation. As pornography became more socially acceptable, hard-core stuff became far more available.

Depictions of bondage, torture, and a wide range of fetishes grew commonplace.

One of the most popular fetishes was pedophilia.

Pedophilia became so popular and accepted in the 1970s that it actually entered the zeitgeist. Child prostitutes were all the rage in films like *Taxi Driver* and *Pretty Baby*. Woody Allen's obsession with young girls, epitomized in *Manhattan*, also reared its ugly head. In the porn world, periodicals like *Lollitots*, *Naughty Horny Imps*, and *Child Discipline*, as well as a plethora of films, offered images of young children performing fellatio, having intercourse, and being gang raped. Remarkably, such merchandise was sold over the counter in Times Square and other cities. In San Francisco, a hard-core kiddie porn festival even ran in a public movie house for five weeks.

The reason child pornography flourished in the 1970s was because, shockingly, there was no federal law to stop it. As a result, child pornography quickly grew into a booming, multimillion-dollar business. By 1977 (the year I met Gary), there were at least 264 different monthly magazines that featured child pornography. The cost for this type of entertainment was high. A typical magazine cost $25 while a short 8-mm film cost $50. Adjusted for today's inflation, these items would cost $89 and $178, respectively. Needless to say, kiddie porn was a very lucrative business.

Because Frank's apartment doubled as a film studio, there was always a lot of activity going on. Various men came in and out to work the lights and cameras, and various people in S/M garb usually seemed to be hanging around. There were always a few pretty (probably underage) girls in the bedrooms. But there were no other kids, and no one seemed to acknowledge the fact that I was only four feet tall.

Life at Frank's involved absolute degradation and authoritarian control. During the day, I worked as an actress, performing whatever perverted sex scene Frank could dream up. This usually involved sex with one or more adult men in one or more positions. I was used to all that. But doing it in front of a crew and a room full of porn actors made the whole thing a thousand times more mortifying.

For the most part, I simply kept my head down and did whatever Frank commanded. I knew it was pointless to resist, so I shut off my thoughts and feelings and did as I was told. One time, though, fear got the better of me.

I was required to do a scene where a male master led me in on a leash. A domme then entered the scene, and the two of them discussed me as if I were a dog about to be bred. I waited on all fours, still held by my master's leash, while the domme went offstage to retrieve her slave. She returned with a man on a leash. Like me, he pretended to be a dog on all fours, but this other dog had on a black leather mask. I don't know why, but the thing scared me to death. I jumped up and backed away, inadvertently ruining the shot. This was the age of expensive film, not cheap video.

Frank was furious. He demanded I get back on the floor.

But I refused. In a ten-year-old's temper-tantrum way, I refused to return to the scene. I doubt I was able to verbalize that the mask was scaring me. Not that it would've mattered. Frank told me to go to his bedroom. So I did and felt relieved.

Not for long. When Frank came into the room, the expression on his face was all business. It was clear that defiance would not be tolerated. Without a word, he hog-tied me and hung me on a hook in his ceiling. For the vast majority of people who have never been hung by their extremities, it's difficult to convey how it feels. The stomach wants to fall to the ground while the arms and legs are being pulled behind the body straight out of the shoulders and hips. Very quickly, the muscles in the thighs and buttocks start to spasm while the shoulders suffer searing pain.

In all my years of slave training, I'd never experienced this particular type of torture. Panicked, I struggled for relief, but it was all in vain. I cried out, and Frank very quickly returned. Silently, he took me off the hook, released the bonds, and left the room. I followed with my tail between my legs. I did the scene where a man in a mask fucks me from behind like we're dogs. I just tuned out everything and did it.

PART II

CONSEQUENCES

For he who loses all often easily loses himself.

—Primo Levi, *If This Is a Man/The Truce*

Scared Selfless

I t's truly astounding what some people are able to endure. Each year more than a million children in the United States are repeatedly neglected, physically abused, and/or sexually abused, yet they get up each morning and go about the business of living life. Victims of domestic violence do the same, as do combat soldiers, refugees, and civilians in war zones. They go to work; they stand in bread lines; they stroll their neighborhoods knowing that at any moment they could very well face pain, dismemberment, death.

According to psychiatrist Judith Herman, author of *Trauma and Recovery: The Aftermath of Violence—from Domestic Abuse to Political Terror,* "The worst fear of any traumatized person is that the moment of horror will recur." For victims of prolonged violence, this fear is realized over and over again. How do victims cope with the sure knowledge that their worst nightmare will return? Simply put, they block out reality. They pretend the truth ain't so. There are many terms used to describe this pretense: *repression, denial, dissociation, doublethink*. While each word may describe a slightly different mental process, they all serve the same purpose: They keep us moving forward and functioning despite our fears.

Fear is an unbearable emotion. No one can stand to feel it. Not for long, anyway. When we are overcome by fear, our bodies instinctively try to combat it through fight or flight. But if circumstances prevent us from throwing punches or running away, we get overwhelmed by terror and freeze up, becoming physically and emotionally petrified. Physiological freezing in the face of fear is inborn and so common that it's the basis of a universal nightmare—the monster is coming to kill us, but we are too terrified to run or scream.

Paralysis also freezes the mind. This is why we usually remember bad events like accidents, disasters, and assaults in slow motion. During trauma, our brain's ability to process information becomes suspended. Our emotions also enter a state of suspended animation. Countless people who have survived accidents, surgeries, and rapes describe the sensation of being whisked out of their bodies and observing the trauma they are suffering with detached calm. The surreal feeling that people experience during trauma is the result of dissociation—a psychological term that describes an altered state of consciousness in which thoughts and sensations are separated from their accompanying feelings. When a person is dissociated, he can witness horrible things and *know* that they are horrible, yet the *feeling* of horror doesn't register. Dissociation of this sort is an ingenious defense mechanism. When we can't fight or flee, our psyche still finds a way to shield us from the full brunt of pain. We become, quite literally, scared out of our minds.

Freezing and dissociation are involuntary responses to terror. But even in the absence of a life-threatening emergency, a person still has an irresistible urge to mentally escape fear. Anyone who has ever sat in a dentist's chair awaiting a root canal knows how hard the mind can work to avoid panic. We hear a drill; our heart starts to pound; and we will our brain to "think happy thoughts." Suddenly, we're taking a mental vacation to a beach in Cabo. And just like that, we've entered a state of altered consciousness.

To a far greater extent, this is exactly what victims do in order to cope with prolonged trauma. They use their minds to create a different reality, one that is less frightening and painful, one that allows them to get through the day. Political prisoners and POWs have often described inducing self-hypnosis and trance states to help them cope with hunger and torture. Likewise, victims of child abuse and domestic violence are notorious for finding ways to repress, deny, or minimize their abuse. Sometimes these efforts are conscious; sometimes they're not. Either way, it's the mind's ability to pretend that allows victims to endure long-term trauma.

While these sorts of mental acrobatics are effective at quelling terror and providing a false sense of safety, they come with a price. Over time, lying to one's self can become a habit. When that happens, the victim can lose sight of reality. In cases where there are other victims present, such as soldiers, prisoners, refugees, and some hostages, victims often rely on one another to maintain a grip on what is real and true. In cases where the victim has no social support, as with battered wives, abused children, and kidnapping victims, the perpetrator's version of reality invariably wins out.

This false reality almost always involves a belief that the perpetrator is good and safe. According to psychiatrist Keith Ablow, victims must adopt this stance because "to maintain one's desperation and grief and rage for many years would be too damaging to the human mind, so the human mind tells itself a story about safety and contentment to safeguard itself."

WHEN I WAS A KID, I would tell myself a story. I told myself that my mom and dad were happily married and that I was their beloved child. In this story, I was a normal little girl from a normal family who had nice, caring parents—the kind of parents who would never hurt their own daughter. I believed so fervently in this fairy tale that I soon thought Gary was my biological father and Lundquist was my real last name. If you asked me about my ancestral heritage, I would tell you that I was Swedish, like Gary, as opposed to the Swiss background of the Brechbills. I was so delusional that I loudly and vehemently talked about my happy family to anyone who would listen. I needed my teachers and classmates to see me as a normal kid so I could see myself that way as well.

In order to maintain this self-deception, though, I had to willfully and repeatedly find a way to block out all the real things that were happening at home. I did this by dissociating—mentally going away anytime anything happened to me that didn't fit my picture of the perfect life. Whenever Gary or the other men abused me, I automatically altered my consciousness. "Normal" Michelle would drift away to her happy place, totally unaware that her body was being used for sex by grown men.

If this is hard to fathom, think about driving long distance, especially at night. Nearly everyone has had the experience of zoning out and missing an exit, then suddenly "waking up" and realizing they've been so engrossed in their thoughts that they forgot they were even driving. Highway hypnosis is a form of dissociation. It demonstrates just how easy it is to get completely lost in a daydream while still performing a vital physical task. The mind has a remarkable ability to divide its consciousness, allowing the psyche to focus its attention on multiple tasks at the same time.

By dissociating during the abuse, I was able to maintain the delusion that I was a normal child living a normal life. I could go to school, socialize with my classmates, and listen to my teachers without dwelling on the horrible things that would happen to me later that night. While in public with Gary, I could act the part of the dutiful daughter unburdened by the knowledge that at home I was really his sex slave.

Leading a double life, though, has consequences—especially when one is not consciously aware of the fact. In time, this duplicity began to manifest in my personality.

Well . . . personalities.

See, I developed more than one.

IT'S HARD TO DESCRIBE what it's like to have multiple personalities, which is technically called dissociative identity disorder. The first thing that comes to most people's minds is *Sybil* or *The Three Faces of Eve*. In books and on screen, alternate personalities are always portrayed as obvious and dramatic. Mild-mannered Norman Bates turns into a cross-dressing killer. Dr. Jekyll turns into the vicious Mr. Hyde. Housewife Tara Gregson turns into just about everybody, from a sexed-up teenager to a beer-drinking good ol' boy. To hear the media tell it, people with multiple personalities are a bunch of gender-confused, sartorially challenged, homicidal nut jobs!

I first realized we multiples had a PR problem about ten years ago. I had just been admitted to a psychiatric hospital because a few of my alternate personalities were running wild. In the ward, I was surrounded by detoxing meth heads, suicidal manic-depressives, and schizophrenics who either pissed in the halls or wore tinfoil on their heads so the government couldn't hear their thoughts.

At breakfast that first day, all the patients shared their stories. The meth head talked blithely about her overdose. The manic-depressive talked proudly of driving her car through the front window of Cartier. But when I simply said I had multiple personalities, the table went silent. Everybody stared at me like I was an alien. Then the schizophrenic who actually thought she *was* an alien said, "Whoa, multiple personalities? That shit freaks me out."

That shit used to freak me out too, which is probably why I didn't even know I had multiple personalities until I was in my early thirties. I'm sure this sounds strange. I mean, how could I *not* know if I was constantly dressing up in outlandish costumes and speaking in altered voices? The thing is: Multiple personalities are not as flamboyant as they seem in movies. Well, not most of the time. In the real world, alternate personalities don't just pop out willy-nilly and announce themselves at the grocery store. That's because alters develop in childhood to protect the main personality from harm. How protective would these personalities be if they constantly drew attention to themselves? So, contrary to Hollywood portrayals, most multiples don't stand out in a crowd. Many have spouses and kids and steady jobs, like football legend Herschel Walker and comedian Roseanne Barr. While their various personalities may appear during the day, the switch is so subtle that others don't notice.

The scary part is that the person with multiple personalities might not notice either. That's because alternate personalities develop without the main (or "host") personality's conscious awareness. People can live for many years without the knowledge that other people live inside them. But that doesn't stop those other people from taking over the body from time to time and running amok. What's worse, some alters are the moral opposite of the goody-two-shoes host. A devout, mousy wife suddenly starts drinking and smoking and shagging every guy in sight. When Suzy Homemaker returns to her own body, she may have no memory of all the naughty things she's done. At best, she'll find a mysterious pack of cigarettes in her purse and feel like she's entered the Twilight Zone. At worst, she'll get an STD, not know where it came from, and be utterly terrified.

Having multiple personalities *is* terrifying. I can tell you firsthand it's awful to "wake up" after a dissociative episode, realize you've lost time, and have amnesia for the things you've done. If little clues appear—a matchbook from an unknown bar or a bus ticket for a faraway city—you rack your brain trying to remember what the hell you've been doing. Was it dangerous? Was it illegal? The uncertainty breeds panic that never subsides because you always fear losing control again. The whole thing makes you feel unbearably crazy, which, technically, you are. It's the stuff of nightmares.

To UNDERSTAND how all of this happens, one must first understand how multiple personalities develop. The generally accepted theory is that they are the result of abuse in childhood. And not just any old abuse. We're talking cruel, consistent, crushing mayhem. On working with multiples, psychiatrist Frank Putnam, author of *Diagnosis & Treatment of Multiple Personality Disorder*, said:

> I am struck by the quality of extreme sadism that is frequently reported by most MPD victims. Bondage situations; the insertion of a variety of instruments into vagina, mouth, and anus; and various forms of physical and sexual torture are common reports. Many multiples have told me of being sexually abused by groups of people, of being forced into prostitution by family members, or of being offered as a sexual enticement to their mothers' boyfriends. After one has worked with a number of MPD patients, it becomes obvious that severe, sustained, and repetitive child sexual abuse is a major element in the creation of MPD.

This does not imply that the abuse has to be sexual. DID can also develop as a result of physical abuse, severe neglect, emotional abuse, or being in an unpredictable, frightening family. What matters is that the situation is "severe, sustained, and repetitive," causing the child victim to repeatedly cope through dissociation. The victim's mind repeatedly "goes away" while the body stays present and functioning—just as happens during highway hypnosis.

In this process, consciousness splits, dividing its attention between the daydreaming "normal" child and the body that is being terrified and hurt. If this happens often enough, the part of consciousness that is being abused begins to develop a tragic personal history—one that is very different than the supposed life of the "normal" child. Identity is nothing more than the sum of our memories. So, in time, the part of consciousness (or parts, as consciousness usually splits multiple times to deal with multiple types of abuse and abusers) that has memories of abuse begins to develop a sense of its own identity—one with thoughts and beliefs and intentions apropos of its traumatic existence. Meanwhile, the "normal" child who "goes away" during the abuse has no awareness that she is being abused or that a dissociative identity is forming. Lost in daydreams whenever bad things happens, she maintains the illusion of the white picket fence.

Dissociation explains why abused children develop multiple personalities. What it can't explain is why those personalities have different names, speak with different accents, claim to be various ages, and may even claim to be different genders than the bodies housing them. To understand this, one must remember that DID always develops in childhood, and children have wonderful imaginations!

According to Rita Carter, author of *Multiplicity*, more than two-thirds of all children use those imaginations to create imaginary companions. These ICs come in a wide array of forms (girls, boys, adults, animals) and display a dizzying array of characteristics (angry, sad, hyper, picky). It's probable the same mechanism that allows children to so brilliantly create imaginary friends who are quite different from themselves also allows children to fashion colorful alternate personalities.

Children are also clearly aware of archetypal figures. For, despite the fact that each child develops multiple personalities on her own, the types of personalities that develop in all people with DID are remarkably similar. Nearly every multiple, for instance, has what is known as a "host" personality. This is the personality that is "out" most of the time and identifies with the information on the person's birth certificate—name, birthday, place of origin, etc. Generally, this host personality has no knowledge of the abuse or the other alters that exist inside. She is dedicated to the delusion that her life is normal. As such, she is most often a traditional, reserved, submissive, "good" girl (or boy, as DID affects both genders in about equal proportions).

On the flip side, nearly every person with DID also has at least one "bad" alter. This bad alter (or alters) is usually the part of consciousness that was present for the abuse, so she knows all about the person's sordid history. Having lived through horrible abuse, this bad alter typically shows the scars. She (or they) is often angry, cynical, suspicious, hard, and promiscuous. In short, she is the absolute opposite of the host personality, whom she usually despises.

In addition to these black-and-white personality types, most personality systems also include child alters of varying ages and genders. There are persecutor types, who rage against the others and are often responsible for suicide attempts. There are helper types, who do everything in their power to help the whole personality system heal. There are also administrator types—emotionless drones who do schoolwork, hold down jobs, and get all the boring business of life accomplished.

DURING MY CHILDHOOD of horrendous abuse, I survived by developing all these types of alters. By scripting a cast of characters who could deal with the abuse, I was able to keep moving forward. I could go to school and make friends unencumbered by the knowledge that I'd be raped and tortured later that night.

This kind of repression, though, comes at a cost. I soon developed some serious physical symptoms. The first notable symptom was headaches—headaches so severe I sometimes thought my head would explode. They started during puberty, right around the time Gary rejected me. I would feel a terrible pressure building up in my head. The pressure made my head feel fuller and fuller until it was an overstretched balloon. Eventually, the balloon grew so big that it popped. At this point, the pressure would dissipate, but portions of my face would become numb. As these headaches worsened over time, they often left one whole side of my face paralyzed, sometimes for a few hours. My parents knew about these headaches; they witnessed my paralyzed face. But despite the seriousness, they never sought medical help.

Another symptom I developed was nosebleeds. I'm not talking about the manageable little nosebleeds kids get once in a while. I'm talking gushers—gushers with so much blood that I would easily go through an entire box of Kleenex. These nosebleeds, which happened nearly every day and often more than once a day, went on well into my teens. In elementary and middle school, I was frequently sent to the nurse, who would try to stop the bleeding with cold compresses. In high school, I became so embarrassed by these unpredictable and unmanageable nosebleeds that I often avoided public events.

Other physical symptoms that I frequently experienced were light-headedness and dizziness. While I can't say for certain what caused all these problems, my best guess is stress. Just living in a house with my cruel parents generated enough stress to cause symptoms. But I think the real stress came from having to hide the sexual abuse and the alternate personalities—even from myself.

IRONICALLY, AT THE SAME TIME that my mind was trying to shield me from the truth, it was simultaneously telling me about it. One way it did this was in the form of daydreams. Daydreams, of course, are a normal occurrence; every child indulges in them. But my daydreams went on for hours unabated, usually for days on end. They were so engrossing that I often lost track of time, forgot where I was, couldn't remember anything that happened to me while I was daydreaming. I'd suddenly find myself going home on the school bus, for instance, and have no recollection of how I'd gotten there. I might not even remember being at school that day at all.

All I remembered was the content of my daydreams—epic fantasies in which I was an unwilling princess forced into an arranged marriage with a cruel prince or a kidnapped prisoner forced to live in a cage while a mad scientist performed horrifying experiments on me. There were several plots, but the theme was always the same: I was physically enslaved by an evil man who used me for his voracious, sadistic whims.

I have since come to understand that these fantasies were my version of "post-traumatic play," a morbid, unchanging type of make-believe in which children repetitively act out traumatic events. Unlike normal play, posttraumatic play goes on for years—well past the time when a child's chronological age suggests it should end.

While an ordinary, untraumatized child probably plays make-believe until the age of twelve, a traumatized child may "pretend" far longer. Personally, my fantasy stories of enslavement, rape, and torture dominated my mental life well into my twenties. Even now, in my forties, I can get lost in these mental plays from time to time.

I also spent much of my life remembering the terrible things that happened to me through "post-traumatic reenactment," a phenomenon familiar to clinicians who work with survivors of trauma. A posttraumatic reenactment involves the compulsion to physically re-create parts of the original horror—as when a war veteran repeatedly roams the streets of a violent neighborhood or a girl with a physically abusive father marries a physically abusive man. In cases like this, the reenactment is completely involuntary; it is beyond the survivor's conscious control or understanding.

From about the age of twelve, I started to do strange things that I didn't understand. I would go to the refrigerator, for instance, in search of large phallic vegetables then stab them into my vagina even though it caused me discomfort. I tied bandannas around my mouth, effectively gagging myself for hours on end. I would take ropes or scarves and tie my ankles and wrists together as best I could, then sit in a dark closet. I would strip naked, lie on my bed, and hold my hands to a headboard, imagining they were tied there.

None of these actions brought me any kind of pleasure—sexual or otherwise. I was reenacting rape. But because of dissociative amnesia, I had no clue what I was doing or why I was doing it. Clearly, my bad girl was trying to send me a message, trying to hint at the abuse. This happened constantly for more than twenty years. My alters, or subconscious mind, habitually left clues about the abuse and dissociation in the form of reenactments, flashbacks, dreams, drawings, and writings. It's as if my mind was slowly and repeatedly feeding me information until, little by little, I was able to accept the whole truth about my life.

MORE SUBTLE PERSONALITY CHANGES were also taking place. Sometime in the seventh grade, as I became more socially aware, I came to the troubling realization that I wasn't very popular. As the host personality, Michelle, I was a shy, quiet, submissive girl. I didn't bring attention to myself and certainly didn't want to be noticed. Then, seemingly overnight, all of that changed. A completely different personality emerged. Suddenly, I was loud, outgoing, and assertive. I stole every opportunity to announce myself to the world. The girl who once hid in corners was suddenly singing on tabletops in the cafeteria. In short, the personality I call Mooch showed up exhibiting traits and characteristics that were completely the opposite of the person I thought of as Michelle.

Later in life, as I learned more about my personality system, I realized that Michelle and Mooch are my two main personalities. They are like twins—of the Arnold Schwarzenegger/Danny DeVito variety! I say this because, in just about every way, they are polar opposites. Michelle is an introverted, submissive homebody who yearns for domestic bliss, whereas Mooch is an extroverted, dominant artist who wants bright lights and big cities. How did these two very different identities develop inside me? My best guess is that when I was a child Gary required me to be different people at different times. At home, he demanded I be quiet and submissive so he could dominate me. Out in the world, though, he insisted I transform into an outgoing, witty performer who could be the star of his drama club. In time, these two ways of being cemented into two different identities who behaved as complete opposites.

The drastic changes in behavior that accompanied the switch in these personalities went unnoticed by my teachers, but they didn't go unnoticed by me. I started to get a sense that there was something very wrong with my personality. I started to get the sense that I had more than one. This was not an explicit thing, mind you. I was only twelve at the time, not old enough to know about dissociation or multiple personalities. I did, however, have a real sense that there were two people living inside of me—an introvert and an extrovert. And, for the life of me, I couldn't figure out which one was really me. I was deeply troubled by this identity crisis and wrote lengthy poems in which I pondered my inauthenticity. One line read:

I wish I could bring myself together, but the two of me divide

Another snippet read:

I was wrong; it was only the beginning
Of a tug-of-war I can never be winning.
One side wants Mooch, happy and gay
The other wants a slave with nothing to say . . .
I can't find myself, and I probably never will.

Another:

I've lost my true identity
It's a big price to pay, I know now.
I'd like to find my real self back, but
How do I do it?
How?
"This isn't me!"
I've shouted time and time in vain.
There are times—frequently now—when I wonder if I'm . . .
insane?

Aside from demonstrating what a terrible poet I was (and am), the personal writings of twelve-year-old me strongly suggest I was already suffering the effects of DID. This is very important evidence, for it flies in the face of skeptics who claim there's no such thing as dissociative identity disorder.

Yeah, that's right. Despite nearly two hundred years of anecdotal and empirical evidence to support the fact that some people develop multiple identities, there's a movement that claims dissociative identity disorder is a bogus diagnosis. The basis for this assertion is the fact that during the '80s—a time when stories of child sexual abuse were all over the news—the number of reported cases of DID shot up exponentially. What was once considered to be an extremely rare condition was suddenly believed to affect tens of thousands of people. (This is very similar to what happened in the '70s and '80s when reported cases of child sexual abuse—the one-in-a-million phenomenon—rose twenty-two-fold.) Rather than accept the simple fact that increased media attention to *any* disorder increases awareness among clinicians and patients and, thus, increases diagnosis, skeptics cried, "Bullshit!" They said the rise in the number of people being diagnosed with DID was the result of overzealous therapists who were implanting the idea of alternate personalities into their unsuspecting patients' heads. (Sound familiar, Dr. Freud?) We patients then supposedly gobbled it up because we're prone to fantasy and highly suggestible (and terribly stupid).

I have no doubt that media stories about multiple personalities contributed to a rise in the diagnosis of DID. It's also safe to assume that the condition may have been overdiagnosed to some extent. But how, exactly, does overdiagnosis suddenly mean the condition itself isn't real? If we accept this logic, then we must also question the validity of every other condition that has seen an exponential increase in diagnosis in the past few decades, including ADHD, autism, bipolar disorder, and erectile dysfunction.

The truth is: Dissociative identity disorder *does* exist. In recent years, neuroimaging has provided fairly irrefutable evidence. Despite this, a quick Google search of the terms *multiple personalities* and *dissociative identity disorder* will reveal that it is still considered an extremely controversial diagnosis. I believe the reason for this has nothing to do with media reports or rising diagnoses. Instead, skepticism of DID is just another way certain people in our society try to discredit, and ultimately silence, victims of child sexual abuse.

A perfect example of this type of hater is "Dr. Fischer" from UrbanDictionary.com, who defines DID as a "dubious diagnosis" in which multiple personality "creation usually involves the suggestion of a sympathetic and charismatic therapist, but it can also occur within groups of 'survivors' on the internet or in self-help groups."

The bad doctor sounds convincing. Except, when I was writing those poems at twelve years old, I hadn't gone to any therapists or self-help groups yet. And in 1980, there was no Internet. I was just a kid expressing how disturbing it felt to be split, to have no sense of a core. This wasn't due to fantasy or suggestion or a desire for "sympathy/attention associated with the victim role," as Dr. Fischer claims.

This was due to Gary Lundquist and his pervert cronies.

This was due to their "severe, sustained, and repetitive" child sexual abuse.

This was due to years of terror and torture.

It scared the self out of me.

Tommy, Can You Hear Me?

Needless to say, being an eighth-grade sex slave with a pathological identity crisis does not make for a happy kid. Despite being fairly successful in school and extracurriculars, I felt unlikable, stupid, worthless. Good grades and compliments from teachers didn't register. How could they? In every situation, I felt like I was playing a role—the good girl, the extrovert, the student. Anytime I received positive feedback, it felt like the kudos were directed at my performance, not me. There was no me. And you can't build self-esteem or self-confidence if you have no sense of self.

Meanwhile things were unbearable at home. If I wasn't neglected, I was treated with utter contempt. When I was on the phone with a friend, Gary ridiculed my laugh and the sound of my voice, saying it resembled a "high-pitched chipmunk." I was regularly called "stupid . . . retarded . . . lazy . . . liar . . . slut." Feeling hurt and unjustly treated, I often broke down sobbing and wailing in desperation. I wanted comfort and kind words to soothe my hysteria. Instead, I was accused of being "overly emotional" and "manipulative." Gary said I was just trying to "get attention," so he ignored me. He also frequently said I had a difficult personality and that no one would ever love me.

Over the years, when I've shared my story, it's often met with disbelief. To some extent, I can understand that the sexual abuse I suffered is inconceivable. What shocks me, though, is people's reaction to verbal and emotional abuse. I once wrote a play that featured everyday conversations from my childhood. There was nothing about sexual abuse; the play featured a run-of-the-mill dysfunctional family. I was disturbed and angered when theater after theater told me the dialogue was "unbelievable" and "over the top." Many of the scenes were taken from my life verbatim!

Anna Karenina opens with the line "All happy families are alike; each unhappy family is unhappy in its own way." With all due respect to Tolstoy, I don't think that's true. I've counseled many people from toxic families and find that verbal and emotional abuse is almost always the same. There's lots of anger, contempt, and ridicule. Unbridled name-calling. Character assassination. The bullies in unhappy families have a total disregard for anyone's feelings, and they're in continuous competition to see who can use words and actions to inflict the most pain. Think *Who's Afraid of Virginia Woolf?* with 2.5 miserable kids, the living room a minefield of injurious words.

Those lucky enough to grow up in less lethal environments might have a hard time being able to comprehend how parents who are supposed to love their children can act so harshly. But the many, many people from venomous families understand exactly how I grew up. Insults, accusations, and callous cruelty marked my daily life. The life of my good girl, that is.

My bad girl was still being prostituted to men on a constant basis. But due to dissociation and amnesia, my host personality had no awareness of the abuse I endured. One of the strange things about dissociative amnesia: You don't have to be aware of the abuse to suffer its effects. And I did suffer. Terribly. The sexual abuse, a horrid home life, and an identity disorder created a perfect shit storm of misery. I felt detached, dirty, depressed. Filled with shame and self-loathing. I felt utterly alone, which I was. There wasn't a single person in my life to protect me. I was completely unloved.

I DID HAVE a soul mate, though. In my loneliness, I found *Tommy* by The Who. *Tommy* is a full-length rock opera about a boy who experiences trauma. After witnessing a murder, the young boy is instructed by the perpetrators (his parents) to block out the memory and pretend he didn't see or hear anything. Tommy represses the awful memory, but it takes a toll on his psyche. He becomes a blind deaf mute, and retreats into a dissociative state that resembles a coma. In this weakened mental state, Tommy falls prey to evil family members. His sadistic cousin tortures him, while his pedophile uncle molests the boy.

Tommy is an opera about trauma and its effects. Tommy is horrified by the murder, making him susceptible to his mother's suggestion to develop amnesia about the event. The physical symptoms he suffers are a classic case of conversion disorder, a psychiatric diagnosis that is closely linked to dissociation. In conversion disorder, patients "convert" their anxiety and unacceptable memories into physical symptoms.

For reasons that are obvious now, *Tommy* resonated with me. At the time, though, dissociative amnesia prevented me from under-standing why I felt so connected to this character. I believe my fasci-nation with *Tommy* was an early indication that my mind was trying to right itself by revealing things about trauma and dissociation to my consciousness. I wasn't strong enough to face the full truth of my life back then; the shame would've killed me. Still, I couldn't get enough of the album. I played it over and over again in the darkness of my bedroom, feeling the pain in every verse.

See me
Feel me
Touch me
Heal me

Tommy was lonely and isolated, abused and unloved. He had dark family secrets to hide. Nobody understood Tommy's real pain. No-body but me.

As I look back, it seems clear that I was depressed. At the time, though, I didn't have a name for anything that was happening to me. All I felt was confusion and unbearable pain. I desperately needed help. I wanted someone to talk to, but no one seemed to care. It felt like no one gave a damn if I lived or died.

THESE FEELINGS WERE HEIGHTENED in the winter of 1982 when, at the age of thirteen, I got pregnant. I don't know by whom. Con-doms were never used when I turned tricks, and I wasn't on any kind of birth control. So it could've been anyone. I'm not sure how far along I was when Gary figured it out. All I know is: One day that winter, I fainted. It was out of the blue and something that had never happened to me before. For Gary, I assume, it was a tip-off. I don't remember any pregnancy test, nor do I remember any queries about the frequency of my periods. (That's not to say these things didn't happen. Again, because of the dissociative amnesia I suffered, there are aspects of my childhood I still can't recall.)

What I have always remembered, quite vividly, is waking up one morning to a nightgown full of blood. Horrified, I tried to get out of bed but fell to the floor instead. I tried to stand up, only to realize I was too weak. Meanwhile, I became aware of the fact that I was bleeding heavily from my vagina, but I had no idea why. Clearly, something had happened to me the night before. But because of the dissociation, I had no recollection of it. I woke up that morning as the good girl—the girl who didn't know she was being sexually abused. Thus, I truly had no idea what was happening to me.

Concerned about the blood and the mess it was making, I some-how managed to crawl across the living room into the kitchen. I pulled a Ziploc bag out of a cabinet, then made my way back to my room. All the while, I felt faint and weak. Back in my bedroom, I propped myself up against a wall, put the Ziploc bag between my legs, and watched in horror as it filled with blood clots. Overcome with shame and disgust, I didn't want to tell my parents. The blood wouldn't stop, though. I was terrified.

Ultimately, I decided that I had no choice but to seek help from my parents, who were both in my father's home office. To do this, I had to crawl across the living room again. But I was weaker by then and starting to lose consciousness. By the time I got to my parents, I was as white as a ghost and could not stay conscious for more than a few minutes. I didn't tell my parents about the hemorrhaging, al-though my mother could see the blood on my nightgown. I told her I was having my period. She got me cleaned up and dressed, then drove me to the local country doctor, an old man with an examination room in his basement. During the examination, I fainted again. When it came time to give a urine sample, I was so weak that my mother had to hold me over the toilet bowl. Blood poured into the plastic cup along with the pee, but my mother explained this to the doctor as menses. After providing my blood pressure and a urine sample, my mother drove me home. Still too weak to walk, I missed school for more than a week.

My mother attributed the whole incident to hypoglycemia, claiming that this was the doctor's diagnosis. Meanwhile, I continued to secretly collect blood clots in Ziploc bags for another full day. I was so scared by the bleeding that I eventually confessed it to Gary. It might seem strange that I would confide in him instead of my mother, but this is the nature of dissociation. While my conscious mind didn't know why I was bleeding, my subconscious mind knew Gary was the cause.

Over the years, there were several times when I sought Gary's help for physical problems related to the abuse, all the while having no conscious recognition of the abuse or Gary's part in it. I would tell him of various contusions or lesions on my genitals. He would then have me disrobe and lie on a bed so he could examine me and perhaps apply some type of medicine. These were murky times for my psyche. My good girl was having her genitals examined by her father—a father she had no idea abused her. Yet somehow denial kept the strangeness of the situation at bay. As I look back, these murky times provide clear evidence that Gary knew about my dissociation and used it to his advantage.

When I told him about the bleeding, for instance, he knew damn well what was happening and why. But my very asking meant that *I* didn't know, that somehow I had blocked out a major event that had happened just a few nights before. So when my good girl worriedly said, "Daddy, I keep bleeding down there," and showed him the Ziploc bags, his response was not to speak of an ended pregnancy. Instead, Gary asked me if I ever put my fingers *down there*. Ashamed, I admitted that I did. My father told me that the bleeding was caused by my own masturbation. This frightened me so badly that my good girl didn't put anything down there for years. Instead, I went on believing that masturbation causes hemorrhaging and that\I was hypoglycemic well into my college years.

Later, as my dissociative amnesia eased and I began to regain my memory, I realized that the bleeding had been caused by a homemade abortion. I remembered my father sitting at the head of our dining-room table while I lay there watching him untwist a wire coat hanger. I distinctly remember him explaining the procedure to me and showing me how the hanger had to be bent on the end just so.

Ten years later, I would be the one demonstrating how to prepare a coat hanger as I sat across a table from Gary, my mother, and our lawyers at a deposition for a civil case I initiated against my parents.

During that deposition, I got the opportunity to review the country doctor's records from that bloody morning. He noted the blood in my urine, my exceptionally pale skin, and the fact that I had fainted during the examination. He also noted my dangerously low blood pressure, which, in a fainting thirteen-year-old, should have been cause for great alarm. There was no mention of hypoglycemia. I don't know what the doctor thought was going on, nor do I know if he suggested that my mother take me to the emergency room.

All I know is: I'm lucky to be alive.

———

AT THE TIME, I didn't feel so lucky. I felt nothing but despair. With no relief in sight and no hope of a better future, I got it in my head that I wanted to die.

Suicidality is common among adolescents and adults who have been abused as children. For those who have never contemplated it, I'm sure that taking one's own life is hard to fathom. It goes against our basic animal instincts as human beings. DNA programs us, above all, to fight for survival. Suicidal people are no different in this regard. Personally and professionally, it's been my experience that suicidal people very much want to live. What they don't want is to be in pain. They see suicide as the only way out.

No one wakes up one morning and decides to kill himself on a whim. Suicide is the solution to a problem, usually a long-standing and dire one. Whether the problem is physical (chronic pain, illness), financial (debt, job loss), social (loneliness, loss), emotional (depression, anxiety), or a combo platter, the suicidal person feels like they have run out of options. They no longer have hope that things can improve.

That's how I kind of felt after the abortion. I say "kind of" because I was on the fence. While there's no doubt I was lonely, isolated, and morbidly depressed, deep down I was still looking for someone to save me. I think a lot of people with suicidal tendencies are like that—at least in the beginning.

In my attempt to find a rescuer, I wasn't shy about sending up flares. At school, I wrote endless dark and brooding poems that weren't subtle.

One untitled poem reads:

My life is not all that I want it to be.
The pressures . . . are too much for me.
I can't help feeling that life must cease
to get that feeling of true, true peace.
Life for me is a burden to bear.
Does anyone care? . . .
I am at the edge of the deep, blue sea.
I can take the final plunge,
and that's what scares me.

Dropping the not-so-sophisticated metaphors, a poem called "The Last Night" reads:

The only way to escape the pressure is to commit—
Suicide.
I want to die.
I cannot deny . . .
I want someone to touch me.
I want someone to hear me.
I want someone to feel me . . .
I'm Tommy, hidden from everyone.
There's no one here to save me now . . .
I really don't have a reason to live . . .
There's no use in pretending.
It's a pre-death note I'm sending . . .
I can't take my life much more . . .
I've reached
The End.

My state of mind was obvious, and in sharing my writing with friends and teachers, I was desperately trying to be heard. Most suicidal people do this; they make the proverbial "cries for help." I did so particularly loudly. In art class, I drew pictures of tombstones, knives, and nooses. In music class, I sang angst-filled songs. I glued pictures of celebrities who had killed themselves to the front of my notebook. But no one seemed very concerned with a morbid eighth grader. Not friends. Not teachers. I never got sent to the guidance counselor or the school psychologist or anything like that.

There's a saying: "People who talk about suicide don't kill themselves." It's entirely false. Most people who attempt suicide talk about it quite a lot beforehand, either indirectly ("Sometimes I wish I'd never been born.") or directly ("I want to kill myself."). I think the problem for would-be helpers is that they don't know what to do. What's more, suicide is taboo. Like rape and sexual abuse, it's not the sort of thing we discuss in polite company. So, feeling uncomfortable and put-upon, bystanders too often choose to ignore the signs.

When I was in high school, I wrote an autobiographical essay about suicide for an English class. It says, "For the first time, I knew of an alternative to all of life's problems—death . . . SUICIDE—it sounds so powerful. It's so glorious, yet so final . . . Once you've experienced anything suicidal, life's already over . . . Anyone who knows suicide is already lying in the pine box." Pretty alarming stuff, but rather than ask to speak with me about this very disturbing piece (or the many other pieces about depression and death that I penned), the teacher chose to critique my prose.

"Somewhere," she wrote, "your piece is misleading to the reader. You start out with this thing about popularity . . . then you move to this friend and are sort of vague . . . then you talk about suicide." I was fifteen years old and expressing a barely shrouded wish to die. Yet this teacher didn't talk to me. She didn't send me to a guidance counselor or the school psychologist or *do anything*. Yet I'm sure that if I'd actually killed myself, she would've been one of the many people saying, "How tragic! If only I'd known!"

What chance do abused, neglected, and/or depressed teenagers have if their own teachers ignore direct pleas for help?

Suicide is the third leading cause of death among kids aged ten to fourteen, and the second among teens and young adults. From personal experience, I can easily see why. In the early 2000s, I began teaching English at an inner-city high school in Los Angeles. The first essay I assigned was a piece about the students and their lives. Most of the stories involved run-of-the-mill stuff about parents, siblings, and teenage love. A few, though, revealed depression and even abuse. Concerned, I told a seasoned teacher who trained all of us newbies. She was well aware of the serious troubles facing many of the students. "That's why I never assign anything autobiographical," she said. "Then I don't have to deal with it."

No ONE WANTED to deal with me or my feelings. Not my friends, not my teachers, and certainly not my parents. At home, I showed ample signs of depression—sitting in a darkened room for hours every day listening to *Tommy* over and over again. I wasn't trying to hide my emotions. On the contrary, just like most depressed and troubled teens, I pulled out all the stops to gain my parents' attention. I didn't really want to die back then. What I wanted more than anything was love. My parents' love. I was still young and naïve enough to believe gaining their love was possible.

All the signals in the world, though, don't mean shit if no one's around to see them. Gary was always out and about with his new child bride. And my mother was gone. This was during the time she left home indefinitely to tend to my dying grammy. I felt abandoned and completely alone.

Once summer came, life got worse. I had nowhere to go and no one to see. The isolation was staggering. With nothing to do from morning till night, I wallowed in depression, spending most days in my pitch-black bedroom. I was a copious diary keeper during this time, leaving a permanent daily record of my worsening mental condition. It shows the struggle and obsessiveness that mark depression and suicidality.

July 4, 1982:

Today at 1:00 pm I don't know if I really would have done it, but I had a knife & was thinking suicide. I just layed in my room and it was totally dark . . . I couldn't even figure out why I was so depressed . . .

July 6, 1982:

Once again I'm thouroughly depressed. It seems sort of scary to only ever think about suicide. I have good reasons though. It would save me a lot of grief to just be dead.

July 10, 1982:

All I think about is suicide and remembering Pete [a boy I liked] *is the only thing that keeps me from it.*

July 11, 1982:

I don't know what's wrong with me. I realized today, when my mom pointed it out, that I'm not good for anything and don't care about anything either. There's only one thing I care about & remembering him stops me from taking the knife out of the drawer.

July 12, 1982:
Suicide frightens me.

July 14, 1982:

I had the knife out and had started to cut my . . . I'm not sure if I would have gone all the way. I might have just stopped after a little blood . . . I still want to die. I feel funny like God's watching me. The knife's in my drawer. It's gonna be a long night.

Around this time, my diary indicates that I traveled with Gary to work at some mall shows. While at one of the malls, I bought a bottle of over-the-counter sleeping pills. I got the idea after watching a documentary on Marilyn Monroe; it said she committed suicide via sleeping pills. In the age before Google searches, I didn't realize that lethal sleeping pills require a prescription. I fully expected these would do the trick.

On August 4—just four days after returning home—I closed the door to my darkened bedroom, put a cassette in my tape recorder, and opened the bottle of pills. In the darkness of my room, I listened to *Tommy* while I swallowed one pill. Then I turned on the tape deck and recorded my feelings for posterity—my version of a suicide note. I waited one hour then took the next pill. Waited another hour, swallowed number three. I'm not sure why I chose to take the pills in such a tentative way. I suppose I was scared and ambivalent. After the first few pills, though, I loosened up. By the time evening fell, I was downing three or four an hour. I did this well into the night.

At some point, my father came home, but he didn't bother to check on me. Not that he would've noticed much. I mean, it was nighttime, and I was lying in bed. I drifted in and out of sleep, but it was nothing like the deep nothingness I had expected. If anything, I felt jittery. My heart was pounding fast; I was sweating a lot. By the next morning, it was clear that my dramatic scene had not played out as planned. There was no unconsciousness, no discovery of my limp body, no rush to the hospital by hysterical, regretful parents who would finally realize the error of their ways. Just me, lying on my bed in a dark bedroom. Nearly a whole bottle of sleeping pills and nothing had changed.

I grabbed the bottle and counted out the remains. Still six left. I went to the kitchen to refill my glass of orange juice. It was already midmorning by then. Gary had left hours earlier for his store. In all the time he was home, he'd never bothered to check on me or say hello. Had the pills been more potent, my suicidal gesture would have become a completed suicide out of sheer neglect. I quickly downed the remaining pills. The fifty-count bottle was now empty. Pale and clammy, I felt like my heart would bust through my skin. It was scary. I picked up the phone and called my friend Pete. He got his mom.

Calmly, Pete's mom asked to speak with my parents. I told her they weren't around, so she promised to come right over. When she arrived, the look on her face was pure kindness. I didn't know this woman well, but from everything I'd seen, she was a nice, normal mom. She asked how I was feeling, then wiped my sweaty face with a washcloth. At first, I was embarrassed, but within a few minutes, I was basking in the unfamiliar warmth of maternal attention.

I would've liked Pete's mom to stay with me. Instead, she insisted on calling my father. His store didn't have a phone, so the operator had to give her the number for a hot-dog stand nearby. The hot-dog guy fetched Gary and put him on the line. Pete's mom (who didn't really know my father) was very brief. She simply said I'd swallowed a bottle of sleeping pills but seemed to be all right. Then she asked if he would please come home and take care of me.

About forty-five minutes later, my father burst through the front door in a panic. He grabbed me by the chin, lifted up my head, and scoured my face for information. I'm sure Pete's mom assumed he was a scared father concerned for my health. I knew different. Gary's fear had nothing to do with my well-being. He didn't give a shit if I lived or died. He was panicked to have a stranger at home with his unstable daughter. God only knows what I might tell her.

My father ordered me to grab the empty bottle and get in the car. As I reluctantly crawled into his Pacer, I noticed him shaking hands with Pete's mom as she got into her car. Oh, how I wished she would get into mine! I was terrified to be alone with Gary, terrified of what he would do to me for embarrassing him. The drugs hadn't killed me, but he just might!

I don't remember anything about that car ride, but I do remember arriving at the emergency room. My father herded me through the automatic doors and pointed to a plastic chair with the unspoken order to sit down and keep my mouth shut. He went to the nurses' station to check me in, handing them the empty plastic bottle.

Within a few minutes, I was lying on a gurney in a room with sheets for walls, terrified the doctors were going to pump my stomach.

My father said they would; he also said it would hurt. A lot. But then a handsome young doctor arrived to appease my fears. He was very kind and gentle, and made me feel safe. Better yet, he said no pumping was required.

Instead, I was held for a few hours of observation. After that, I was released back into my father's care. There was no social worker, no psych intern, no one to ask me why I took the pills. Apparently, the person they asked was my father. He said my suicide attempt was a juvenile bid to gain Pete's affection. The hospital suggested I see an outpatient therapist, and an appointment was made for the following week.

AT FOURTEEN, I didn't know much about therapists. The only time I even heard the word *therapist* was from my neighbor Maria, a foster child with anorexia. Her social worker made her see a therapist—some fat lady, according to Maria, who sat on the floor of her office and burned incense. Maria pointed her out to me once when we were walking down Main Street. The woman had long brown hair, baggy clothes, and seemed, well, weird. Still, before my suicide attempt, the thought of having a therapist to share my feelings with had been intriguing.

By the time Gary drove me to the appointment, however, all that had changed. I had staged my suicide attempt in the hope of getting my parents to notice me—and Gary sure did. But not in the way I intended. Instead of evoking his sympathy, my cry for help only raised his ire. He made it very clear that if I chose to attempt suicide in the future, I had better fucking succeed. So much for the adolescent delusion that I could scare my parents into caring about me.

When I showed up for my first therapy session a few days later, the whole idea of talking about my feelings seemed pointless. Nevertheless, the appointment had been made, so Gary and I sat side by side in the waiting room staring silently at the clock. I don't know what Gary was thinking during that wait, but I have to imagine he was pretty damned nervous. It can't be fun dragging your child sex slave to a shrink. Even though I had been well trained, there was no telling what I might say. Still, to his credit, Gary did all he could to control the situation. Before I went into the session, he insisted on speaking to the therapist privately. He also made it clear that he expected a debriefing from the therapist after every session.

As the parent of a minor—and the guy footing the bill—Gary was entitled to this. That's one of the problems with treating kids; there's no confidentiality.

So, before I ever stepped foot in my first psychotherapy office, it was obvious that I shouldn't tell the therapist shit. Not that it mattered. I didn't want to talk anymore.

The guy who came to get me was a short middle-aged man. I can't remember his name anymore, but I vividly remember his office. It was smaller than a walk-in closet, with the decorative panache of a storage shed. I don't recall much of what transpired during that first session. I do remember that we talked about the suicide attempt. He asked me point-blank why I wanted to die.

"I don't want to die," I told him. "I just did it 'cause I wanted attention."

"Oh, c'mon," he said. "That's a cop-out."

The guy was right, of course. But at that moment in time, I couldn't see it. I wasn't capable of seeing much of anything. And since successful therapy requires a willing patient, this go-round was doomed from the start.

I don't know if this fellow was a good therapist or not. Right away, though, I didn't like him. He asked me a question then questioned my answer.

Who the hell was he to tell me how I felt?

Later in the session, the guy's tone changed. He lightened up and tried to act chummy in that lame way adults sometimes talk to kids. He was trying to connect with a difficult teenager, which is nearly impossible and certainly can't be done in fifty minutes. There was something about his tone and his phony teenage demeanor that felt like he was making fun of me.

There were a lot of presumptions going on—the presumption that he knew how I felt, that it was okay to joke with me, that we shared some kind of instant intimacy. This is all standard operating procedure for a therapist, but it won't work on a patient who doesn't want help. Nothing does.

After the session, Gary went in for his debriefing. The same scene replayed for a few more weeks. At the end of the fourth session, I told my father I wasn't depressed anymore and didn't need a shrink. He gladly agreed.

Thus ended my first go at psychotherapy.

But it wouldn't be my last.

Not. Even. Close.

Rebel Without a Core

While my cry for help didn't make Gary any nicer, it still had a big effect. It brought my mother back from Maryland. Life changed markedly for me after that. Since my mom had quit her job when she left, upon her return she was unemployed and home 24/7. Her presence made it impossible for Gary to whisk me off to motels. So, after nearly six years, my involvement with the ring finally ended.

As for the depression, I abruptly decided after my suicide attempt that there was no point in having feelings. So I boxed up my sadness, my anger, my loneliness, my angst and filed them away deep inside my psyche—right next to the box marked BAD MEMORIES. This was not a process. It didn't happen gradually over time. After two years of ever-darkening depression, one day I simply said to myself, "I'm not going to be depressed anymore." And I wasn't. Just like that.

If this sounds fishy, it is. It's a classic example of the denial of feelings. Harmful pathological stuff in most cases. During prolonged trauma, however, denying one's feelings can be beneficial and adaptive. What's the point of focusing on how rotten life is if you can't do anything to change it?

I was stuck with Gary and my mother. By way of youth, I was held captive in a house of physical, emotional, and verbal cruelty. Sometimes I thought about running away. But I'd met enough runaways during my time in the ring to know that was a dead end.

At the tender age of fourteen, I already knew I wanted more from life. I wanted a rewarding career with decent pay, a nice house in a pleasant neighborhood, interesting friends, some kind of family. Most of all, I wanted to be *happy*. From my perspective, that meant being *normal*. Kids from normal families went away to prestigious four-year colleges. So I set my sights on achieving that goal. Instinctively, I understood that college was not only the best way to escape my parents, it was also the only means to rise above my circumstances. I didn't just want out; I wanted out and *up*.

It was with this mind-set that I started high school.

FINALLY AWAY FROM Gary's omnipresent gaze and surrounded by several thousand new faces, I seized the opportunity to reinvent myself. Every adolescent does this to some extent. Teenagers are biologically wired to ask, *Who am I?* In response, most will try on several different identities—the Jock, the Stoner, the Nerd—before settling on how they see themselves. The identity that the teen eventually settles on is usually a blend of both internal and external influences.

A seventeen-year-old may describe himself, for instance, as an "outgoing, funny nerd who's good at math." Once that identity has been formed in adolescence, the brain rewires itself accordingly, allowing the person to have a stable sense of himself for the rest of his life.

Having multiple personalities, though, screws all of this up. As a teenager, when I asked *Who am I?* confusing answers came back. I was outgoing or introverted, funny or serious, a good student or a bad student. I was polar opposites on just about everything, depending on which of my personalities was "out" at the time.

This is the nature of dissociative identity disorder. Because alternate personalities are basically fragments of one whole personality, they tend to develop extreme all-or-nothing traits. An angry alter, for instance, is always angry. She will appear when hostility is called for. When the situation changes, my angry alter doesn't grow calm. She simply goes away. Instantaneously, another alter emerges—one with the feelings, skills, and background necessary for the situation at hand.

Being a multiple feels a lot like being an actor who is always on stage. Depending on the needs of the scene, my psyche casts me in various roles. Frequently, this makes me seem moody and unstable. In the morning, when one personality is out, I'm shy. By lunch, when another comes out, I'm the life of the party. Yes, yes, I know. Everyone feels more or less outgoing at times. But I'm not talking about gradations here. I never feel more or less of anything. If I'm shy, it feels like I've always been and will always be shy. Two hours later, when I'm outgoing, I can't conceive of what being shy might feel like.

Everything about me—my feelings, traits, behaviors, goals, memories, preferences—can change completely with each personality. One morning I'll crave scrambled eggs. The next morning I'll hate eggs and claim that I have hated them all my life. (This drives my wife nuts, as she does most of the cooking.) Nowadays, since I don't black out when my personalities switch, I can remember that I ate eggs the day before. Still, my mind-set tells me I hate eggs, and it's inconceivable that I ever stomached them.

Now that I'm aware of my DID and have had considerable therapy, I'm able to notice when my personalities change, and to a certain extent, I can control them. My condition is greatly exacerbated by stress, which I try to monitor. As a teenager, though, I had no awareness of my dissociation or alternate personalities, and my home life kept me in a relentless state of anxiety. As a result, my personalities switched constantly, leaving classmates baffled. In first period, I might profess my undying allegiance to a friend. By fourth period, I'd stare at her coldly in the hallway as if she were my worst enemy. Two hours later, on the school bus, I'd be chummy again—and wonder why my friend was mad at me.

Despite all the craziness, my host personality, Michelle, attempted to define herself in adolescence. Holding traditional values, she reinvented herself as the Preppy—an identity gleaned almost entirely from *The Official Preppy Handbook,* a best seller at the time. It was a joke book poking fun at WASPs, but Michelle didn't know that. She thought it was a how-to manual for achieving all the things she wanted—happiness; prosperity; a traditional, normal life. Suddenly, as Michelle, I donned headbands, kilts, and crocodile shirts. Not unusual. Everybody at my school was doing that in the early '80s. But I also donned an upper-crust East Coast accent and started calling my mother Mummy. Instead of being from my Podunk town, I started thinking I was from the posher Princeton, which was about fifteen miles away. If a person didn't know better, I would actually claim to live in Princeton. And just as my mind could deceive itself into believing that my parents were actually married and Gary was my biological father, it accepted this lie as well.

Embodying this personality required blatant fronting and deplorable social climbing. So what? The Preppy personality was beneficial for me. As I pored over the pages of the *Preppy Handbook*, I got an education in how to dress, act, and think like a higher-class person—a person who seemed normal to me. It was the Preppy who decided she must go to a good college. It was the Preppy who pooh-poohed would-be downfalls like drugs and promiscuity. The Preppy believed one must secure a good profession and a good marriage. I was taught none of these values through my family, which goes to show the importance of a teenager's milieu. Had I grown up in an urban environment like Queens, I probably would've become the Punk, embraced antiestablishment values, dropped out of school, and gotten into drugs, which would have led to a very different life.

Aside from suicidality, I never fell prey to overtly self-destructive behaviors. I didn't sleep around, never did drugs, wasn't a cutter, or anything like that. This was largely due to DID, which protected me from excesses. When naughty alters came out to smoke, drink, troll for men, or get into other mischief, my psyche quickly switched to a goody-two-shoes personality like the Preppy. Most of the time, this kept me out of serious trouble.

My feelings, though, had to come out somewhere. As I was unable to express my unhappiness in obvious ways, my emotional outbursts became more subversive in high school. For one thing, I started stealing. Not big stuff. Small stuff like sheet music, books, pens. One time I found a nice new backpack sitting on the curb. Inside were gym clothes and a pair of pristine Nikes. I didn't need these things. I already had a backpack and sneakers. Still, I took the bag home. What's more, in my clueless state, I wore the stuff to school the next day. A girl on the bus spotted me; she asked if I'd found the items. "No," I lied. "This stuff's mine."

The girl got flustered and explained that she'd lost the bag the day before. "That *exact* backpack with those *exact* sneakers inside," she insisted.

"Well, I don't know what to tell you." I shrugged. "My parents bought me this stuff."

The girl complained to the bus driver, who also questioned me. I stuck to my story with blasé conviction. The bus driver frowned and told the girl that without proof there was nothing she could do. The girl started to cry. She was frustrated, I guess, but I didn't mind. I mean, if she cared about her shit so much, she should've put her name on it.

I know that sounds callous, but that's how I was back then. I'd lie or cheat or steal without conscience if I thought I could get away with it. When I got caught—as I did after cheating on an assignment or stealing from various employers—I didn't feel guilty. I felt persecuted. To me, stealing and cheating were justified. I had a right to even the playing field by screwing the world over just the same as it screwed me.

Here's a warning about little kids from messed-up families: One day they grow up. And all that shit they seemed impervious to, all that crap that supposedly rolled off their backs, is gonna come back with a vengeance. Parents who put their kids through messy divorces or complicated stepfamilies or alcoholic spouses or any manner of upheaval love to be in denial about this. "It was a horrible custody battle," a mother will say. "But little Timmy's just fine. It hasn't affected him. Kids are so resilient!"

To these delusional statements, I always have the same response: "Just wait till the kid turns thirteen." I've seen it time and time again; children seem to weather divorces, new stepfamilies, alcoholic parents, and abuse with little reaction. Then in middle school all hell breaks loose, and every bad parenting decision comes back to bite Mom and Dad in the ass. This is when the acting out starts. Drinking. Drugs. Promiscuity. Formerly good students start flunking out of school. Formerly docile kids grow moody.

On the other end of the spectrum, some kids become hyper-responsible, turning into rigid, perfectionistic control freaks. Cutting, eating disorders, and kleptomania all generally begin in these years, as does a proclivity for violence.

While not every teenage rebellion can be blamed on a bad childhood, serious problems are often a delayed response to earlier trauma. The delay happens because as kids reach adolescence their brains undergo a big shift in cognitive development. Unlike children, teens are able to think and reason abstractly. This allows them to analyze situations in ways they weren't able to before. Suddenly, they are able to reason, think hypothetically, and grasp cause and effect. They also gain the ability to reflect on their lives. Becoming introspective, adolescents are able to see for the first time how traumatic childhood experiences adversely affected them. And just like that, an angry teen emerges.

I was an angry teenager. But like most troubled kids, I was unable to effectively express my ire to the people who had wronged me. Instead, I felt rage toward the whole world. I hated everyone—my parents, every adult who never helped me, every kid who didn't recognize my pain. I especially hated people my own age who seemed to come from normal families. I resented how their parents gave them love and attention and support, how life was so fucking easy for them.

In my experience, most kids who don't feel enough love and nurturance carry around this kind of inner rage—a rage that often lasts throughout adulthood. The people who should have cared for them didn't. The lesson to take away: All people are shit. This is why troubled youth walk around with chips on their shoulders and why they are so hard to help.

Early on, they learned that people can't be trusted. They often spend the rest of their lives embracing this damaging belief. Seeing the world through shit-colored glasses, they are hypersensitive to every possible slight or judgment, and they believe anyone friendly or kind must have an ulterior motive. How does one ever find help or love with this mind-set? Possible helpers are viewed with suspicion and ultimately pushed away. This reinforces the notion that no one will ever care enough. "People are shit" becomes a self-fulfilling prophecy.

Despite all this, wounded people desperately want and need love. But, terrified to trust, they constantly do things to test and sabotage their relationships. This push-pull dance is well-known to anyone who's ever been close to a victim of abuse, neglect, or abandonment. In its most extreme form, it's the hallmark feature of borderline personality disorder (BPD), a diagnosis that describes people who routinely have "intense, unstable, and conflicted close relationships, marked by mistrust, neediness, and anxious preoccupation with real or imagined abandonment." Those who suffer from BPD are hypersensitive to perceived slights from others and can grow notoriously hostile when they feel dissed. Within the mental health field, borderline patients have a reputation for being particularly hard to treat because they come off as demanding, manipulative, and difficult. Underneath all the shenanigans, though, is primal pain. Like a wounded animal on the side of the road, the person with BPD lashes out self-protectively at anyone who tries to help.

While I never suffered a full-blown case of BPD, I definitely had a hard time with relationships. I didn't trust people. At all. But back then I didn't know it. How can you know you're missing something if you don't know what that something is? Desperately wanting a normal life, I started out high school pursuing the usual goals of adolescence. I tried to make friends, get good grades, participate in extracurricular activities.

In the beginning, things seemed to work out. I got into honors classes, earned the leads in school plays, and gained acceptance to elite musical groups. As a result, I became well known and had my pick of friends.

But every success in every arena always ended badly. Usually, this was because someone made me feel slighted or hurt, and I lashed out—often at my own expense. For instance, I befriended two girls, and the three of us had great fun. We went shopping together, hung out at one another's houses, and sat together at lunch. These were kind and caring girls; neither ever acted maliciously toward me.

One day, one of the girls referred to the other as her "best" friend. It was an offhand comment, certainly not meant to cause harm. But harm me it did. I felt degraded, jealous, and filled with rage. I never expressed any of these feelings to my friends, never gave them a chance to make amends. (At the time, it didn't even occur to me that I could do such things.) Instead, in order to protect myself, I decided the girls couldn't be trusted and never spoke to either of them again.

In addition to ditching good friends, I also had a habit of giving up prime opportunities. For example, after three years of toiling away as a staff writer on the school weekly, I'd been awarded the job of features editor. This was a key position for my future, as I would soon be applying to college writing programs.

During the first few weeks of the semester, I made friends with my new editor in chief and a romance started to develop. We went on a few dates, but Mr. Editor never let it get serious. In the kindest way possible, he broke it to me that he'd begun a relationship with the news editor instead. While they were both decent people who tried not to hurt me unnecessarily, I felt betrayed nonetheless. Unable to handle rejection, I quit the newspaper. College applications be damned.

Little by little, I gave up all of my precious extracurricular activities because I couldn't handle even the most minor slights. I'd competed in the New Jersey Teen Arts Festival for years and routinely placed as a top singer in the state. One year I decided to perform the song "Nothing" from *A Chorus Line*, not realizing that part of the R-rated lyric was unacceptable. After my performance, the music teacher reprimanded me harshly for "embarrassing" her. Mortified, I hid under a grand piano for a few hours. At the age of fifteen, I vowed never to compete as a singer again.

As a junior, I was cast as the lead in *The Bad Seed*. This was a plum part in the main school play, so I was very, very proud. Determined to behave like a professional actress, I learned all my lines two days after getting the script and never missed a single rehearsal. Opening night was on a Friday. That morning I could feel a cold coming on. Not wanting to be sick for the weekend performances, I stayed home from school. In the evening, I went backstage as scheduled for costumes and makeup. When it came time for the director's opening-night pep speech, I was blindsided by a public chastising. Apparently, my photo from the play had been on the front page of the school paper that day and some alert secretary had noticed. There was a rule at the school, meant for athletes, that barred students from playing on any day they were absent. Massive drama ensued while the entire administration tried to decide if I should be allowed to perform in the play. I was unaware of all of this. The director, an English teacher, didn't call me to ask what was going on. He just laid into me that night in front of the whole cast. I was so shocked and shamed that I burst into tears and could barely catch my breath. I went on that night despite the fact that I wanted to crawl into a hole. I went on for the second performance too, and people said I was good. But I never acted again. Never. There was no way in hell I was going to let myself get hurt like that again.

The thoughtless ways these teachers shamed me were reprehensible, and I hope to God none of my former students have any stories like that about me. Being publicly criticized at a proud moment when one is expecting praise is bound to mess with anyone's head. The difference between a wounded person like me and a healthy person is that I could never let any slight go. The English teacher later apologized (kind of), and that music teacher was usually one of my biggest advocates. But none of that mattered. For survivors of abuse, who you trust is a matter of survival. It's black-and-white. There can be no apologies. There can be no gray. There are no exceptions.

Had I enjoyed a better home life, perhaps I could've talked out my feelings and weathered these episodes in less damaging and eduring ways. But my parents were MIA in the "Ozzie and Harriet Sage Advice" department—or any other department, for that matter. Kids who don't have the support of a loving family are continually disadvantaged in innumerable ways. But I don't think I truly realized I was disadvantaged until I took a class in stagecraft.

It was junior year, and I was totally stoked. Stagecraft was an elective, one I'd been looking forward to for years. We were going to learn about lights and costumes and sets and direction. I loved the theater and was hoping to make a life in it. So this class was important for me. Our first assignment was to create a shadow box—a miniature wooden stage complete with backstage walls and a fly space. Terribly eager, I rushed home from the bus that first day and went straight to work. Following the directions, I measured and cut four squares of wood. After nailing them together, I used a knife to make notches in the top for dowels. I got no help from my parents on this project. It never occurred to me to ask, and they wouldn't have helped anyway. I couldn't drive and had no money to go to a hardware store. I used what I could find around the house. But I'd followed the instructions, and I thought it looked damned good.

When I took it to school a few days later, it didn't look anything like the other kids'. They'd all used thin, graceful balsa, while I'd used thick, clumsy plywood. The balsa stages were all perfectly cut and glued together by dads who clearly knew what they were doing while my ugly stage was misshapen—the result of a teenager using a hacksaw for the first time. When the grades were given out, all the balsas got As, while my monstrosity received a C. I was devastated and deeply enraged. All the other kids freely admitted that their dads had made their projects. For the first time in my life, I really understood that I was a victim of deprivation and injustice.

On the next assignment, I vowed to level the playing field. We had to design a series of costumes and present them as painted sketches. Unfortunately, I can't draw or paint although I've always had an eye for fashion. I asked the teacher if I could design the costumes and get an artist friend to render them. She said no. I tried to abide by this, but my attempts at drawing drew laughter from the class. Feeling the situation was unfair, I asked my artist friend to paint the rest of my designs.

When I handed in the assignment, the teacher immediately knew the work wasn't mine. She confronted me, but I denied it. Out for blood, she officially accused me of cheating and plagiarism, triggering a meeting with the principal and guidance counselor. Since I was in danger of suspension, my parents were notified. They didn't seem to care, and they didn't accompany me to the disciplinary shindig. I sat alone facing the firing squad and freely admitted to my sins. But I expressed no remorse. Why would I? I didn't feel I'd done anything wrong. I couldn't explain about the plywood or the C or the injustice. I didn't have words for all that back then. When they tried to disgrace me, I refused to let them.

"I don't really care what you people think," I told them.

Despite my brazen defiance—or perhaps because of it—I was spared suspension and was simply kicked out of the class.

That was little consolation as I'd once again lost something that mattered to me.

The lesson I learned?

People are shit indeed.

EVEN AFTER MANY YEARS and much therapy, remembering unkind teachers still stings. I think that's why I became an educator and, later, a therapist—because I wanted to give teens and young adults the understanding I never received. Troubled kids need encouragement, support, and guidance. They need people to notice their strengths, teach them how to set goals, and believe in their futures. They need role models to entice them toward happy, healthy, productive lives.

Teachers, coaches, and other youth mentors are the best hope for troubled teens. But in order to help, they have to see past the teenage shell of protective anger. Too often adults can't see past it. They take the yelling, lying, stealing, cheating at face value and dub the kid a "sociopath" or some other hopeless label. I guess it's easier to judge bad behavior than take the time to understand the pain causing it.

Feeling judged and misunderstood was the story of my life in high school. To this day, I'm dumbfounded by the lengths to which teachers went to avoid making a personal connection and outraged by how quick they were to judge me. In my sophomore or junior year, I took a creative writing class, another highly anticipated elective. In it, we were told to write a fictional story. Mine was about a fifteen-year-old rebel girl fighting against a sadistic tyrant who rapes, beats, and kills a different woman every night. (My subconscious was already trying to put my story on the page.) When the tyrant captures the rebel, he has her brought to his bedroom dressed in a virginal white nightgown and handcuffed to the bed. The two engage in some verbal sparring before the tyrant loses his temper and beats her. Eventually, the girl begs for mercy. Her submission softens the tyrant, who begins to caress her in soft, sexual ways. The girl expresses gratitude to her abuser, and the two begin to make love.

If a fifteen-year-old student handed me a story like that, I'd be concerned, to say the least. Graphic S/M novels are not a usual genre for adolescent girls. So I would wonder if something terrible was going on at home. Suspecting this, I'd take extra care with the student—engaging her in conversation, trying to get her to open up. Understanding that this girl probably shoulders a terrible burden, I'd try to be especially nice so as not to make her life any worse. I would also immediately notify her counselor and the school psychologist.

My teacher never did any of that. Instead, she wrote a brief comment to express her disapproval.

Michelle, this story is well written, but it is a bit frightening because it reads like a classic defense of a wife abuser. It almost defends the man who gets sexual pleasure out of beating a woman, and it portrays the woman as being the sick person who loves it.

Personally, I think ignoring signs of the assault and rape of a young girl is what's "sick."

MY TEACHERS' lack of compassion becomes far sicker when you realize that by the time I was a junior they all knew my father was a child molester! How did they know? Because in the spring of 1985 Gary Lundquist was charged with three counts of child molestation.

The whole thing started quietly. After one little girl made an accusation, the prosecutor's office in our small town conducted a discreet investigation. They found two other girls who were willing to come forward and testify. All three victims were former students at my father's school.

I vividly remember the day I learned Gary was in trouble. I got home from school to find my father and mother pacing the living room. I immediately knew something was wrong because they both should have been at work. The minute I walked in, my mother hysterically announced the news. My father had been indicted and needed to present himself at the police station immediately for formal arrest. They'd waited until I got home, so I could ride along.

At the police station, I watched my father give fingerprints and get mug shots. Meanwhile, in the waiting room, my mother ranted about the financial ruin that was sure to befall us if he went to jail. We would lose the house, the cars, everything. We'd be out on the street.

Once my father's processing was complete and he'd posted bail, our family walked across the street to meet with a defense attorney. Because the victims were minors, only their birth dates were listed in the police report—no names. The lawyer feared this might hinder a defense, but Gary was able to provide a name for each victim based solely on the accusation and birth date. When the attorney asked my father about the validity of the charges, Gary denied everything. Instead, he portrayed the whole investigation as a witch hunt propagated by the school board to retaliate for his work on behalf of the teachers' union.

According to former FBI agent Kenneth Lanning, child molesters who are arrested typically attack "the reputation and personal life of the investigating officer; attack the motives of the prosecutor; claim the case is selective prosecution or a witch hunt." Gary's all-too-common defense became the official family line.

The next day at school, I was summoned from class by a guidance counselor. She ushered me into a dark teachers' lounge and instructed me to take a seat at the conference table. Already seated was a woman

I didn't know. She stood up and introduced herself as the investigator on my father's case. She asked if I was aware of the charges pending against him.

"Yes," I said. "I was there when he got arrested yesterday."

"And is there anything you want to tell me?" she asked matter-of-factly.

The question made me anxious. "I . . . I don't know what you mean . . ."

"Well"—she stared at me—"has he ever done anything to you?"

The room seemed to grow dim.

I started to feel fuzzy. I wanted out of there.

"Michelle," the woman pressed on. "Has your father ever done anything to you that you want to tell me about?"

"N-n-no," I stammered. "I don't know what you mean."

This seemed to agitate the lady. "You know, Michelle, if there's something you want to tell me, you really need to do it now."

"I don't have anything to say." I shrugged. "I don't know what you mean."

And the truth is: At this point in time, I didn't. My dissociative amnesia was still in full force. All I knew at that moment was a palpitating heart, pressure in my head, the dim lights growing darker and about to go pitch-black. These are telltale signs of panic. It was a panic I felt any time my denial system was threatened and my good-girl identity was in danger of learning the truth about my life.

"Can I go now?" I whispered, as my eyes scanned the floor, the walls—anything but the lady's face.

"Yes." The woman sighed. "If you want to . . . But if you ever want to tell me anything, just call."

She handed me her card. I took it with a trembling hand and raced out of the room.

I was terrified.

Knowing what I know now, I'm perplexed by the way the investigator chose to question a teenage witness. On the day she came to talk to me, she already knew Gary was a child molester. (He also had a prior conviction in another state on a weapons charge.) Three girls had accused him; it wasn't much of a stretch to presume he had molested me too. Yet to think I would simply disclose such information to a total stranger on our first meeting was ludicrous.

Even in the most supportive circumstances, children rarely disclose their abuse. I define a "supportive circumstance" as one where a child from a loving home is seduced, but not threatened, by an acquaintance molester who is not close to the parents. In such instances, even if the child is likely to be believed and supported, even if the abuse is suspected by the parents, even if the child has no reason not to tell, most children will never disclose abuse. Even when they are confronted with irrefutable evidence like photographs or videos, child victims still vehemently deny that abuse occurred.

We don't know precisely why kids are reluctant to report, but it's probably a combination of things: embarrassment, guilt, fear of parental reaction, positive feelings for the abuser, amnesia. Keep in mind here that we are talking about molestation by an acquaintance who has not threatened the child. When threats and coercion are involved, or if the perpetrator is a family member, the cost of disclosure goes way, way up. Children in these circumstances routinely face the fear of bodily harm to themselves, their families, or their pets. They may be ostracized by family members or forced out of their homes.

I faced all of these risks and more. Yet a complete stranger, who was threatening to undermine the only security I knew, questioned me only one time and asked me only one question! Looking back, I wish I'd been questioned in a way that made me feel more at ease, but this was 1985—long before law enforcement realized the massive scope of child sexual abuse and began training personnel in how to investigate these types of crimes and interview child victims. Nowadays, investigators understand that if a person is accused of child molestation he is likely guilty of multiple offenses, including possession of kiddie porn. That's why any good investigation should include a search of the perpetrator's home.

Had investigators searched my family home, they would've found the handgun, the stun gun, the wooden paddle, and various S/M devices that were routinely used to terrorize and control me. They would have also uncovered pornographic pictures and videos taken of me and other children by my father, as well as the child pornography produced by Frank. Most important, they would have obtained the names and addresses of Gary's pervert friends.

The authorities had a chance to uncover a major child sex ring.

Instead, by questioning me in such a cut-and-dry manner, they completely terrified their best potential witness and lead.

On a conscious level, I was afraid of Gary and my mother and what they would do to me if I betrayed them. On a subconscious level, I was afraid of Frank and the ring and being labeled a snitch. Surprisingly enough, though, the people who most terrified me were the police. I feared they would send me to jail for prostitution. Like many victims of child sexual exploitation, I didn't see myself as a victim. Due to brainwashing, I sincerely believed I was Gary's willing accomplice. I thought I was guilty of horrible crimes and would be locked up if the truth came out—a belief Gary was all too eager to support.

When I got home from school that day, I wrote a letter to the judge on Gary's case. In it, I said my father was a good and loving man who'd never done anything to harm me or anyone else. Gary obviously encouraged me to do this, as he's the one who provided the name and address of the judge—not to mention the stamp and envelope. He didn't coerce me into writing the letter, though. In my brainwashed and terrified state, I felt it was my duty to protect my master, much like abused cult members protect their leader.

I wasn't the only one who rallied behind Gary. At his elementary school—the school I had attended—a petition was created to support his innocence. Nearly every teacher signed it and, in doing so, essentially accused their own students of lying. One teacher who refused to sign was Nancy Bennett, by far the most dedicated, supportive, encouraging teacher I ever had. She had been my middle school English teacher and was singularly responsible for steering me toward academic success. While she didn't know about the abuse, she cared enough to notice my suffering.

A few years ago, she told me, "I just couldn't sign that petition. I didn't know what, exactly, was going on, but I knew you were a very unhappy kid."

As for Gary, at first he pled not guilty to the charges against him. In fact, he was so adamant about his innocence that he offered to take a lie detector test—a testament to his unbridled arrogance and narcissism. Not surprising, he didn't pass. Based on those results, as well as the testimonies of the victims, he decided to accept a plea bargain in which he admitted guilt on two of the charges. Nowadays, a person convicted of molesting two children under the age of twelve might serve serious jail time. Back in 1985, Gary got the requisite slap on the hand. He was sentenced to three years' probation and lost his teaching license. He was also ordered into court-appointed psychotherapy. During the time that I lived with him, though, I don't remember him seeing the probation officer or the court-appointed therapist more than once.

Financially, the conviction created some hardship for our family. Gary lost his annual salary and pension. My mother, who'd become a bus driver at Gary's school, lost her job too. Much of their savings was eaten up by legal fees. Still, they were able to make ends meet through Gary's various businesses—businesses where Gary continued to employ young girls.

Other byproducts of the case weren't so easy to overcome. We lived in a small town. The case was big news in the local paper, turning us all into social pariahs. One might think that the daughter of a convicted child molester would be treated with an extra dose of kindness, especially by the adults around her. But nothing was further from the truth. I expected all the jeers and snide remarks I received from other students. What I didn't expect was the seeming indifference of every adult I knew. No parent of a friend ever asked me how I was doing. No social worker or school guidance counselor ever met with me. Even close friends and teachers erected a wall of shaming silence.

THANK GOD, by the time the whole thing was over, I was already seventeen and a senior in high school. I had completed most of my credits and had to go to school for only a few hours each morning. I had my driver's license and Gary's old '77 Pacer, which I used to get to my job at the local copy shop. I worked there every day from about eleven a.m. to five thirty p.m. At six p.m., I started my night job as a grocery-store cashier, a shift that lasted until midnight. In the morning, I had to be in school by seven a.m., and the whole thing started all over again. While this schedule allowed no time for school work or extracurricular activities or a social life, I didn't really care. I felt that everyone at that high school had let me down. I wanted nothing to do with them or my family or anyone else in my life. I just wanted to get away.

My dream was to move to New York and reinvent myself. I wanted to be a writer and was grateful to be offered a partial scholarship at New York University. In August of 1986, I packed up my typewriter and escaped to Greenwich Village. It was time to start a new life and forget all about the old one.

Memories, though, are hard to erase. And the bad ones have a way of sticking around, rearing their ugly heads long after the horror has passed. I thought that in getting out of New Jersey I could get away from Gary. What I couldn't comprehend at the time was that the damage had already been done. Gary had left his hideous mark on my mind, body, and soul. And no matter how far I ran, I would never fully get away from him.

The Village Idiot

In the Broadway musical *42nd Street*, a young dancer named Peggy Sawyer hops a bus for Manhattan to seek fame and fortune. Cast as a chorus girl in a big new show, Peggy is soon plucked out of obscurity and given the leading role. When the show becomes a hit, Peggy magically transforms from a broke nobody into a celebrated star. Her talent and moxie have made her the toast of New York.

As I drove through the Lincoln Tunnel to start my new life in the city, I figured that's just how things would happen for me.

I wasn't a dancer, nor did I harbor ambitions to act or sing professionally. But I was a writer with visions of making it on the Great White Way. I was going to be the next Neil Simon, minus the hair loss and the Jewish mother. First stop, Greenwich Village. Next stop, the Tony Awards.

Of course, anyone who's ever opened the *Preppy Handbook* knows that my low-brow show-biz ambitions are nowhere to be found on its plaid pages. As the Preppy, I should've been headed to Vassar with dreams of winning a tennis tournament, not a Tony. But the Preppy wasn't in charge anymore. During high school, the identity I call Mooch had taken over as the dominant personality and was now running the show.

In DID, the alternate personality who can best handle a situation is usually the one who is "out." In high school, as I began to experience personal conflicts, it made sense that the hardened Mooch started to take charge. When a person has multiple personalities, distinct emotions like joy, contentment, or rage are often divvied up among the alters. Mooch holds anger and ambition. She's the fighter in my personality system. So when it came time to fight my way to the top, she naturally took charge.

Mooch, like Michelle, was a teenager. Like all adolescents, she went through the natural process of defining herself, of asking, *Who am I?* In Mooch's case, she was an outgoing, outspoken diva who thrived on drama. So she set her sights on the stage. She defined herself as the Writer—a witty, urbane New Yorker, blunt and street smart, who liked big sweaters with patches on the elbows, used bookstores, and black coffee. Like the Preppy, the Writer was pure stereotype. She was based on writer characters in plays like *Deathtrap* and *Brighton Beach Memoirs* and movies like *Manhattan* and *Hannah and Her Sisters*. (My father was a big Woody Allen fan. Hmm.) Never mind that all these characters were middle-aged men. Never mind that their experiences in the city had nothing to do with my rural white-trash life. The Writer didn't come from white trash. She was a Manhattan sophisticate. At the age of sixteen, she already had a subscription to the *New Yorker* and scanned the real estate section of the *New York Times* on a regular basis to ascertain which Upper East Side apartment she would soon buy.

Remembering this now, I can chuckle at my airs and naïveté. As teenagers, we do and think some silly things while figuring out who we will be in life. With DID, though, things get out of hand. Having no core sense of self, I didn't try on affectations; I became whatever role was necessary to get through life. These roles were cast subconsciously by my psyche to ensure my safety. As I contemplated adulthood, life felt precarious. I had no money and was keenly aware that even a minor crisis could render me homeless. In order to feel safe, I needed money. Idiot that I was, I thought the road to riches was paved with words. (Oh, how I wish my mind had created the Investment Banker instead!)

There's another reason I felt unsafe. Having been a victim, I believed that people were generally malicious. In my mind, everyone was out to hurt me, and I felt powerless to protect myself against a cruel world. Young people who feel disempowered, as I did, are at a serious disadvantage. In order to alleviate our feelings of weakness, we tend to glom on to others who seem strong. This makes us susceptible to abusive partners, charismatic cult leaders, gangs, even hostile political and religious movements. Those who lack the social skills to team up with stronger individuals—loners—often attempt to take back their power by seeking revenge on whoever they believe stole it. Most school shootings are committed by these types of people. Many serial rapists and murderers are also motivated by a need to exert power over the types of people they once felt powerless against.

I never wanted to hurt anybody, but I couldn't stand feeling powerless either. In my mind, I was a Nobody, and Nobodies are vulnerable to all manner of ill treatment. In order to be safe, I subconsciously deduced that I needed to become a Somebody. In my teenage world, Somebodies were entertainment types—actors, singers, writers. So my psyche created the Writer, an identity hellbent on acquiring fame and fortune. She was ready for a fresh start, one unencumbered by the baggage of the past.

IN THE SITCOM VERSION of the story, that plan might have worked. But in the real world, trauma is not so easily overcome. Violence has psychological consequences for victims. And a whole lot of violence has a whole lot more. When you see the happy faces of people who have just escaped atrocities—kidnapping victims, Holocaust survivors, soldiers returning from war—their smiles are just the start of a long road ahead. Relief before reality sets in.

The reality is this: Violence changes a person in permanent, profound, existential ways. Once you experience the horrible things one human being can do to another, it's hard to trust anybody ever again. Once you've faced death, you never really feel safe. And once you know that atrocity exists, it shatters your faith in God and humanity. As a result of this darkened worldview, people emerge from trauma with predictable symptoms. They are detached from others. They feel that they are in constant danger, and they fear that life has no meaning.

So, despite my desire to magically morph into a carefree college student, I was anything but. The problems started the minute I walked into my dorm room, a ridiculously small space that was not built for the three girls it was going to house. Being the last to arrive, I was forced to take the top of a bunk bed. The normal bed—already claimed by the first girl to move in—was pushed against the only window. I could've lived without the view and probably made peace with the bunk. What I couldn't stand was my roommate's television. From the minute I walked in the room and heard the blare of amplified voices, my heart sank. My stomach twisted into knots.

I already knew I hated the sound of TVs. At home, my mother kept one on nonstop. The incessant noise bothered me, especially when I tried to sleep, and I often begged her to turn the damn thing off. Irritation, though, was not what I was feeling on the first day in that dorm room. The small room, coupled with the noise of the television, made me feel like the walls were closing in. My heart raced; my body shook. I started to feel nauseated. I dumped my bags and got the hell out as fast as I could.

I spent the first few weeks of college avoiding the room as much as possible. I hung in the rec room or the laundry room or the hallways—anywhere I could feel calm. The problem was: The sound of a television wasn't the only thing that freaked me out. I could be in class, in the cafeteria, out on the street when, seemingly out of nowhere, I'd be crawling out of my skin. My breath would quicken. My vision would narrow. The whole world would turn darker, as if an ominous cloud were about to envelop me.

I didn't understand what was happening at the time, nor would I for many years. But what I was feeling was anxiety—so severe that it often escalated into full-blown panic attacks. Never knowing why or when these attacks would occur became a terror of its own. I found myself doing anything to avoid them. That meant drastically restricting my life. I couldn't join clubs. I couldn't go to parties. Hell, I could barely go to class! My failure to assimilate made me lose hope in the future. I sunk into a cavernous depression.

These are classic symptoms of post-traumatic stress disorder, the disorder soldiers bring back from war. I'd been through a war on the domestic front, so PTSD made sense. Except I didn't know I'd been through a war. I still had traumatic amnesia. So instead of recognizing the effects of abuse, I just thought I was crazy.

Eventually, my inability to live with roommates forced me to give up my bed in NYU's coveted dorm in the Village and move to a hotel the school was renting nearly thirty blocks from campus. The Hotel Seville was in a dicey neighborhood filled with drug addicts and hookers. But, hey, I got my own room.

I thought living alone would be easier, and in many ways, it was. I didn't have to deal with the blare of a television or the gum snapping of a roommate. The hotel, which was in the process of being remodeled, was practically vacant, so there were no loud parties and hardly any talking in the halls. As long as I stayed alone in my room, I felt pretty safe.

UNFORTUNATELY, IN THE ABSENCE of anxiety, depression took center stage. How could it not with my sitting alone day after day in a dingy hotel room? I had no friends back home to call and no family. There were no more early-morning coffee runs to the dorm cafeteria and no late-night talks with other coeds. I just sat in that room feeling empty and lost and hopeless. Was this the great college experience in New York I had dreamed about? Was this my big escape? All of the drive and determination I had mustered to get away from Gary seemed to disappear. Without his control, I felt like a hollow shell.

I needed something to occupy my time. I needed pleasure. Comfort. I found all of these things in food. There was a twenty-four-hour deli across the street from the hotel. It was filled with cookies, candy, ice cream, cakes. At first, I bought these things because I was hungry. Then I started to buy them because I was lonely and bored. But after voraciously downing an entire bag of Vienna Fingers one day, I found that the old panicky feeling returned. I was worried about gaining weight. So I went to the bathroom, put my head over the toilet, and put my finger down my throat. I threw up the cookies, which made the panic go away.

Almost immediately, this became my daily routine. First once, then twice a day. Pretty soon the entire day felt like a nonstop binge. Go to the deli, pick up the food, bring it back to the privacy of my room, shove it in my mouth fast and methodically, wait for the nauseous feeling to wash over me, go and throw it all up. Exhausted, sleep for a few hours. Repeat. This is how I spent my days during freshman year. It gave me a way to occupy myself and allowed me to hide the deeper hunger inside.

It wasn't a panacea, though. I was still battling anxiety and depression—although I had no words for what I was feeling at the time. No self-awareness. I only knew that I felt awful and lost. Moreover, I was gaining weight and flunking out of school. Desperate for help, I made an appointment at NYU Mental Health. After a brief assessment, some lady in a tiny room told me I had bulimia. I was vaguely familiar with the term, though I hadn't realized it applied to me. Again, zero self-awareness. They put me in a group that dealt with eating disorders.

Groups were not my thing, though. People were not my thing at that time—especially girls my own age. I didn't know how to relate to them and their seemingly white-bread worlds. When they boohooed over Mommy and Daddy's divorce or the ballet teacher calling them fat, I couldn't help but roll my eyes. I had come from so much violence, so much deprivation, that the problems of normal people were foreign to me.

You're sad that Daddy doesn't call you as much since he got a new family? Try not having a father at all, even on your birth certificate. You're upset that Mommy suffocates you? Try having a mother who throws shoes at your head.

I realize now that I was being terribly callous. My parents had never shown me empathy, so I was incapable of feeling it for others. Instead, all I felt was jealousy, anger, and contempt for these girls and their perfect little lives. I also felt shame because I knew that deep down I was way more fucked up than anyone else in the group. My family, my life experiences, my mental health problems were so extreme that I felt like an alien. The other girls started to make friends with one another and get better. I just got more depressed.

The facilitator of the group noticed. Dr. Taylor was a psychiatry resident at Bellevue who also worked at NYU. I don't know what, specifically, made him flag me. But one day he pulled me aside and said the group wasn't a good fit. He offered to see me privately for psychotherapy. Sure. Why not? He seemed like a nice enough guy. A few days later, I found myself walking east on Twenty-ninth Street toward the infamous Bellevue Psychiatric Hospital.

BELLEVUE, CIRCA 1986. What can I say? It made the place in *One Flew Over the Cuckoo's Nest* seem like a resort. Outside, it was an old Gothic building. The grimy windows were covered by metal bars, and there was soot an inch thick on the crumbling stone walls. The place looked like it hadn't been cleaned since it was built two hundred years ago. No one had bothered to tend the grounds either. The sorry shrubs were either overgrown or dead, and there were more weeds than cement on the sidewalk. Off to the side of the building, I found a nondescript door with a small sign that read OUTPATIENT SERVICES. I entered to find a dimly lit waiting room with flickering fluorescent bulbs, broken plastic chairs, and cracked linoleum floors. It felt like the set of a horror movie. Some nurse-type women were behind bulletproof glass. They gave me a couple of forms to fill out and told me to pay seven dollars. I sat down in one of the plastic chairs. In front of me was a wild-haired old woman yelling at no one. To my right was a twentysomething guy who kept twitching and smelled like urine. For a girl from the sticks, Bellevue was shocking.

Shit, I thought. *If I'm here, I must be really nuts.*

Eventually, Dr. Taylor came out to fetch me. I followed him through the foul-smelling hallway to his office. I don't remember much of what we talked about, just that it felt awkward. At some point, he told me I felt "sad." This was news to me. I mean, I didn't want to cry or anything. My problem was that I felt nothing at all. But he said I was depressed and gave me a prescription for the antidepressant imipramine. After filling my prescription at the Bellevue pharmacy, I walked back to the Seville, stopping at a deli along the way. I took a bag full of junk food back to my hotel room, downed it, and threw it up.

In the following days, I continued to do the same. The only difference was the little white pills, which I started to take faithfully.

I began seeing Dr. Taylor on a regular basis. Once a week, I'd make the trek over to First Avenue for our fifty-minute session. For the life of me, I can't remember anything we talked about. School, I guess. The bulimia. We should've been talking about the abuse I'd suffered. Unfortunately, I couldn't talk about something I didn't remember. I had all the symptoms of abuse—anxiety, depression, self-esteem problems, trust issues, eating disorder—but no clue why. As long as my psyche was committed to self-deception, psychotherapy was pointless. There was nothing to talk about. Nothing real, anyway. And try as he might, Dr. Taylor could never make an in. I couldn't let him because subconsciously I knew I couldn't handle what he would find.

Nonetheless, I kept going to the appointments. I kept taking the pills. And little by little things began to change.

Unfortunately, they got worse.

In the fall, I'd been panicky and lost. By spring, I was downright suicidal. I don't know if it was the pills or therapy or what, but everything careened downhill. I was bingeing and purging constantly. I almost never left my room, causing my GPA to plummet. I had very little social contact and no desire to do or accomplish anything. What was the point? No matter what I tried, it was bound to turn to shit.

Like so many people who have been held captive, I'd spent my time dreaming of escape. In my fantasies, I assumed that freedom would be easy and wonderful and perfect, but that was magical thinking. When we are stuck in prolonged crisis—war, slavery, domestic abuse, kidnappings—we are forced to focus on survival. In order to muster the strength to stay alive and get away, we have to believe that escape will bring unbridled happiness. What we can't imagine is how hard it will be to adjust to a world of normal people who don't understand what we've been through. Nor can we comprehend how much the crisis has changed and damaged us. When we realize that life after trauma can be just as hard, or harder, than life during trauma, our fantasy of carefree happiness is shattered. That's when a deep, immutable hopelessness can set in.

AT FOURTEEN, I'd been quite dramatic about my suicidality. There were lots of dark drawings and morose poems, lots of moping around the halls. I'd been crying out for help back then, hoping someone would stop and take notice. At eighteen, the experience was different. I was truly and utterly hopeless. I couldn't delude myself into believing anyone gave a shit whether I lived or died. So I kept my urges to myself. I didn't even tell Dr. Taylor how bad I really felt. I didn't tell him how I'd lie in the dark for hours trying to imagine what it would be like to not exist. I didn't tell him how often I counted out those little white pills he gave me, just to make sure I had enough.

As spring came to a close, I knew my time was running out. The semester would be over soon, and I'd made no living arrangements for the summer. That meant I would have to go home to New Jersey. To my mother. To Gary. Thinking about it made my stomach turn. The only thing that gave me solace was the fact that during my high school years I had gone to great pains to fix up one of the barns in my parents' backyard. The two-story structure, once storage for hay and equipment, had fallen into disrepair. Wanting some privacy and peace, I had personally taken on the work and expense of remodeling it. With help from some DIYer friends, I'd put up Sheetrock and laid wall-to-wall carpeting. I'd even bought myself a little sofa bed and an air conditioner so I could sleep there at night.

On the day I packed up my belongings and boarded the bus back to New Jersey, I knew it would be a rough summer. I'd barely talked to my mother or Gary since I left for New York, a silence that suited all three of us. The only thing that would make the summer bearable was the fact that I would not actually be living with them. I would be in my little barn. Alone. Safe.

When I got to the barn, however, there was a rude surprise. My mother, a bit of a hoarder, had filled the entire place with junk. Old furniture and dusty boxes were piled floor to ceiling. It was so packed that I could barely open the door, much less live there. My mother knew what the barn meant to me; she knew how much time and money I had poured into it. She knew I planned to live there. Yet she gave me no warning about its condition. This was my mother being her typical immature self. The crap in the barn was a game—her way of saying she was glad to be rid of me and didn't want me back.

But I had nowhere else to go. I felt trapped and frantic—not a good combo when one is depressed. I ran into the house and demanded that my mother move her things. With smug satisfaction, she refused. Desperate for sanctuary, I begged and pleaded. Tears streamed down my face as I implored my mother to show mercy. The scene was reminiscent of ten years earlier when at the age of eight I had begged my mom not to move in with Gary. She ignored me this time as she had before, with a contemptuous countenance that screamed, *How dare you presume to inconvenience me!*

Distraught and enraged, I went crazy, impetuously grabbing my purse and pulling out the imipramine inside. In a nanosecond, I popped off the cap and swallowed the entire bottle in front of my mother.

I suppose there are a lot of emotions a mother can have when watching her daughter down a lethal dose of pills. Shock. Panic. Horror. Disbelief. Distress.

My mother was pissed. She demanded I throw up the pills, adding in some snide comment about my bulimia. I refused to throw up. I didn't want to. I didn't want to live. Frustrated, she turned to Gary, who'd been ignoring the scene silently from his La-Z-Boy, and told him to drive me to the emergency room. Gary refused, saying, "If a person wants to kill themselves, we should let 'em."

Still raging, my mother picked up her keys and told me get in the car. I was already feeling groggy and lacked the energy to resist. The car ride is a blank; I guess I was already blacking out by the time I got to the emergency room.

That's when I slipped into cardiac arrest and died.

Unlike the mild over-the-counter sleeping pills I'd taken five years earlier, imipramine is an old-school powerful antidepressant quite capable of causing fatality. Had I not been in the emergency room when its effects kicked in, I doubt I'd be around to tell this tale. I'm grateful to the doctors who resuscitated me. But at the time, not so much. When I woke up in the CCU, in fact, the first thing I did was yank the IV out of my arm.

I wanted to die all over again.

ON FEBRUARY 21, 1944, a twenty-four-year-old chemist was sent to Auschwitz along with 650 other Italian Jews. Eleven months later, when the camp was liberated, 620 of those people were dead. By a stroke of luck, the chemist survived and, within a few months, resumed his former life. Neither his family nor his property had been lost, allowing the young man to quickly proceed with life. He married, had children, and enjoyed a thirty-year career in chemistry. By all external measures, Primo Levi not only survived but also thrived.

Despite all this, the chemist, who would eventually become a world-renowned author, did not walk away from Auschwitz unscathed. He brought back a darkness that stayed with him throughout his life—and may have eventually ended it.

In his memoirs, *Survival in Auschwitz* and *The Reawakening,* Levi expressed that darkness while describing the horrors of the Holocaust and its aftermath. For the next forty years, nearly everything Levi wrote was about his relatively brief time in the camp. Clearly, he remained preoccupied and troubled by the trauma he'd endured as a young man, and by middle age, he began to suffer serious depression. He was suffering from depression even forty years after the war and was certainly suffering on the day he took his own life. While there are myriad reasons for one to commit suicide, Levi's family and friends feel he was never able to shake the darkness of the Holocaust. As fellow survivor Elie Wiesel noted, "Primo Levi died at Auschwitz forty years later."

It seems contradictory that someone would struggle to survive a death camp only to take their own life after escaping. Nonetheless, it's a common phenomenon. Among the elderly, Holocaust survivors have been three times more likely to attempt suicide than their peers, and there's a long list of notable Holocaust survivors who have taken their own lives. Art Spiegelman, creator of the graphic novel *Maus,* lost his survivor mother to suicide. Later, in attempting to understand her death, Spiegelman visited psychiatrist survivor Paul Pavel, who told him, "The only thing a survivor can do is to kill himself . . . After the optimism of liberation all the optimisms fail."

While I disagree with the notion that the only thing survivors of horror can do is kill themselves, I know firsthand the pull of suicidality. We who go through trauma, especially long-term trauma, come out the other side with a host of symptoms that can make liberation its own living hell. That's mostly because our bodies don't get the memo to calm down after the peril has passed. Instead, we remain in a state of hypervigilance, always ready for the next attack.

We startle easily, especially at things that remind us of the original trauma (e.g., vets who duck and cover when a car backfires), and suffer insomnia in our misguided efforts to stay alert. Always on edge, it's no wonder we become emotionally exhausted, making us irritable, detached from others, and disinterested in things that used to be fun. In addition, our minds seem unable to let go of the terrible things that have happened, causing us to experience distressing recollections, nightmares about the trauma, and terrifying flashbacks in which the event seems to actually reoccur. Naturally, we try to block out these upsetting memories, leading us to avoid talking or thinking about the experience, but avoidance only makes symptoms worse.

Of course, not everyone responds to trauma the same way. Some people can endure a traumatic event and come out the other side only mildly affected; others become psychologically crippled for life.

Why does trauma cause long-term problems for some people and little or no symptoms for others? The age, background, and coping skills of the victim have something to do with it. Not surprising, the type of trauma a person suffers also seems to make a difference. While there's no magic formula to measure this stuff, in general, the more severe a trauma, the more severe its effects. Natural disasters are usually easier to cope with than violence, and a single violent event (e.g., a rape) tends to be less damaging than something long-term (e.g., sexual slavery).

Long-term repeated trauma—the kind that happens in wars, imprisonments, kidnappings, cults, domestic abuse, child abuse, and ongoing sexual abuse—is generally the most psychologically damaging. For, unlike single episodes of violence, captive victims are assaulted again and again and again. The person who gets mugged may be terrified, but he has the ability to get away, connect with loved ones, and eventually reestablish a feeling of safety. For the person enduring long-term trauma, *there is no safety*. There is only the constant threat of more injury and possibly death. As a result, these victims and soldiers are always on alert. Fear becomes the new normal, and that fear rarely dissipates once the danger has passed. It subconsciously stays with the survivor, making her feel that she is constantly in danger. In an effort to feel safe, the survivor restricts her environment, relationships, and activities. She grows more introverted, more neurotic, less open to new experiences, and less agreeable. Basically, long-term trauma can actually change a victim's personality.

SINCE MY ABUSE STARTED at such a young age, it's hard to know how it may or may not have changed my inherent personality. What I do know is that by the time I reached puberty, I was already exhibiting classic symptoms of long-term sexual abuse. The severe depression that began to plague me at the age of thirteen, for instance, is quite common among adolescents and adults with a history of sexual abuse. Likewise, suicidal ideation and suicide attempts happen far more frequently in those who have been molested versus those who have not. Bulimia, while not specifically listed as an effect of trauma, has been highly correlated with sexual abuse. And I certainly doubt I'd have developed dissociative identity disorder and dissociative amnesia if I hadn't had awful memories to block out.

Anxiety, on the other hand, is not so easily blamed on trauma. About 18 percent of the U.S. population has a diagnosable anxiety disorder, making it the biggest mental health issue by far. The reason for this is simple; we are genetically predisposed to fear things. It was our neurotic caveman ancestors, after all, who probably noticed the saber-toothed tiger in time to run! Our brains have remained hard-wired to constantly look out for danger. It is so automated, in fact, that our bodies will instantly jump back from a snake on the ground before our cerebral cortex realizes it's just a rope. Whew! And we are not only preprogrammed to look for every potential danger but also to remember those dangers forever. That's why we can't drink peach schnapps ever again after that time it made us sick in college! (Perhaps I'm divulging too much.)

Fearful mammals that we are, it's no wonder we're prone to anxiety. For many, many people, neuroticism is a birthright. For others, though, anxiety disorders are a direct result of trauma via classical conditioning. Most people know of classical conditioning through the work of Ivan Pavlov, the guy who discovered he could get dogs to salivate on cue. Salivation is the body's automatic response to the sight and smell of food—just as fear is the body's automatic response to danger. Pavlov found that when he made a specific sound at dinnertime the dogs learned to associate the sound with food. Eventually, the dogs' bodies would react to the sound by salivating even if the food wasn't there.

The same thing happens during trauma. While terrified, our minds tend to take in not only the danger but also everything else associated with the moment. Our brains remember the "everything else" as dangerous and tell our bodies to react in similar situations. If a person is shot while walking alone down a dark alley, for instance, he will almost certainly be afraid of being shot again. He will fear the sight and sound of a gun as well as anything that looks or sounds like a gun. What's more, he may generalize his fear to include everything else that reminds him of the assault—alleys, being alone, the dark. He may even become fearful of seemingly innocuous things such as brick walls (like the one in the alley) and neon signs (like the one he saw in the distance just as he was losing consciousness).

Obviously, one act of violence can create a lot of fear triggers for a victim, triggers that will cause anxiety and phobias down the road. In cases of long-term trauma, there are multiple acts of violence, often in multiple settings. Unfortunately for the victim, this means there are exponentially more fear triggers to contend with.

The chronic anxiety that I began to notice in college was a direct result of such triggers. Having been abused by so many different people in different ways in different places for such a prolonged period of time, my brain had learned to fear just about everything.

The sound of a TV made me panic, for instance, because johns often used them to drown out sounds while they raped me in motel rooms. I was similarly panicked when I heard highway traffic (which could be heard in motel rooms) and stereo music (which played during sex parties). I felt anxious every time I entered a motel room or a shopping mall. Worst of all, I suffered a panic attack every single day at dusk because that's the time of day Gary usually molested me.

With so many subconscious fear triggers in my head, it's no wonder I was in a constant state of panic. Having complete amnesia for the abuse, though, meant I didn't realize the anxiety was being triggered by external stimuli. On the contrary, I had no idea why I felt so jumpy all the time, nor did I have any idea how to control it. My solution was to block out every stimuli I possibly could by having complete control over my environment. This is why I chose to live alone off campus. It's also why I needed so badly to live alone in my barn that summer.

What I am describing—distress at exposure to traumatic stimuli followed by frantic attempts to avoid such stimuli—is the very definition of post-traumatic stress disorder. Having no conscious memory of being traumatized, however, I had no way of connecting my anxiety to the abuse I had suffered. Instead, I attributed my trauma symptoms to inherent character flaws. I thought of myself as highstrung, overly sensitive, and a control freak. These negative assessments were also used by my family to describe me. Because I had frequent emotional outbursts that were triggered by trauma stimuli that appeared innocuous to others, I was also labeled as "moody." My desperate attempts to regulate my affect through external change, such as demanding to sleep in the barn or insisting that a TV be turned off, got me branded as "manipulative." Believing myself to have all of these innate negative qualities, it's no surprise I suffered from feelings of shame, guilt, and deep self-loathing.

Psychologist John Briere calls these unwarranted negative perceptions "cognitive distortions." They are nearly universal in those who have been abused as children and, because they form our subconscious belief system, are notoriously intractable. In addition to having cognitive distortions about myself, I entered college with cognitive distortions about others and the world.

Due to my repeated victimizations at the hands of men, I assumed all men were dangerous and generally felt threatened every time I was in contact with them. My view of women was not much better. Based on my experience with my mother, as well as the female teachers at school, I believed women were, at best, heartless and, at worst, backstabbing bitches just waiting to throw me to the wolves.

Needless to say, I entered adult life with a severe distrust of all people. I was incredibly sensitive to the slightest sign of aggression, betrayal, manipulation, criticism, or judgment. I assumed the world was a dark and threatening place where human beings existed only to hurt and exploit one another. This made it impossible for me to form intimate relationships, be they with friends, sexual partners, or therapists.

Perhaps most damaging, the abuse altered my perception of God. Before meeting Gary, I'd been raised in a Christian church that was warm and inviting. In Sunday school, I'd been taught that Jesus loved me and would always protect me. I took these lessons to heart and had held an unflinching faith in God. But when Gary came along, we stopped going to church. He mocked Christianity and said it was for idiots. I didn't believe him.

I still prayed to God every day. First, I prayed that my mother wouldn't move in with Gary. Then I prayed that we would move out. I prayed for the abuse to stop. I prayed for my mother to be nice to me. I prayed for all kinds of things, but none of my prayers were ever answered. Surprisingly enough, this did not shake my faith in God. It just made me think He had it in for me. For some reason, I'd been forsaken. This led to a deep and lasting belief that no matter what I attempted to do in life my plans would ultimately be doomed.

Psychologists refer to this perception of impending doom as a "sense of foreshortened future." But words cannot really describe the insidiousness of this particular symptom, this deep-seated belief that one's life will never work out. When one truly feels that their life will end in ruin, every relationship, every career move, every endeavor is tainted before it starts. The worst part for me was an enduring belief that I would never achieve happiness—that happiness was simply not in God's plan for me. Because this belief was so ingrained, anytime happiness approached, I would start to panic. I was always waiting for the other shoe to drop. Waiting, though, was uncomfortable and felt too much like being a victim. So I would usually find some way to sabotage my happiness before God could do it for me. This made me feel less helpless. But it also made it impossible for me to build any kind of satisfying life.

MY LIFE FORCE, though, remained inexplicably strong. I survived my suicide attempt, and while still in the CCU, I had an epiphany. It came to me as I was lying in the hospital bed—a strong, clear thought that I knew was not my own. I didn't know if it was God speaking to me or what. All I know is: The message was very authoritative and very wise. It said, "You keep trying to get your parents to love you, but they will never give you what you need." That's all the message said. But in that moment, I understood. It was absolute truth. A great shift immediately took place in my psyche. Everything seemed clearer. A giant weight lifted off my soul.

In all the days I was in the CCU, my parents never came to visit. But after the epiphany, I didn't care. As I'd done five years earlier after my last suicide attempt, I made a decision to block out everything negative in my life and focus on moving forward. Suddenly, I forgot all about my crappy family, depression, and anxiety. Even the bulimia that had dominated my life magically disappeared. This was not a gradual remission of symptoms as a result of therapy. I'm saying that I went into the hospital a total wreck and came out a changed person. All the doom and gloom wafted away, and suddenly, I could enjoy people and activities in a way I never had before. My motivation and ambition returned in spades. My head and life path were instantly crystal clear.

A miracle? Yes. Absolutely. A miracle of the human mind.

Once again, in the face of grave danger, my psyche used dissociation to help me survive. This time, of course, the "danger" came from within; I had nearly killed myself. So my mind did what it was wont to do. It kept me safe by blocking out all the icky thoughts and feelings that were making me suicidal.

In order to do this, a new personality emerged. The Student was a responsible, even-tempered adult who was driven by duty. Utterly sensible, she didn't succumb to self-pity or indulge in fanciful daydreams. She is what is commonly referred to as an "administrator" alter, an emotionless identity who can cross off the to-do list, stick to the schedule, and get the job done.

The job, at that time, was getting through college. My heroic feats of truancy had nearly tanked freshman year. The Student decided she would never miss another class no matter what. She also resolved to earn outstanding grades. A survey of my past academic performance, though, suggested that the Student was nuts. I mean, I'd rarely taken school seriously and had the piss-poor grades to prove it. In high school, I'd stopped taking science and math as soon as I could, opting for easy classes like choir. (This was in the days before weighted grades.) My SATs pronounced me painfully average. Even my guidance counselor, in attempting to sell me to colleges, could say only that I had the "ability to work hard" if I felt like it.

Exactly where this straight-A-seeking student came from, I don't know. I can't recall a popular image that grabbed my psyche the way the Preppy or the Writer did. The Student seemed to spring forth from my subconscious with an edict to get real and get on with it.

And get on with it she did. Just days after being released from the hospital, I found myself a full-time summer job, earning enough to return for sophomore year. I chose to live back in my original dorm and was blessed with a roommate who hated TV as much as I did. Naomi and I became good friends, and I made lots of other friends too, many of whom remain friends thirty years later.

I kept my promise to never miss another class or assignment—sticking to the straight and narrow for the remaining three years of undergrad as well as all eleven years of my various grad schools. For the first time in my life, I actually read the novels and plays and textbooks that my instructors assigned and found that I liked studying. It was a pleasant surprise to learn that doing homework and showing up for class could improve one's grades. Before the Student came along, I had no idea that hard work and effort were directly related to success. The realization was empowering.

The Student opened me up intellectually the way the Writer had opened my creativity. But the Student, built only to complete day-to-day tasks, didn't feel like a full identity. She had no image of herself, so she didn't prefer certain clothes or have an elaborate back-story. She didn't have interests or hobbies or long-term goals, feelings or memories. The Student lived entirely in the present moment, ever ready to accomplish the work at hand. She was more like a robot than a person.

BEING A ROBOT has its advantages. Mostly free of depression, anxiety, or any other negative emotions, I truly began to flourish. My work at school was such that NYU gave me a special scholarship and award for academic achievement. One of my plays was chosen for a run off-off-Broadway. I was offered a job as assistant editor of a theater-themed newspaper where I churned out countless articles and reviews. Within two short years, I'd not only conquered the school thing but also seemed well on my way to a career as a writer.

My personal life was also flourishing. Sophomore year, I began dating a film student who lived in my dorm. By senior year, Steve and I were sharing a studio on Jones Street. It was right in the heart of the Village and had hardwood floors and a fireplace. I absolutely adored waking up in the morning and going for coffee at Patisserie Claude. Steve and I took long walks around the park and explored every inch of the neighborhood. In the evenings, I spent hours writing at the Washington Square Diner.

By the time I turned twenty-one, I felt like life was right on track. Good job. Good boyfriend. Good apartment. My old life in New Jersey seemed a million miles away.

Gary? My mother? My past? I hardly ever thought about any of it.

That all changed in the fall of 1989 when my past suddenly came back to haunt me via a medical crisis called AIDS.

IN 1989, THE AIDS EPIDEMIC was still in its infancy. The disease had first been identified in 1981, and by 1983, researchers figured out it was caused by HIV. Both Rock Hudson and Liberace made big headlines when they died of the disease in the mid-1980s. So I, like everyone else, was aware of it. But despite a lot of press, AIDS remained a niche issue. Most of the reported cases involved gay men, drugs users, and hemophiliacs. For a straight woman who didn't do drugs and didn't sleep around—even a straight woman in Greenwich Village—AIDS didn't seem like a threat.

That is: I was oblivious until I heard that a childhood friend had contracted it. It was Madeline, the girl Gary had courted after me. When I heard the news, I took it hard. That old sense of impending doom returned with a vengeance, and I became gripped by a panic so thick I could hardly breathe. The anxiety continued unabated for weeks. Suddenly, I was imprisoned in a soggy dark cloud. The thought running through my head night and day was *I must have AIDS too. I must have AIDS too.*

On the surface, this made no logical sense. As far as my conscious mind knew, neither Madeline nor I had been abused. I'd only slept with a few boys in college, most of whom were virgins. This meant my chances of contracting HIV were practically nil. But my subconscious mind knew better. It knew about all the various men I'd been forced to have sex with in the late '70s and early '80s when AIDS was silently breeding.

The life-and-death nature of the AIDS threat put so much pressure on my psyche that my rock-hard denial system began to fissure. The truth of my past was oozing through the cracks. It told my conscious mind that I must get tested.

Back in those days, the HIV test was fairly new and available only via a blood sample. Appointments had to be made weeks in advance, giving me plenty of extra time to panic. When the day of the test finally came, I was so terrified that I fainted as the nurse thrust the needle into my arm. When I came to, the nurse informed me it would take several weeks to get the results.

Those weeks were some of the darkest of my life. I was sure that, like Madeline, I had AIDS and was destined to die a horrible death.

I couldn't eat. I couldn't work. I couldn't sleep. I could barely speak. Believing my risk was nonexistent, my faithful and trusting boyfriend tried to reason with me. But I couldn't be reasoned with because my subconscious knew my risk factors were through the roof.

Once again, my justifiable anxiety appeared to be completely unjustified. Once again, I looked and felt nuts.

Finally, I was called in to receive the results of the test. To my great surprise, I was HIV negative. Miraculously, I had dodged death. (Although at the time, I didn't yet realize what a true miracle it was.) At first, I was immensely relieved, but the cloud of doom soon reemerged. AIDS or not, something felt terribly wrong. Bad things were going to happen to me. I could feel it in my gut. I walked around in a constant state of terror. But terror of what? Everything was the same as before. Same job. Same boyfriend. Same apartment. Underneath, though, a great change had occurred.

AIDS MAY HAVE SPARED my immune system, but my denial system was now compromised. The Cloak of Invincibility I'd been wearing since the last suicide attempt suddenly had holes in it. Through those holes, tiny bits of feeling and memory started to escape.

In a recurring dream, for instance, I stood naked on a busy street corner. Then Gary came to me, and we had sex in the gutter as people watched. For my senior thesis, I wrote a play about an adult daughter who returns home to seduce her father, oust her mother, and claim her rightful place as the family wife. Pretty on the nose, I know.

But the crazy thing is: I didn't realize my play was autobiographical! My subconscious memory was feeding my conscious mind lots of sick and twisted plot ideas and characters and dialogue that I thought were coming from my imagination. God only knows what my professors thought of me!

Senior year, I also experienced my first body hijacking. For people with DID, body hijackings are a common occurrence as one identity takes over the body from another. If a person is in complete denial about their DID, this switch happens outside of the person's conscious awareness. But when the mind can't or won't hide DID, the hijackings sometimes feel like out-of-body experiences.

My first one happened while Steve and I were having dinner at a restaurant. We were having a mundane conversation when I suddenly felt light-headed. It was as if I were floating up to the ceiling. Steve seemed far away, and all the restaurant noise hushed. Then I heard someone say, in a barely audible voice, "I think my father molested me." I was aware that the voice was coming out of my mouth; I could even sort of feel my lips moving. But I had no connection to being the source of the information or even having the intention to speak. It was crazy body-snatcher stuff.

It was the first time I had ever acknowledged being sexually abused. Steve, who had spent time with my parents and disliked them, did not seem surprised by the revelation. But for me—a person who believed a fictional version of my childhood—the admission was shocking.

Why would I say such a thing? Why did I feel so weird when I said it?

Disturbed and confused, I thought it might be a good idea to get help. Dr. Taylor, now in private practice, was out of my price range. So I went back to Bellevue and played shrink lotto, the fun game where poor people are forced to go to clinics and bare their souls to whatever trainee flies out of the machine.

This go-round, I got a fat, balding psychiatrist who was doing his residency. Unlike Dr. Taylor or the first guy I'd seen in New Jersey, this one didn't have a soft, empathetic, *Free to Be . . . You and Me* vibe. Instead, Dr. A. Hole reeked of old-school psychoanalysis: aloof, judgmental, chauvinistic, arrogant.

I can give this assessment now because I've been around the mental health block and know what makes for a good or bad therapist. At the time, though, I was just a mixed-up girl looking for some direction. On the surface, I was confused about what to do after college. I had always planned to stay in Manhattan, but Steve was from Los Angeles and wanted to move home. When he left, rent would become a burden, but that wasn't the real problem. The dilemma between New York and LA came down to a fear of being alone.

I had no siblings, hardly any relationship with my parents, and no other family to rely on. Steve was the only person I could count on in the whole wide world. If I lost him, I'd have no one to call in an emergency, and any tiny crisis was sure to leave me shaking a can on Sixth Avenue. Most people, thank God, don't ever know what it's like to be that alone. Most people have some family somewhere who will bail them out in a pinch. Former foster kids, runaways, and others estranged from family because of abuse or homophobia, though, are at terrible risk because they live with no safety net. That's why so many end up living on the streets.

Of course, I didn't have any of this perspective at the time. When I talked with Dr. A. Hole, I'm sure I sounded more like "Blah-blah-blah LOVE New York, blah-blah-blah La-La Land has no seasons." To tell the truth, I don't really remember much about these sessions except that it was difficult to talk with Dr. A. Hole. He made me feel like a bug.

Nonetheless, in one session, I experienced my second body hijacking. I was sitting in a hard plastic chair babbling on about the lack of theater in LA when I drifted away and heard a voice speaking.

"My father molested me," it said. I knew it must be me talking, but I had no idea how I was doing it.

I can't really remember what happened after that. But I doubt it was very enlightening as I stopped seeing the doctor after only seven sessions.

AFTER MUCH ANGST AND DEBATE, I decided I must leave New York. It killed me to give up my job, my contacts, my perfect apartment, theater, seasons, decent bagels. But what choice did I have? Being alone in the world terrified me. It was a matter of survival.

So a few months after graduation, Steve and I packed all of our belongings into my new used car. We ordered a set of TripTiks from Triple A and headed west. For my sacrifice, Steve promised we'd rent a huge two-bedroom apartment so I could have a dedicated writing room. He also promised I'd learn to love sunny, seasonless, theater-challenged LA. I tried to be optimistic about the future. But it was hard losing my school, my home, and my dreams all in one day.

What I didn't yet realize was that I was bringing all sorts of things with me: buried memories, toxic feelings, psychopathology, and a whole host of ready-for-prime-time inner characters. If Steve had known what he was in for, I doubt he would've been so keen to stay together. I suspect he would've hopped a yellow cab, bought a one-way ticket to LAX, and ripped out his home phone.

Instead, we drove across the country, past picturesque farms and the St. Louis arch. Through flat cornfields in Kansas and Technicolor rocks in New Mexico. We visited the "Home of the 72 ounce Steak" in Amarillo and the Grand Canyon in Flagstaff. We had an adventure. The good kind.

After traveling through Las Vegas and Death Valley, we stopped in Barstow for the night. When I woke in the morning for my first day in California, I was so excited that I ran to the motel window and threw open the curtains. The sun that poured in was the brightest and strongest I'd ever seen. It was blinding.

Little did I know that the California sun would soon be shining a light on my very dark past and finally set me on the long road to healing.

PART III

HEALING

———

The truth will set you free. But not until
it is finished with you.

—David Foster Wallace, *Infinite Jest*

Daze of My Life

P lease, God," I prayed. "Please. Please, I'm desperate. When I get home, you have to make the phone ring. You have to make them call today. Please, God, you owe me this."

I was walking back from a grocery store on Ventura Boulevard, having just spent my last five bucks on ramen noodles and frozen burritos. When the food in my grocery bag ran out, I would starve to death. After everything that had happened to me, I didn't have much faith left in God. But He was my only option now. Getting my life back on track was going to take a miracle.

The miracle I sought was a job, which doesn't seem like the sort of thing that should require divine intervention. But a year into California dreamin', things felt more like a nightmare. Steve and I were living in a craptastic one-bedroom apartment in the Valley that shared a wall with the 101 freeway. The few pieces of furniture we owned were all procured via Dumpster. I knew absolutely no one, which was probably for the best, as a gazillion streets with crazy names made it impossible to find anyone or anything anyway. I suppose transitioning to postcollege life in a new city is challenging for everyone. But being penniless, estranged from family, and preprogrammed with endless fear triggers really turned up the heat for me.

So did having undiagnosed dissociative identity disorder. Try as it might, my psyche just couldn't get a handle on what identity was going to help me triumph in LA. The Preppy was too traditional and uptight to hang with laid-back Angelenos, and the Student had lost her one and only purpose in life. The Writer should've been able to fit in; lots of Hollywood writers are former theater-loving New Yorkers who eventually grow up and move west in search of grown-up wages. My alternate personalities, though, are not real people. They are caricatures drawn from external images. Like cartoon people, they never seem to age, change, or grow. They are trapped in time. (My wife, in fact, calls me Homer Simpson because I continuously make the same stupid decisions!) As a result, the Writer, who was originally conceived as a New York playwright, had a hard time envisioning herself in La La Land.

Despite all this, things in LA started out well. Within a few days of arriving, I scored a job interview with the head writers of the NBC soap *Days of Our Lives*. The meeting went well, and I was asked to intern in the writers' offices, which is the common launch pad for budding TV scribes. It was a dream opportunity, the kind every young writer wants after college. Things were going great, and within weeks, I was asked to write my first script. By all objective measures, I was on the fast track to a lucrative career as a Hollywood writer.

But it never happened.

I started having flashbacks.

And just like that, my bright future got snuffed out by my dark past.

MY BREAKDOWN WAS TRIGGERED by the move to LA. People with DID are prone to psychological decompensation when they are removed from the original traumatic situation. Once I was three thousand miles from home, I started to feel a sense of danger that I couldn't explain. Needing to feel safe, I decided to cut off all contact with my parents. I went so far as to get an unlisted number and a post office box. I didn't know why, but I wanted to hide from anyone I'd ever known.

Once I felt safely disconnected from my old life and assured that no one could find me, I started to see things in my mind. The first image was of the American flag hanging above the blackboard in Gary's classroom. After that, other images would randomly flash: the sign for the Revolution Motel, a man's calloused hand, my parents' green bedspread. These pictures were seemingly innocuous and random. They held no meaning for me. So why did they fill me with dread?

Dread turned to horror as the images became more explicit. Genitalia, blood, and scenes of torture would randomly pop into my head like persecutory Whac-A-Moles. I had no idea why I was seeing these things, nor could I explain the phantom sensations that were happening in my body. Often, I'd feel like my wrists were tied together by a rope that was pulling me along, or I'd feel like my arms were tied to the headboard of a bed. I'd have the sensation of being gagged or held down. But, of course, none of these things was actually happening. What's worse, I started having violent mood swings.

Most of the time, I felt terror or sadness, but there were also flashes of crazy rage. One time, I screamed at Steve and threw a six-pack of yogurt across the apartment because he'd bought the wrong brand. Other times—many times—I curled into a frightened ball and begged him not to leave me.

When this all started, I had no idea what was happening to me. It felt like I'd completely lost control of my mind and was going insane. Terrifying. As different visions, feelings, and shards of knowledge started to coalesce, and I realized that what I was experiencing were memories, it only made things worse. Imagine waking up tomorrow and learning that the whole life you thought you had lived was a lie. Your loving grandma really beat you senseless. The older brother you idolize stuck his dick in your mouth. This is how it was for me. While I certainly knew my parents were mean, I had no idea I'd been molested. And by my own father! The truth was a total shock—like finding out Dr. Huxtable was a rapist.

The whole thing sent me into a tailspin. I became obsessed with figuring out what else I didn't know about my own life. In order to document the things I was remembering, I started to write in my journal.

11/19/90
What I Remember So Far
They are all vague. They are all dreamlike, and they are not all. But I have memories. I must get them all out, every single one.
I remember wrestling on the bed. I remember him putting his hands on my ass. I would tense up. And he would go "la dee dah" and laugh. So amused . . . I remember him forcing his hand down between my thighs . . . I remember a motel in King of Prussia. I

remember swimming in the pool at night. I remember him holding
me. Maybe touching my breasts. Maybe pulling off the top of my
bathing suit . . . I remember another motel in New York. The
Revolution Motel . . . I remember more about the hotel in King of
Prussia. I remember the room. The inside of the room. I remember
him teasing me when I undressed. Telling me I was silly to act
modest. What hadn't he seen before?

THIS IS HOW my memory started coming back to me. In strange bits
and pieces. Some things, little things, just seemed to suddenly appear as normal everyday memories—Gary's hands on my ass, a time
he put ointment on my genitals. They were so obvious, so complete,
that I wondered how I ever could have forgotten them. Other things,
bigger things, were more hazy—sexual play on my parents' bed, being fondled by Gary in his classroom. These were more dreamlike
and foggy. They didn't feel like normal memories at all. And then
there were the teasers, the little shards of knowledge that seemed to
foreshadow memories to come. Like suddenly remembering certain
hotels but not knowing why. Or certain men my father had known.

It's important to know that the recovery of my memories didn't
happen all at once. They came in clumps over a period of about fifteen years. In this first round, I didn't yet realize I'd been used in
prostitution or kiddie porn, nor did I remember any of the S/M stuff.
Hell, I hardly remembered anything! All that came to me was the
daily run-of-the-mill molestations by Gary—in his classroom, in
motel rooms, on my parents' bed. But that was plenty to freak me
out! I can't say for certain why the memories came back in stages or
why I generally remembered the more "normal" abuse long before

the really kinky stuff. I assume my psyche gave me what it thought I could handle, which was very little at the time.

I realize that for someone who has not experienced the recovery of repressed memories the whole thing must seem bizarre. It was bizarre for me too.

One minute, I was a normal college grad trying to start a career. The next, I was some incest victim. What the fuck?

TRYING TO MAKE SENSE of what was happening to me, I went to the source of all knowledge in the days before Siri: the bookstore. Prominently displayed was a recent bestseller called *The Courage to Heal: A Guide for Women Survivors of Child Sexual Abuse*. It provided answers in plain black-and-white. It said I was a survivor of childhood sexual abuse like countless other women, and that my flashbacks and mood swings were par for the course. It explained that my history of depression, anxiety, and suicide attempts were means of coping. Most important, it said I could heal and told me how.

Nowadays, there are many books about child sexual abuse. In 1990, though, when I began to regain my memory, talking openly about incest and molestation was still very new. In the '70s, the women's movement opened the can of worms when it dared to speak out against rape. Speak-outs on incest soon followed, and the movement to publicize and prevent child sexual abuse was born. By the mid-1980s, child sexual abuse became a major focus of American culture.

Groups popped up to help victims while law enforcement cracked down on perps. Sensational stories about satanic cults and abusive preschools dominated the news. In short, child sexual abuse became a very big deal—some say to the point of national hysteria.

In a bizarre twist of fate, my personal history coincides precisely with America's "discovery" of child sexual abuse. In the 1970s, at the height of the kiddie-porn market, I was forced into those films. In the 1980s, during the fervent hunt for child molesters, my father was prosecuted. By the 1990s, when the term *recovered memories* hit the mainstream, I was just beginning to have flashbacks. Yet despite being the poster child of an era, I was completely unaware of the larger political and social machinations surrounding child sexual abuse.

So when I bought *The Courage to Heal*, I didn't know there was a controversy surrounding its discussion of repressed and recovered memories. In the book, the authors, who don't hold degrees in psychology or any other mental health field, encouraged readers to unearth their repressed memories of abuse through regression therapy. They urged readers to trust the veracity of their recovered memories even if there was no objective proof of abuse. Most controversial, the authors told readers that if they *felt* they were abused they probably were even if they had no memories of abuse.

This loosey-goosey approach didn't sit well with some people. A few readers claimed that upon following the advice in the book they recovered memories that later turned out to be false. Around the same time, an organization called the False Memory Syndrome Foundation was formed by a group of parents who claimed that their adult children had falsely accused them of child sexual abuse. The FMSF worked hard to build skepticism about recovered memories of abuse—claiming such memories were either the result of media influence or misleading therapists who implanted ideas in their patients' heads.

While there is certainly evidence that false memories can be created under certain conditions, the idea that hordes of women are routinely duped by self-serving therapists reeks of an Oliver Stone–style conspiracy theory. It harkens back to the 1890s when Freud's colleagues accused him of implanting false memories in his patients, as well as the 1980s when skeptics claimed therapists were creating false cases of multiple personality disorder. There's a theme here: In all of these instances, people uncomfortable with the divulgence of widespread child sexual abuse try to discredit and silence victims. They do this by calling us "confused" or "manipulated," but what they are really calling us is "liars."

To this day, many people believe that recovered memories of child sexual abuse are never real. Upon hearing my story of recovered memories, I have no doubt that skeptics will try to discredit me. At worst, they'll say I'm a charlatan who's making the whole thing up for money. At best, they'll say I'm confused, that my "memories" are false and were implanted by *The Courage to Heal* or some Rasputin-esque therapist.

The thing is: My memories started coming back to me *before* I ever bought any books about child sexual abuse or sought any kind of therapy to deal with the memories I was recovering. In addition, while pursuing a civil case against my parents, my lawyer managed to collect quite a bit of evidence of the crimes committed against me, including medical records and eyewitness accounts.

Is it possible for people to repress and later recover the memory of a horrible event? The *Diagnostic and Statistical Manual of Mental Disorders*, all mainstream organizations that specialize in the study of trauma, and a vast clinical literature say yes. In contrast, false memory syndrome is not recognized as a diagnosis by the American Psychiatric Association or any mainstream psychological organization.

If one needs more proof that a person can repress and later recover traumatic memories, there is also ample anecdotal evidence. Take, for instance, the case of Alicia Kozakiewicz. When Kozakiewicz was thirteen years old, she was abducted outside her Pittsburgh home by a man she had met on the Internet. She was held hostage, tortured, and sexually assaulted for four days before being rescued by the FBI. When agents entered the dungeon where Kozakiewicz was being held, they discovered her chained to the floor with a leather collar around her neck. Despite this acute trauma—probably because of it—Kozakiewicz could not remember the horrors she endured during her ordeal. In addition, the teen also suffered huge chunks of memory loss for the years before her abduction. By the age of nineteen, Kozakiewicz said she had come to recall "bits and pieces" of her life and the trauma. Slowly, over time, she appeared to be recovering the memories of what had happened to her.

KOZAKIEWICZ AND I SEEM to have suffered similar traumas. We were both taken by sadistic men, locked in basement dungeons, bound, tortured, and raped. We both dealt with the trauma by blocking out the memory of it, by repressing it. Repressed memories, though, rarely stay that way. They creep in as frozen images, phantom pains, confusing dreams.

When my memories started coming back, I was thrown into an emotional crisis. Some days, I felt so terrified that I would hide inside my closet for hours. Other days, I cried uncontrollably and couldn't get out of bed. Unable to function, I was forced to quit my internship at *Days of Our Lives*. I could barely write a grocery list, much less a script!

Recognizing that my life was falling apart, I knew I needed help.

Exactly how to get help, though, was a bit of a mystery. I knew I needed a therapist, but good ones cost good money. Now unemployed, I was SOL. This is one of the catch-22's of severe abuse. Healing from it takes a lot of time and money, but traumatized people are often too damaged to work steadily.

Eventually, I found a nonprofit counseling center in Van Nuys that offered low-cost therapy to poor folks. These sorts of clinics are all over the country and are the primary source of care for the sickest patients, who generally lack money or decent insurance. The way these clinics are able to offer cut-rate fees, however, is by staffing green therapists. These are mostly students in their first or second year of graduate school working for free to earn the hours they need to become licensed.

It's a sad reality that therapists with absolutely no experience and very little training are routinely thrown into rooms with patients suffering from serious mental health issues, including borderline personality disorder, dissociative identity disorder, and other forms of dissociation. New to the game, these therapists often have no idea what they're dealing with, which helps explain why patients are routinely misdiagnosed for years.

I was paired with a therapist in her midfifties. Ethel (Therapist #4) was a second-year student in a master's program who was starting her second practicum. Despite her grandmotherly looks, she was cold and hard. Like most graduate psychology students, Ethel was probably overworked, undersupervised, and overwhelmed by the serious cases being assigned to her. As an older person, she also seemed to resent being forced to work for free. Ethel clearly lacked knowledge about psychological problems. Her biggest shortcoming, though, was a complete lack of empathy. The ability to be empathetic and nonjudgmental is essential for a good therapist, yet it's stunning how many I have met who lack these qualities. Ethel was certainly lacking. When I tried to tell her about the awful flashbacks I was having, about my crippling anxiety and dark thoughts, she couldn't seem to grasp the pain I was in.

Week after week, as I tried to share the anguish I felt about memories of molestation, she offered dumb platitudes about nothing being as bad as it seems and looking on the bright side of life. One evening, when I told her I was feeling gravely suicidal, she suggested I try knitting to distract myself. (I'm not kidding.) After that, I decided to stop seeing Therapist #4.

Instead, I started attending a free group for survivors of child sexual abuse. Still shocked and struggling to believe that I *was* a survivor, I initially found the group comforting. As time wore on, though, it became difficult to relate to most of the other women, who seemed to lead far grittier lives. Many of the unmarried twenty-somethings already had a few kids, and one had an extensive criminal record. None of them had been to college, nor did they seem interested in bettering themselves through education or careers. It was a pessimistic bunch, and, frankly, their lack of ambition and hope scared me to death. I'd joined the group to hone my identity as a survivor, but what I found were people who saw themselves as victims of circumstance.

At twenty-two, I didn't have words to describe any of this, but I instinctively understood that this kind of negativity was a dead end. You can't get well and find happiness if you don't believe it's possible.

One woman in the group did impress me. She was in her forties and married. She'd been steadily working all her life until, in her late thirties, repressed memories of abuse started to emerge. Shaken, the woman had to quit her job and take some time to heal. For the past few years, she'd been seeing an experienced private therapist, and it really showed. Unlike the rest of us, she seemed to accept her past and had real insight into how it had affected her adult life. What's more, she was able to cry freely when she felt sad, which was something I couldn't do.

In the group, this woman eloquently expressed her regret at facing her demons so late in life. In her twenties and thirties, she'd been afraid to deal with her past, choosing instead to distract herself with work and relationships. Lost in self-deception, she'd made some poor choices. One was her husband, whom she'd sought for protection, not love. The two were in the midst of a divorce. The woman's biggest regret, though, was never having children. Always running from her feelings, she'd never looked inside to realize she wanted to be a mother. Now it was too late, and she cried about it with such anguish that it scared me. At twenty-two, I couldn't comprehend the finality of menopause. Still, I could see that an unwillingness to face one's demons in a timely fashion was a recipe for misery.

STRUCK BY THIS WOMAN'S PROGRESS, I asked for the name and number of her therapist. She was seeing a guy in Altadena, about thirty miles from my house. Despite the distance, I called him. Clinic-style shrink roulette had rarely worked out for me, so I was willing to go out of my way for someone who came recommended and whose good work seemed to be evident by what was in front of me.

After chatting on the phone, Javier scheduled an initial appointment. A few nights later, I drove east on the 134 with high expectations. Javier's office was in a small medical building mostly filled

with dentists. His waiting room wasn't plush, but compared to Bellevue and the clinic in Van Nuys, it felt like a palace. After a few minutes, the door opened and a tall, sturdy man stepped in. He was in
his late thirties, with a mop of dark hair and a shaggy moustache.
His jeans, moccasins, and sweatshirt all gave off the impression of a
laid-back dude.

Javier's office was an enormous space with vaulted ceilings, beat-up
couches, and an oversize desk. On one side, there was a fish tank sitting on a dark wood stand. The whole look reeked of the 1970s. Javier
seemed like something out of the 1970s too. He had a relaxed, warm,
whatever-goes vibe—another *Free to Be . . . You and Me* therapist.

Because Javier seemed so open, it instantly made me want to be
open too. Truth be told, I was so overwhelmed that I was dying to
pour my heart out to someone who might understand what I was
going through. I told Javier about the hard move to California and
my sudden flashbacks. I told him about the awful memories, skin-
crawling anxiety, debilitating depression, and dark thoughts of suicide. I told him how desperate I was to find a good therapist who
could really, truly help.

During all of this, Javier listened patiently. He nodded at appropriate moments and offered comforting, empathetic comments. He
seemed to understand the hell I was going through, and he clearly
knew a bit about child abuse and trauma. I silently prayed a thank-
you to God for finally sending me the right therapist.

Then we talked about money.

When Javier found out I wasn't working, had no savings and no
insurance, he abruptly cut off my monologue. He told me his hourly
fee, which I already knew. But I was so desperate that I had decided
money shouldn't be an impediment to getting good help. I asked

him about a lowered fee or seeing him on credit until I could find work. Javier's warm demeanor immediately gave way to a business-like iciness. He started shuffling papers on his desk; his body language told me it was time to go.

Distraught, I burst into tears. I rushed over to Javier's desk and begged him to take me on, promising I'd pay him back when I could.

Javier sighed, looked me straight in the eyes, and spoke with a weary resolve. "Look, Michelle, healing from sexual abuse is hell. It requires a lot of time and strength to get through it. You're not in a position to deal with this right now. You've got to get your life together."

I RETURNED to the free group at the clinic. But shortly after, I got a phone message one day from a member named Amy. While I knew who she was, we'd had no private conversations, no personal relationship of any kind. Amy said she was calling at the behest of her therapist and that she was seeking information. It seemed Amy had something called multiple personality disorder and couldn't remember parts of her day-to-day life. Amy was calling all the women in the group because she wanted us to tell her what she'd said and done. I didn't know much about multiple personalities except that it was some crazy, weird shit.

I didn't call Amy back. In fact, the whole thing freaked me out so much that I never returned to the group.

I mean, what could I possibly have in common with a nut job like that?

Unable to find the help I needed to heal, I did what I'd done many times before: I walled off my feelings and tried get on with life.

Pulling myself up by the bootstraps was definitely more difficult now that I remembered some of the sexual abuse. Still, I had to do it. I had to earn money to surivive.

Finding a job after *Days of Our Lives*, though, proved difficult. I applied for a playwriting fellowship at the Mark Taper Forum and didn't even get an interview. An agent suggested I become a sitcom writer, so I penned a *Doogie Howser, M.D.* script to act as a sample of my work. It was so bad, she refused to send it out.

Around the same time, a short film I had written the year before finally had its industry screening. Some important people came, which was unfortunate as the film totally sucked. Unable to catch a break in entertainment, I returned to journalism as a theater reviewer for the *Los Angeles Reader*. But the *Reader* didn't pay much. Sorry, did I say "much"? I meant "nothing"! I was now knocking out six hundred words a week for the privilege of a free ticket.

Since I couldn't make money as a writer, I applied for any sort of job I could get. I sent resumes to every appropriate want ad in *Variety*, the *Hollywood Reporter*, and the *Los Angeles Times*. However, on the few occasions when I actually scored interviews, I tanked. This wasn't like me. In the past, I'd always been able to ace meetings. One of the great things about having multiple personalities is the ability to subconsciously summon whatever identity will do well in a given situation. It's how I got through life. But once the flashbacks started, everything changed. I lost my mojo.

That's why I was praying hard as I walked back from the grocery store. After much searching and several interviews, I was waiting to hear back about an entry-level clerical job at the Los Angeles

Theatre Center. While typing and filing and running packages around town was no dream job, it now felt like one to me. Feeling this was my last shot at a job with any kind of growth potential, I turned to the Almighty for help. "Please, God," I prayed, as I rounded the corner in front of my building.

"Please, God," I begged, as I entered my building and climbed the stairs.

"Please, God," I pleaded in desperation, as I entered my apartment and homed in on the answering machine. There was no blinking light. No job offer had miraculously appeared. As usual, my prayers went unanswered. God hated me; that much was obvious.

I was just starting to drown my sorrows in a cup of ramen noodles when the phone rang.

"Hello?"

"Michelle! Hi! It's Lynne from the Theatre Center. Congratulations! You got the job!"

I was ecstatic and thought God was finally coming around . . . until I heard the salary. But beggars can't be choosers, so I accepted enthusiastically. I was genuinely excited to get a job at a theater. I just had to figure out how to make ends meet.

As luck would have it, the Broadway musical *City of Angels* was about to start an open-ended run at the Shubert Theater in Century City. I managed to get a minimum-wage job as an usher. Suddenly, I was commuting an hour every morning to downtown LA, working nine to five at the Theatre Center, driving an hour and a half across town at rush hour, and working six thirty to ten at the Shubert. On weekends, *City of Angels* ran twice a day, so I worked from about noon to ten.

With such a hectic schedule, there was no time to focus on the past. The constant barrage of flashbacks and feelings that had plagued me since moving to LA blessedly stopped. This would become a pattern for years to come. In times of extreme stress, usually brought on by life changes, my psyche would unleash a storm of new memories, throwing me into emotional instability. Then, as I pulled my life back together, the memories would stop coming, allowing time to process and integrate the new things I'd learned about myself.

The new jobs made denial easy; I was too busy to think about the past. The Los Angeles Theatre Center turned out to be both boring and stressful. I spent my days at the office doing mind-numbing tasks like answering phones and stuffing envelopes. The other part of my job involved delivering packages all over LA, which, in the age before GPS, involved the use of a three-hundred page map. (Again, not kidding.)

The biggest problem with LATC, though, was not the work. It was the lack of pay. Literally. Just a few months into the gig, I stopped receiving paychecks. I worked for more than a month without pay before the theater finally announced it was bankrupt. Just like that, I was out of work again. The job hadn't even lasted long enough to qualify me for unemployment.

Unaware of the theater's financial woes, I had already signed a lease on a more expensive apartment. My ushering gig had already ended, leaving me broker than broke once again. Any peace I had made with God got flushed down the toilet with my job made in heaven. To offer up a blessing only to take it away was cruel. God was an asshole, and I hated Him for it.

But that was the feeling of a young girl who had yet to see the bigger picture. I now understand that the Lord really does work in mysterious ways. Looking back now, I can see that losing my job at

LATC was a blessing. It turned out to be the thing that led to the thing that eventually fixed my whole life.

At the time, though, I couldn't see the silver lining. I needed money, so the morning after the theater closed, I bought a newspaper and vowed to find a new job. In the want ads, I found a job that seemed strangely alluring. It offered a high hourly rate and an immediate start date. The good news: It was walking distance from my apartment. The disturbing news: It involved phone sex.

In my head, this didn't seem like a big deal. You get on the phone. You talk to guys. You say dirty things. Blah. Blah. Blah. I have no moral objection to it, nor did I then. On the contrary, I held a weird fascination for sex work and assumed I might become a prostitute someday. On the surface, such thoughts were strange coming from a good girl like me. Underneath, though, my fascination with the sex trade made perfect sense. Unfortunately, I had not yet remembered my history as a child prostitute, so I had no idea why I was so keen to be a phone-sex worker.

I don't remember much about my first night on the job except walking into an office space filled with cubicles and seeing lots of women in sweats and jeans with phones in their hands. As I was ushered through the room, I overheard one woman saying, "Oooo, baby, you making me so hot, I gotta get off." Then, she picked up an electric toothbrush, turned it on, and let the vibrating sound entice the listener.

After filling out my W-2 forms and getting an education on how to physically work the buttons on the phone, I was shown to my cubicle. Since it was my first night, I was assigned to a "chat" line—

meaning I was to flirt with guys, not get them off. When a button on my phone lit up, I grabbed the receiver.

"Hello?" I said, in a voice I barely recognized.

The voice on the other end sounded like a young man in his twenties. He had a southern accent and was shy and polite. I can't say what we talked about because I wasn't really there. Some other part of me had taken over the conversation while I listened passively from a far-off distance.

The voice—my voice—was flirtatious and giggly with a slight drawl, which delighted the young man. She spoke of her riding lessons, her love of horses, and the grand farm where she lived. The details suggested a life in the southern aristocracy.

The customer was so charmed by this girl that he stayed on the phone for the full half hour allowed by his credit card preauthorization. When the phone cut him off, he called back again then again. He did this for my entire five-hour shift.

During those hours, the young man remained polite. He was flirty but not overtly sexual, as that was beyond the scope of the "chat" service. He did, however, seem obsessed with figuring out where his new love interest lived. He asked over and over, offering to drive or fly anywhere to meet her—me—in person.

It was harmless enough. There was no way the man could ever figure out where I lived; we used fake names on the phone. Still, when I went to bed that night, I had horrible nightmares that he was after me, abducted me, and held me as a sexual hostage.

The next day, I quit my job as a phone-sex worker. The dreams were too terrifying and, though I didn't yet realize it, too close to real life. The part where I wasn't really me was weird too, but I didn't think much about it. My mind had a way of letting me see things about myself without wholly allowing me to be conscious of them. That's the nature of denial and dissociation.

A FEW DAYS LATER, out of the blue, I got a call from Center Theatre Group, the biggest and richest theater company in LA. They got my name from a former LATC colleague who had recently started working there. Without so much as an interview, I was offered a job in the fund-raising department. Lucky for me, it paid just as well as phone sex.

The next morning, I began working for one of the country's most important theaters. CTG ran both the Mark Taper Forum and the Ahmanson Theater, and routinely sent its plays to Broadway. Every day, the halls were filled with notable actors, directors, and playwrights. Within a few months, I'd set eyes on many of my idols, including Stephen Sondheim, Neil Simon, and Marvin Hamlisch. If I couldn't be in New York, this was definitely the next best thing.

So was I finally happy? Of course not!

Although the job offered financial stability, free theater tickets, lavish opening-night parties, and a chance to hang with world-renowned artists, it didn't require *me* to be artistic at all. I spent my days in a windowless cubicle typing donor names into a computer. It was soul-crushingly boring. It didn't help that in my free time I wasn't writing. Since leaving *Days*, I'd been blocked, and I lacked both the drive and the hope to change.

Lacking is actually an apt term to describe this period in my life. Although I had a job that could've led to greater things, I lacked the self-confidence to take full advantage of my luck. I also lacked friends but lacked the social skills to make them. It's not that coworkers didn't try to befriend me. In the beginning, people invited me to lunch. But I was so awkward and self-conscious that I rarely got a second invitation.

I could also be downright rude. After a few days on the job, for instance, the woman who had put me up for the position invited me to lunch. We had worked together before, so I knew her a little. I certainly knew that she'd done me a big favor, so the proper thing to do was invite *her* to a nice lunch, foot the bill, and thank her profusely for her kindness. Instead, we went dutch. I talked very little and asked her nothing about herself. Worst of all, I don't think I ever thanked her for getting me a job!

My bad behavior frequently led to self-sabotage. A few months after starting my job at CTG, I was accepted into the BMI Lehman Engel Musical Theatre Workshop. In New York, this well-respected training ground for musical theater writers includes alumni who wrote *A Chorus Line*, *Little Shop of Horrors*, and *The Book of Mormon*. While the LA group wasn't quite as venerable, getting in was still a coup and gave me a solid shot at getting my writing career off the ground. In the workshop, lyricists like me are paired with composers to write a series of assigned songs. I got paired with Rob, a recent USC grad who worked as a reporter for the *Los Angeles Downtown News*. Right from the start, we were a good match. Our first few assignments garnered high praise, and Rob and I began to form a friendship.

Things were going so well, in fact, that we were invited to participate in the workshop's 15 Minute Musicals festival. Our short original musical would receive a full production, complete with professional actors, lights, costumes, props, the works. It was an incredible opportunity. So what did I do? I quit. Rob didn't show up for a writing session one day. He was usually a reliable guy and had simply forgotten the appointment, but I felt slighted and turned into the hypersensitive, chip-on-her-shoulder psycho from high school. How dare he disrespect me! I will not be ignored!

When I finally calmed down, I realized that I'd made a terrible mistake. I told Rob I wanted to continue our collaboration, but he had already found a new librettist for the project. Kindly, the new partners offered to make it a threesome. I gladly accepted, then spent the next few weeks being difficult and complaining bitterly about anything and everything Rob's new partner did. I hated her script, her song cues, the way she parted her hair. I was acting out my anger at having been replaced so easily, but I had no awareness of this. I just played the part of a prima-donna douche bag while Rob tried helplessly to keep the peace. His reward for the effort was that I quit again, just a few days before dress rehearsal. As money was now involved for actors, costumes, musicians, and sets, the director of the workshop stepped in. He told me that if I dropped out at such a late stage I'd be barred from the group forever. I loved the workshop. It was my only artistic outlet at that time. So true to form, I dug in my heels and ditched the group. I could always find a way to ruin anything good that came into my life.

BACK IN THOSE DAYS, I came off as either a weirdo or an asshole. It wasn't my intention; it just didn't occur to me to act any other way. When people are aloof or impolite, others often judge them harshly, saying it's a sign of poor character. We think, *He's cold* or *She's rude* or *He's odd* when, in actuality, the cold, rude, odd person doesn't always realize they're being that way. Social skills are learned, not inherent. No one is born with the knowledge that they should chew with their mouth closed or say thank you when they're given a job or treat their collaborators with respect. We pick up these rules of human behavior through direct instruction and by watching others. The patterns we learn can be changed, but we often believe they are who we innately are.

Having been raised by a narcissistic psycho, I had a lot of patterns that needed changing. My poor manners, suspicious nature, and chip on the shoulder, as well as the self-consciousness I felt at not fitting in, all combined to make me not so great at relating to those around me. I was a hard worker, though, and highly driven to succeed. So despite my social shortcomings, I began to work my way up in the theater world—from a data-entry temp to Equity stage manager to assistant director. I even toured with a show that had a run at the New York Shakespeare Festival, allowing me to achieve the dream of working professionally in Manhattan.

During those years working in theater, I began the long process of healing from my childhood. As I was now safe from abuse, some of my worst fear triggers naturally subsided, and I was able to enjoy malls, motels, and sunsets again. Through work, I made friends and began to experience something like a normal social life.

I began to write again, selling three short stories to anthologies and penning a play about my experiences with the legal system.

Most of the time, I got up in the morning, went to work, came home, and lived an uneventful life. For most people, this isn't something to write about. But for me, normalcy and predictability were very new experiences.

One day, I was washing dishes at the kitchen sink when a warm, calm, happy feeling enveloped me. *This is contentment*, I thought. It's the first time I'd ever felt it. I was twenty-five years old.

Credit for that contentment and any other progress I made to that point must be given to Steve. We'd known each other for seven years by then and had been living together for four, so I'd had a lot of time to soak in his lessons. Steve comes from about as normal a family as one can imagine: working dad, stay-at-home mom, two kids, two cars. He grew up with nightly family dinners and annual family vacations where no one hit one another or even yelled much. As a result, Steve developed a steadfast, even-keeled, patient personality. When trouble comes along, he's able to think things through rather than act things out, and he spent countless hours teaching me to do the same.

Every night, as I histrionically relayed the crisis of the day, Steve would calmly talk me through it—asking how things made me feel and why I felt that way. Most people take knowing how they feel for granted, but the ability to recognize and name one's feelings is also learned, not innate. Generally, children learn these lessons when they're very young.

On the first day of kindergarten, a nervous child might say her tummy hurts, and the mother responds with "Are you feeling scared?" Over time, the child learns to associate her bodily sensations with the names of feelings. This is the beginning of emotional intelligence.

Like social skills and emotional intelligence, moral values are also learned at a young age. That works out fine if your parents are on the up and up. But when you're raised by a sociopath, basic issues of right and wrong get kind of fuzzy.

Steve possesses an impeccable moral code. He knows right from wrong and knows himself, so he can't be manipulated into doing things he doesn't believe are good. In our nightly conversations, Steve tried to help me develop my own sense of ethics. I'll never forget the first time he asked me what the "little voice in my head" was telling me to do. Little voice? What the hell was he talking about? It took a long time and a lot of late-night talks before I developed the inner voice that most people recognize as their conscience. Whatever good that conscience possessed was due to Steve, who taught me what it meant to be a decent human being who treats others with respect and kindness. That's why, when I decided to stop using Gary's last name, I chose to honor him by changing my name to Stevens.

WHILE MY FRIENDSHIP with Steve remained solid, our romantic relationship did not. As the years progressed, I grew to love him more and more—but not in *that way*. As a couple, we were not compatible. We were both too introverted and staid. I yearned for more adventure. I wanted to explore the world, and I needed to be with people who would coax me out of my shell. For a long time, I kept my feelings to myself. I was deeply attached to Steve and didn't want to hurt him in any way. But I was also bored and increasingly lonely. I felt stuck and didn't know what to do.

Then one day as I was exiting an off-ramp on my way to work, I had another epiphany. That clear, strong, authoritative voice that had helped me out in the past said, "Michelle, you're gay, and today's the day you're going to deal with it."

This came as a bit of a shock. I mean, I'd been living with Steve for years, and before him, I'd gone out with a few other guys. But I'd never dated a woman. Hell, I didn't even know any lesbians! (Though I certainly enjoyed the Victoria's Secret catalogue more than any straight girl should.)

Truth be told, I think that I'd simply been too preoccupied with surviving to think much about my sexuality before that moment. Most people start to become aware of their sexuality and sexual preferences during adolescence, but I was being raped and prostituted during those years. Later, I was trying so hard to look and act "normal" that I dated boys just to fit in. It was only after I began to heal that I gained the energy necessary to focus on my sexuality. It's not unusual for survivors of child sexual abuse to deal with their sexuality later in life. But I'm guessing most people don't figure it all out in one moment as they're exiting the 101!

Sitting at my desk that day, I wondered what to do with the new knowledge I had gained about myself. Oddly enough, I knew right away that it was true. I was gay; I just *knew* it. I also knew I had to do something about it that very day, so I picked up the phone, called Steve at his job, and asked him to meet me for dinner later that night. Sitting together at Bob's Big Boy, I watched him chow down on a burger, completely unaware of the storm about to hit. I knew that telling him would be a major blow and that he would probably want me to move out of our apartment that very night.

I waited till he was halfway through his chocolate cream pie before breaking the news.

"Steve," I said. "I have something to tell you. I'm gay."

He pulled the fork out of his mouth mid-bite, then spat chocolate pie into his napkin. "Are you seeing somebody?" he asked.

"No, of course not! I would never cheat!"

"Then how do you know?" he asked.

"I just do." I shrugged.

Steve started to cry.

I felt awful. Here was the first person ever to treat me well, the first person to teach me anything about love, and I was breaking his heart. God, I was a real shit!

"Look, Steve," I said. "I know you're upset, and I don't blame you. I don't want to make this any harder on you than it has to be. I'll move out tonight."

"Nah," he said, shaking his head. "You don't have to move . . . I think I'm gay too."

Searching for Judd Hirsch

Coming out as a lesbian was a giant leap in my healing process. Through the Los Angeles Gay & Lesbian Center, I quickly made new friends and started hanging out with them at parties and bars and coffeehouses. Soon enough, I started dating, and I enjoyed getting to know a great variety of women who introduced me to lots of new activities, neighborhoods, and ideas. For the first time in my life, I began to feel that I was actually living my life—the normal life of a twentysomething. Before then, my need to feel safe had always trumped my desire for adventure. But after nearly a decade away from Gary, I was finally feeling more sure of myself and my ability to protect myself from harm.

After a few years of dating, complete with all the usual stories of heartbreak and stalker chicks and romances gone bad, I grew tired of the revolving door of girlfriends. I yearned to meet someone substantial, someone I could be serious about. I was ready to settle down.

I was looking for someone who was smart and funny, talented and ambitious, trustworthy and mature. I wanted someone who shared my fairly traditional values regarding marriage, money, education, and child rearing. Unfortunately, these were not the kind of women I was meeting at Girl Bar.

They were not the kind of women I seemed to be meeting anywhere in LA, and I started to blame it on the city. "I'm from the East Coast," I reasoned. "Perhaps I need to meet East Coast women." I seriously started to contemplate leaving my job, my friends, everything I had built in Los Angeles just so I could move back east and meet a decent girl! I became so convinced that moving was my only hope that I once again bargained with God. "God," I prayed. "If you don't send me somebody decent, I'm outta here. I mean it! I'm moving by the end of the month!"

A few days later, I was sitting in my office at Center Theatre Group when I started catching pieces of the conversation next door. My friend Monica was on the phone with one of her friends—a guy who worked at the Directors Guild of America and had, apparently, suffered a disappointing date the day before. "Oh, I'm so sorry, Bob!" I heard Monica saying. "I know you liked her a lot. I can't believe she turned out to be a lesbian."

I don't know what came over me, but like a shot, I popped my head into Monica's office. "Lesbian?" I asked. "What lesbian? I want to meet her!"

And despite not knowing Bob or his lesbian in question, I was soon set up on a blind date with a woman I knew nothing about.

It was my first blind date. I had no idea what to expect.

The night before, I couldn't sleep, but it wasn't because I felt nervous. I was electric with anticipation. I just knew this mysterious woman was going to change my life.

Meeting Chris certainly did change my life. Right from the start, we were inseparable, and it was clear that we were meant for each other. Not just because she was smart and fun and adventurous and ambitious and made me laugh on a constant basis, but because there were all sorts of freaky signs.

One day, for instance, she opened the trunk of her car to reveal a bunch of Broadway sheet music. *Evita*. *A Chorus Line*. *They're Playing Our Song*. All the shows I loved. She could play my favorite Marvin Hamlisch songs on the piano and had spent her childhood performing in music and theater groups just like I had.

When I stayed at her apartment for the first time, I took the obligatory browse through her bookshelves. Prominently displayed—and lovingly preserved in a plastic book cover—was *The Official Preppy Handbook*. She could recite every word of it.

Despite these odd similarities, Chris and I came from completely different backgrounds. She was born in Cleveland, the daughter of Filipino immigrants. Her parents were both doctors and worked hard to earn their place among the American middle class. They sent their only child to prep school and paid her way through college.

In many ways, Chris was like Steve. They were both children of well-to-do families, accustomed to expensive lessons, foreign travel, and parents who expected their offspring to be successful professionals. The difference was: Steve was a part of the culture he inhabited; he fit right in at the club. Chris was an outsider in her very white-bread world. Kids called her Chink on the playground and made fun of the stinky Filipino food she brought for lunch.

That's why the *Preppy Handbook* mattered to Chris. Like me, she devoured its lessons in how behave like a successful American. Even though it was a joke book, we both read it at impressionable ages—and it sure did make an impression! We both grew up dreaming about the day we would own Labrador retrievers and Volvos to tote them around.

Needless to say, the part of me that was the Preppy latched right onto Chris. We shared the same traditional views on money, children, and marriage. (I understand that the word *traditional* might sound strange when speaking about a gay couple, but we grew up wanting to be in *The Brady Bunch* just like everyone else.) The part of me that was the Writer was also smitten. Chris had graduated from a college writing program before moving to Hollywood to pursue a career in television. In her job as a TV executive, she worked with writers every day and helped them fine-tune their work. I soon realized that Chris was like the Einstein of story structure, making her the perfect sounding board for my writer's creative ideas.

Did I mention she's also really cute?

EVEN THOUGH it was clear from the start that Chris was the One, we still had big problems. Couples' counselors usually like to say that both partners are equally responsible, but I take most of the blame. I entered the relationship with more issues than *People* magazine and a cast of characters in my head more changeable than Doctor Who.

My myriad problems had crept into relationships before. When I met Chris, they seemed to decide it was time for a fiesta. I've seen this phenomenon happen in the lives of my clients; all their insecurities and bad behaviors come to the forefront when they finally meet

M. Right. I think this is because as a mate starts to feel like family we wounded people assume they will be just like the crappy families we had before. In order to protect ourselves from the sequel, we start to look for problems and test our mates relentlessly. We think, *I know he'll hit me if I mouth off (just like my father did)*; *I know she'll leave me if I demand all of her attention (just like my mother did).* Then we act badly until our mate has no choice but to prove us right.

With Chris I acted badly in so many ways! A few months into dating, I remember a fight I picked while driving to Idyllwild for our first romantic weekend. Chris was talking about her friends from high school, college, and Hollywood when she realized they mostly came from wealthy families. "Of course they come from wealthy families," I pointed out. "People tend to associate with people who are just like them."

"But I'm not from a wealthy family," Chris said innocently. "My dad came to this country with forty bucks in his pocket."

Instead of honoring Chris's family and the obstacles they'd over-come, I became infuriated. All the rage I felt about coming from poverty, having to pay my way through college, and having no family to fall back on exploded in a tirade against "rich kids" who were "given everything in life," had it "so easy," and never had to "worry 'bout nothin'!" Chris tried to protest, but I went apeshit, accusing her of being a spoiled rich kid who had no idea what it was like to have a hard life.

Lost in self-righteousness, I conveniently forgot that Chris too had a tough childhood. But unlike me, she did not grow bitter from her experiences. Chris was a humble, thoughtful, generous person who generally liked everyone. I was the one with the black heart. I was the one who was spoiled.

I was also the one who demanded *Fatal Attraction* levels of devotion. An intense need for attention and reassurance is common in adults who were abused or neglected as children. We are running at such a deficit in the love column that when we find it we can't get enough. Unfortunately, other adults—no matter how much they love us—can't provide the kind of selfless, unconditional love we didn't get from our parents. In grown-up relationships, our partners have their own lives and needs.

When I met Chris, she had a demanding job, hobbies, friends, and a large extended family to tend. I loved that she led a full and active life, yet I also viewed it as a threat. I needed to be Chris's numero uno. Truth be told, in order to feel secure, I yearned to be the only person in her life. Anyone who's ever dated someone codependent (or is codependent) knows the kind of conflict that ensued. I would pout when Chris tried to leave the house, even for work. I would whine when she tried to make plans with friends. I would demand that she take me to after-hours work functions. I needed to keep her close. I had to know she was mine, mine, mine.

Even after nearly three years together, I remained intensely insecure and demanding. Things came to a head one Memorial Day when Chris went to a family barbecue. We had fought about her family many times. It was large and close-knit and prone to constant gatherings. Chris was not out to her family yet, so there was no way she could bring along her girlfriend! Instead, I tended to stay home alone while she fulfilled an endless stream of family obligations. This particular weekend, I'd had enough. Chris had already spent Thanksgiving, Christmas, Easter, and even New Year's Eve with her kin. I didn't feel she should spend Memorial Day with them too.

Chris needed to cut some apron strings, no doubt about it. But that's not the point of the story. The point is what happens when a person with abandonment issues flies into a psycho rage. After Chris left our apartment on that holiday morning, I felt so angry and helpless that I went into her closet and wildly started ripping at her clothes. Screaming and crying, I tore everything she owned off hangers and left it all in a giant heap on the closet floor. I probably would've set fire to the pile, burning the apartment and myself in the process, but Chris came home early and stopped me.

She was very upset about her clothes.

But she was relieved that she didn't own a bunny.

DESPITE MY CONSTANT DRAMA, Chris and I stuck it out. I give her all the credit. She's the most loyal, thoughtful, dependable, generous mate imaginable. Right from the start, Chris was sympathetic to all I'd endured. She understood the rotten hand I'd been dealt in life and how it handicapped me emotionally, socially, creatively, and financially.

Chris's love couldn't fix me, though. Nearly thirty, I was becoming increasingly frustrated by the problems in my life that never seemed to get better, like writing regularly, building a career, or learning how to get along with people. My emotions were a nonstop roller coaster of depression, anxiety, manic enthusiasm, and rage, and I always seemed to be in some kind of crisis or fight. The ups and downs drove those who loved me crazy. I was so unpredictable that Chris often joked that I must have multiple personalities or something.

I drove myself crazy too, because no matter how hard I worked or how much I accomplished, I never seemed to achieve any traction in life. Anytime anything good came my way, I managed to ruin it. In time, I began to feel like a real loser and lost all hope that I'd ever reach my potential or find lasting happiness.

In hindsight, it's easy to see that my inability to move forward was the result of not dealing with my past. I spent so much mental energy running from my memories and feelings that I had nothing left over for the present or the future. This is common in people who have endured childhood trauma. In order to survive, we become so adept at hiding our feelings that denial becomes a way of life. But over time, the denial of our true feelings and experiences prevents us from growing and moving on. We stay stuck in the past.

This all sounds very obvious, I know. But it's not so apparent when you're in it. Every day in my practice, I see clients who feel frustrated and hopeless. They've been repeating the same unhealthy patterns over and over again, sometimes for decades. But they can't see the patterns that are holding them back—nor can they accept that their problems might stem from some long-ago trauma like their mothers' neglect or their fathers' alcoholism. All they can see is that they are unhappy. Nothing ever seems to work out for them, and they sincerely don't know why.

That was me in a nutshell. I was constantly trying to find happiness by changing my circumstances—new jobs, new friends, even new houses (I moved ten times in six years!). But the problem wasn't with my circumstances; the problem was with me. I didn't know who I was. How could I? I didn't even have full access to my memories! The fear of facing my past kept me from facing my feelings about it, and it kept me from recognizing all the ways I'd been damaged mentally and emotionally.

To quote Dr. Phil, "You can't change what you don't acknowledge." I wasn't acknowledging anything! Not the extent of my abuse nor my feelings about it. Not insane behaviors and mood swings. I didn't acknowledge how badly I treated people, especially Chris and Steve. I didn't own any of my own shit, but I sure as hell was outraged that the world kept shitting on me!

DURING THESE DIRECTIONLESS YEARS, I drifted in and out of therapy the same way I drifted in and out of jobs and apartments. It's a testament to my low self-esteem that the therapist I chose to see was Javier, the guy who callously told me to come back when I could pay. I did go back to Javier, on and off, for about six years. We talked about my love life, my creative aspirations, my personal problems with friends and coworkers. We talked a bit about the memories I'd had and the rage I felt at my parents, but we never did very deep work. Part of the problem was me; I didn't yet have the courage to fully face my demons.

But after six years, I'd have to say a lot of the problem was Javier. He simply lacked the Right Stuff.

The Right Stuff for a therapist is the ability to create a therapeutic environment where the client feels safe to expose their true self in order to heal and grow. To achieve this, the therapist must be open and genuine, empathetic and nonjudgmental, and treat the client with unconditional positive regard. Seems simple, right? Well, it's much harder than it sounds, which helps explain why most therapists overrate their abilities.

I think Javier overestimated his abilities. At the time, I overrated him too. He seemed friendly and warm, knew some things about child abuse, and was generally a nice fellow. That made him better than any other therapist I'd seen. But looking back, I realize that I never fully trusted Javier, probably because I sensed that he didn't trust me.

In order to help people overcome trauma, it's imperative to believe that they can do exactly that. I know I sound like Captain Obvious. Yet it's sad how often therapists don't believe in their own patients, especially if they appear to be all-out crazy like I was back then. I was impulsive, moody, anxious, angry, unpredictable—all the qualities that spell i-n-c-u-r-a-b-l-e to many therapists. These were symptoms of the abuse I'd suffered, but Javier made a common mistake. He assumed my symptoms were me. As a result, he was often patronizing, judgmental, and disrespectful of my choices. For instance, he assumed that both Chris and Steve must be bad for me despite any evidence. In Javier's mind, I couldn't possibly attract loving, healthy relationships. Despite all that I'd already survived and overcome, the guy had no faith in me.

A therapist who secretly doesn't believe his client can heal is like a teacher who doesn't believe his student can learn or a coach who doesn't believe her athlete can win. For the client/student/athlete trying to succeed, their guide's pessimistic attitude is poisonous. Unfortunately, I couldn't see things so clearly back then. If changes weren't happening in therapy, my lack of self-esteem made me believe that the problem must lie with me. Javier didn't dissuade me of this opinion. Like many arrogant therapists (and teachers and coaches), he believed any lack of progress was due to his pupil's unwillingness to learn his valuable lessons.

Those who loved me didn't see it that way. Over the years, both Chris and Steve urged me to find somebody new. Eventually, I gave in and made an appointment with a marriage and family therapist I found in the Yellow Pages. She was in her midthirties and newly out of school. She had a simple, pleasant office and a simple, pleasant mind to match. Before every session, she would pour herself a cup of hot tea, curl up in an armchair, and sip while I laid out my problems, as if we were having a sisterly chat. She was nice enough but not very bright. In grad school and internships, I've met lots of therapists just like her: well-meaning people from humdrum backgrounds who have never experienced much of life and certainly don't think philosophically. As a result, they have no wisdom. This might be fine for some clients, but it definitely wasn't right for me.

For anyone counting, that was the end of Therapist #6.

I KNOW I'M HARD on my profession, and I'm probably ruining my chance of being crowned prom queen at the next convention of the American Psychological Association. But after seeing six therapists over the course of fifteen years, I think I have a right to be angry at a string of helpers who didn't help! I'm sure my former therapists would blame me for the lack of progress. We shrinks like to point out that people don't change until they're ready, which is true. But I think being in the presence of a brilliant, dedicated, passionate therapist can also *make* a person ready. Great therapists, like great teachers or coaches, inspire people to want to learn and grow.

Think of the movie *Good Will Hunting*. In it, a young man named Will cannot reach his full potential because he is plagued with symptoms from a traumatic childhood. A foster kid who was frequently beaten, Will grows up suffering from low self-esteem, fear of the unknown, generalized rage, and a severe inability to trust. Forced into therapy, Will demonstrates his unwillingness to change for a string of therapists who all throw up their hands. Then Will meets

Robin Williams's character, a psychologist who not only recognizes Will's resistance as a symptom of trauma but also cares enough to push him to change.

Thank God entertainment is ripe with stories of passionate therapists who are able to save tortured souls. If not for these fictional depictions of therapist as hero, I might have given up hope. Instead, despite the string of mediocre shrinks who made me feel incurable, I knew that someday I'd get my Hollywood ending. I just had to find the right therapist—the one who would be skilled enough and smart enough and dedicated enough to pull me back to health.

I had a vision in my head of this perfect therapist. It was Judd Hirsch in *Ordinary People*. I saw *Ordinary People* as a kid, shortly before my first suicide attempt. The story of a teenage boy who is suicidal after the death of his brother resonated. I could relate to his pain and the loneliness he felt inside. In the movie, Judd Hirsch plays the boy's therapist—an intelligent, extremely kind, but no-bullshit kind of guy. I was immediately struck by his skill and empathy, but what really sold me was his dedication. Near the end of the film, when the boy is desperate, he calls Judd Hirsch after hours. Sensing the boy's distress, the therapist doesn't stand on protocol. He doesn't tell the boy to call back during office hours or go to the nearest emergency room. Instead, understanding that the boy really needs him, Judd Hirsch cares enough to meet with the boy in the middle of the night.

At thirteen, I didn't know anything about therapy, but I instinctively understood that in order to heal I would someday need a therapist who was as dedicated as Judd Hirsch. My secrets were so dark, my suicidal tendencies so strong, that I'd never be able to face them without a therapist I could trust with my life.

———

Unfortunately, we don't always get to choose when we'll face our demons. Shit happens. And in 1997, it happened to me. I got a call one day from my mother. We hadn't spoken in more than five years.

"Shell?" she asked, in a tentative voice.

"Yeah?" I answered warily.

"I just wanted you to know that Gary's dead!" I could hear her breaking down in tears.

I thanked her for the call and got off as quickly as possible but not before learning he'd died of a stroke at the age of fifty-four. Gary had a long history of diabetes. I would later learn that in the years since I'd last seen him he'd lost a toe, then a foot, then a whole leg to the disease that eventually killed him.

Getting the call was very strange. I didn't know how I was supposed to feel. Throughout my childhood, I'd prayed for Gary to drop dead. Now he finally had, but I wasn't sure how or if it even mattered.

One thing I knew for certain: Hearing my mother cry for that man, mourn that monster, sickened me.

Even though I hadn't had much to do with him in more than a decade, the death of Gary Lundquist pried open a dusty crypt in my mind. All the memories and feelings I had walled off for years came pouring out. It was like the *Days of Our Lives* days all over again.

I guess some people might wonder why my abuser's death created an emotional crisis. I mean, the guy was a monster; I should've been celebrating. While I was certainly relieved that Gary was dead, that relief was indicative of the problem. Even though Gary hadn't been in my life for years, I still feared him and what he might do to me someday. That fear stood like a sentry over my psyche, keeping all sorts of sordid memories at bay. Now the fear of Gary was gone. There was no longer an outward threat to remembering the past, and that was the greatest terror of all.

Frightened of my own mind and all it had to show me, I became gripped by debilitating anxiety. For the past several years, I'd been living with Chris at her Studio City condo, and we'd been quite happy there. After Gary died, though, everything changed. The neighbor two floors below liked to practice guitar during the day. He'd been doing it for a while, but it suddenly drove me crazy—so crazy that I couldn't stand to be in the apartment and would prowl the halls waiting for the noise to stop. In the evening, I began to hear the television of the neighbor beneath us. Then I noticed that his dog barked in the middle of the night, suddenly ruining my sleep. The insomnia got so bad that I demanded we move our bed from the recently redecorated master bedroom to the tiny guest room down the hall.

My instant, and seemingly nonsensical, hypersensitivity to noise made no sense to the all-too-sensible Chris. She'd never seen my PTSD in full swing and couldn't comprehend why I was suddenly so jumpy. In order to avoid noise, I constantly demanded that we change rooms or turn on white noise or leave the apartment, which made her think I was a crazy person.

I was crazy, although I couldn't understand why. I didn't realize that I became frightened and anxious every time my memories saw an opportunity to emerge—when I left home for college, when I moved to LA, and now when Gary had died. Since the first memories of Gary and the abortion had overwhelmed me seven years earlier, I'd worked valiantly to keep the rest—the S/M, prostitution, and pornography—under wraps. This wasn't a conscious choice. You can't consciously choose to block memories if you don't know they exist. But my subconscious mind knew they were there. And just like Jack Nicholson in *A Few Good Men*, it knew I couldn't handle the truth.

So my subconscious sent me constant fantasies instead, much like the fantasies I'd experienced in my youth. The nature of these fantasies was always dark and sexual with detailed, unchanging plots. In one plot, I was taken to a remote cabin where a deer head hung over a fireplace. The cabin had a basement where I was subjected to all sorts of S/M tortures by various men. In another fantasy, I was imprisoned by a mad scientist who kept me in a cage and used me for painful experiments that included the use of needles and electric shock. A third involved a group of men who abducted me, held me captive in a motel room, and gang-raped me repeatedly.

Obviously, these "fantasies" weren't fantasies at all, just thinly veiled memories. They remained veiled because I wasn't strong enough to face my past. Still, I understood that the stuff running through my mind wasn't normal. I mean, as far as I knew, I'd never had any kind of kinky sex or even watched a porno film. So why was I always thinking about such nasty stuff? I figured I must be some kind of pervert.

Unable to function, I had to seek help, and the person I instinctively turned to was Javier. I'd seen him the longest; he knew me the best. I was in crisis; I had no time for shrink searches or backstory bullshit. Right away, Javier and I got to work.

I told him about my daydreams—about the cabin with the deer over the fireplace and the basement used for torture. Suddenly, I had an epiphany. I remembered that Gary's old house had a fireplace with a deer head over the mantel. I remembered it had a big basement! For the first time, it dawned on me that my "daydream" must be a memory.

The vision of a torturous tool kept popping into my mind during this time. I could see it, and I knew I was afraid of it. But I didn't know what it was. Javier asked me to draw a picture of what I was seeing. I drew a rectangular box with two spikes on the end. I told him that when the spikes touched my skin they caused unbearable pain. Looking at the drawing, Javier immediately recognized it as a Taser, and it made perfect sense. As a child, I knew Gary owned a Taser. I had heard the word *Taser*, but I'd never heard the word used in relation to the dreaded little box. Now, through therapy, the word and the image and the memory all blended together to make sense.

This is the deep work of trauma-focused therapy. The therapist and patient work together to process all sorts of images and feelings and thoughts as they arise in order to establish the survivor's story and help her make sense of it. In a case like mine, where there is dissociation and a lot of painful abuse involved, the process is slow and agonizing. Given my history of suicide attempts, it is also incredibly dangerous.

For the therapist, the main focus during trauma work has to be safety, which is achieved by containing the patient's emotional reactions. If the memories start coming too fast or the feelings get too strong, the patient is likely to get overwhelmed by the pain and be retraumatized. The therapist's job is to constantly monitor the patient's emotional temperature and teach her how to cool things down when they get too hot. This is extremely difficult to manage when one is dealing with volatile memories, which is why trauma work is sometimes likened to waking a tiger.

In my case, containment had always been a serious issue. Every time the abuse broke into my consciousness, it erupted like a volcano, burning everything in its path. Flashbacks would play nonstop; I'd get overwhelmed with feelings and completely lose the ability to function in everyday life. This time was no different. When the memories came, they were fast and furious, and brought along all the usual fear, pain, rage, and sadness. In addition, it is the nature of dissociative identity disorder that different memories are "owned" by different alternate personalities. So every time a repressed memory popped into my consciousness, an alter popped in along with it. The rapid switching of my personalities was extremely disconcerting, and I'm sure it made me look even crazier than usual.

I was thankful that there weren't a lot of people around to see me during this time. Because of the breakdown, I wasn't working—again. Meanwhile, Chris was supporting us both by clocking eighty-hour weeks. Isolated from prying eyes, my alters felt safe to come out completely and "take over" my body. This would happen without my conscious knowledge, but the switching left plenty of signs.

Chris would often come home late at night to find the stereo blaring, the TV playing, and all the lights on. A half-made dinner might be on the counter or a half-potted plant on the patio, but I was nowhere to be found. It was so bizarre and so frequent that Chris started calling these incidents "alien abductions." It drove her crazy that I would leave the house in such a state. She complained constantly that I was being thoughtless when I didn't turn off the lights or leave a note. How could I explain that I didn't know I was leaving the house? How could I explain that I wasn't even sure where I'd been all day . . . or *who* I'd been?

As the weeks wore on, I became more and more disturbed. The flashbacks kept coming, the feelings kept bombarding me, but Javier wasn't helping to contain them. When a client is in crisis, the first thing a therapist should suggest is more frequent sessions. Once a week is fine for ordinary therapy, but desperate times call for desperate measures. I should've been seeing Javier two or three times a week.

Unfortunately, Javier was no Judd Hirsch. Instead of offering more sessions, he started canceling them. He'd often call just an hour or two before our weekly appointment to say he couldn't make it because he was too busy with another project. One time, I drove all the way to his office at our scheduled time and sat in the waiting room for the whole hour before realizing he'd neglected to show up!

When we did have sessions, I made it very clear that my mental state was declining. As in the past, my anxiety eventually morphed into depression, and I became suicidal. I spoke to Javier about my suicidal feelings, and he suggested I go on antidepressants. I met once with a psychiatrist who prescribed a fairly new drug called Effexor.

In many circumstances, psychotropic drugs are excellent at alleviating symptoms related to trauma. Over the years, they have been an absolute lifesaver for me. Finding the proper medications and dosages, however, can take time. It can also take time to work through a drug's initial side effects.

Unfortunately, at this point in my life, I lacked the maturity and patience to follow up with my shrink and manage my medication responsibly. As a result, Effexor was not nearly as effective as it could have been, and I needlessly suffered from a multitude of side effects, including headaches, nonstop yawning, and dry mouth that was so bad I couldn't speak.

The worst side effect (which could have been avoided entirely, had I called my doctor), was nightly insomnia. Insomnia is toxic to a disturbed mind. Up all night, I would pace our apartment and battle a voice in my head that was telling me I should "Die! Die! Die!"

When a client is suicidal, it is customary for a therapist to offer emergency support. In general, that means reminding the client that they can call between sessions if there's an urgent need. The therapist isn't trying to encourage overdependence but wants the client to know that in an emergency a trained professional is around to talk her off the ledge. After a session in which I confessed to strong suicidal feelings, Javier followed protocol by reminding me that I could call him in a jam. I'd never called any therapist in an emergency, so the offer seemed pointless. But then I'd tried to commit suicide twice. Maybe this time it might be better to try something different.

Maybe this time I should ask for help when I need it.

Maybe this time I should trust someone.

THE FIRST TIME I called Javier I was in a terrible state. Obsessed with the past, I'd pulled out some old letters from my parents. As I read through them and saw all their lies and half-truths in black-and-white, I got very, very agitated. Feeling I was about to fall into an abyss, I left Javier a message. It took him six hours to call back.

During those hours, something strange started happening in my head. Instead of "Die! Die! Die!," I got an urge to flee. I became convinced that I should grab some money, hop on a Greyhound, and go somewhere new. It didn't matter where; I just had to leave. I had already stuffed a bag and was nearly out the door when Javier finally called me back. He explained that there's something called a dissociative fugue, a state in which stressed people take off and forget who they are. Javier said he thought I was in danger of a fugue. He recommended that I stop reading the upsetting papers and give them to him at our next appointment.

I did give the papers to Javier, but it didn't matter much. My problem wasn't a few letters. My problem was a childhood of torturous memories and feelings that were trying to break free. They overwhelmed me day and night, and I felt helpless to stop them. My mind was a weapon I couldn't fight, so I had to flee. Whether it be a Greyhound or a grave, I had to escape. I just couldn't take the pain anymore.

SO, ONE FRIDAY AFTERNOON, I got it in my head that it was time to call it quits. I already had the means—a full bottle of Effexor—and I was more than ready to take it. But I'd promised to call Javier before I did anything dangerous. So I did. Then I sat in a dark room and waited for him to call back.

I waited the rest of Friday and all of Saturday before I finally realized that Javier had no intention of returning my call. He had offered to be available, had basically urged me to trust him. Then he'd let me down just like everyone else in my life. He didn't really give a shit about me or my feelings or whether I lived or died. In my troubled mind, Javier was no better than my crappy parents.

This was more than my battered soul could bear. I'd prayed for a therapist who would care enough about me to stick it out through the dark times and pull me back to health. Javier didn't care enough to return a fucking phone call. It was devastating.

On Sunday evening, I downed the pills. There wasn't a lot of thought put into it. I was in a very dark place, and I swallowed whatever was left in the bottle. Chris wasn't home. No one was scheduled to visit and "accidentally" find me. I had given up on being helped. I had given in.

Ironically, this was the moment when Javier finally called. The first thing I did was berate him for taking so long. Two days! He got defensive and explained that the timing of phone calls was his prerogative.

"Well, you should've called a little sooner," I said flippantly. "You might've caught me before I took the pills."

"Pills? What pills?" Javier asked.

Oh, yeah, *now* I had his attention.

After assessing what, when, and how much I'd taken, Javier asked if anyone else was around. He wanted someone to take me to the hospital. If I couldn't find someone, he said he'd call the cops. I thought about walking out of the apartment into the night. The cops couldn't find me if they didn't know where to look. But ultimately, my good girl kicked in, and I did as I was told to do.

I called my friend Dan, who lived about a block away.

When he arrived, Javier told me to hand him the phone.

"Dan," Javier said. "Michelle just took an alarming number of pills. I need you to drive her to the emergency room."

At the emergency room, it was the same old scene. Get assigned to a cubicle, tell the doctor what I took. They made me drink charcoal to soak up the drugs. (Yes, it's as gross as it sounds.) But there was really nothing to worry about. Turns out Effexor is rarely lethal even in large doses.

That was small comfort to the people who loved me. Dan called Chris and Steve, and all three stood vigil throughout the ordeal. This was very different than the other times I'd tried to commit suicide—the times my parents had displayed wanton disregard for whether I lived or died. Now there were people in my life who seemed quite upset by what I'd done.

Realizing that my actions affected other people made me feel guilty and ashamed of a suicide attempt for the first time in my life.

Another difference this time around was the hospital staff. When I was a kid, all the doctors and nurses felt sorry for me and were kind. When an adult goes to the emergency room after a suicide attempt, I learned that the staff has little sympathy. They believe suicidal patients are histrionic and selfish and wasting their valuable time.

The doctor was cold, the nurses were curt, and the social worker who was sent in to talk with me displayed outright contempt.

"Why'd you do it?" she asked.

"I'm in pain," I said. "I just can't take life anymore."

"Well, that's just dramatic," she countered. "Things always seem better in the morning."

The person I really wanted to see in the emergency room was Javier. Even though I was angry at him for not returning my phone call in a timely manner, I was still desperate to believe he cared about me. I was experiencing a lot of transference, which is a fancy shrink way of saying I saw Javier as a parent. Transference happens a lot in therapy. When a client has been neglected or abused by their own parents, it's a force to be reckoned with!

That force can be used to great advantage if the therapist is caring, dependable, and trustworthy, like a good parent. In this type of healthy relationship, the client gets to experience what it feels like to be nurtured and loved—often for the first time. And just like a child who is nurtured and loved by their parents, the client begins to heal and grow.

I did my part; I put my faith in Javier. After seven years together, I trusted him. Unfortunately, Javier was not the kind of therapist who cared about honoring that trust. He couldn't bother to show up for scheduled sessions; he couldn't bother to return urgent phone calls; and he sure as hell couldn't bother to visit me in the emergency room after I attempted suicide even though Chris got on the phone and begged him.

Javier's apathy was devastating, but it was also a wake-up call.

For the first time, I saw him for who he really was and realized his brand of "therapy" did more harm than good. I vowed never to see him again.

Instead, all I wanted to do was get back to my apartment, hug my dog, and crawl into bed next to my girlfriend. With my nonemergency emergency winding down, I got off the gurney, turned to Chris, and said, "I'm really tired. Let's go home."

She nodded, opened the privacy curtain, and scanned the hall for a nurse who could sign us out.

Just then the social worker accosted me. "Where do you think you're going?" she asked.

"We're trying to find someone to release me," I explained. "I'm ready to go home."

"Home?" she snickered. "Oh, you're not going home. You're being transferred to a locked-down mental facility. You've been committed."

All You Need Is Love

I have to go to the bathroom. I don't think I can hold it much longer. A pint of heavy charcoal has worked its way through my body, and it wants out. Now.

The bathroom is just a few steps away. I can see the toilet. It's just sitting there. But in order to get to it, I have to get out of this bed. That means acknowledging to the nurses that I'm awake. More upsetting, it means acknowledging to myself that I'm here, locked in a fucking looney bin.

They brought me by ambulance the previous night. Everything about it was humiliating. The way the social worker pronounced my sentence with hardened glee, the way the nineteen-year-old EMTs got dramatic when Chris asked to ride along. "No way. Uh-uh. You can't go where *she's* goin'." The way the admitting nurse handed me a cheap toothbrush and cheaper socks while reminding me that it was my right to wear my own clothes on the ward, but I couldn't go on outings with the patients because my stay was "involuntary."

The most humiliating part of all was the cause of this involuntary stay. It was all Javier's doing, as it turned out. While he'd ignored me at the ER and pretty much blew off Chris, he did talk to the social worker long enough to tell her I should be committed. Now I'm not saying this was a baseless recommendation. I did try to kill myself. But committing someone—taking away their power and their freedom—is a very harsh move and terribly traumatic, especially for someone who spent their childhood enslaved.

Now that I'm a therapist, I take my power to commit someone very seriously and would never use it unless absolutely necessary, which it never has been. Anytime I've had a patient who needed to be hospitalized, I've spoken with her and suggested she voluntarily admit herself. Taking this approach allows a wounded patient to maintain her dignity and sense of control during a dark time. It also works to strengthen, rather than destroy, our therapeutic relationship.

Javier, unfortunately, was not the kind of therapist who understood the emotional and psychological sway he held over his patients, nor do I think he wanted to be that involved. Javier was a by-the-book kind of therapist. And the book says: If someone is a danger to herself, best to lock her up.

So there I was, a certified crazy person. A ward of the state. This new status was shocking and mortifying. How the hell had I sunk so low?

Freaked out, I refused to get out of bed, which seemed to piss off the nurses. Several times already they'd been in to rouse me, saying it was time for breakfast, time for group, time for lunch. But the thought of getting up, walking the halls in my dirty clothes, and eating with a bunch of mental patients was too much for me.

I wasn't some mental patient. I didn't belong.

Adding insult to injury, the charcoal couldn't wait any longer. Feeling I was about to have an accident, I was forced to rush to the toilet, which soon looked like a campfire grill. I don't mean to be disgusting, but I need to convey the utter degradation of writhing in pain on some mental-ward toilet while shitting briquettes.

In some ways, I know I deserved these indignities. I had tried to kill myself, after all, which legally deemed me incompetent to make my own choices. But being locked in a hospital wasn't going to help. If anything, it made me feel more desperate.

THE SOUND OF FLUSHING brought a nurse into the room. She was standing in front of me before I could pull up my pants. "Lunch is ending," she said, a bit snippy. "You better go get something. It's a long time till dinner."

I was hungry, but I just couldn't bring myself to leave the room. Being locked up and abased and treated unkindly by people who were supposed to care all felt way too much like my childhood. And just as in childhood, the only thing I wanted to do was hide. Spotting the narrow space between the side of the bed and the wall, I did what I'd done countless times in motel rooms: I plopped myself down on the floor, drew my knees into my chest, and began to rock back and forth.

Hidden from view by the mattresses, I felt safely invisible, and the rocking had a soothing effect. While I didn't realize it at the time, this rocking motion is one of the ways I put myself into a dissociative trance.

I don't know how long I sat rocking on the floor, but I'm sure I looked like a total whack job to the nurses and patients who walked in.

The funny thing is: Had anyone asked me, I would've vehemently denied the need to be in a mental hospital. Yet to the outside observer, I probably looked like the most disturbed patient on the ward!

Hours passed by, the light through the window changed, but I never moved—not to eat, not to stretch, not for anything. It's hard to say what was going on internally during those many hours. I was a zombie. But underneath all that, I suppose I felt terrified—of being in the hospital, of course. But I was also terrified of being totally alone.

Now that Javier had betrayed me I had no one to help me.

Who the hell could I find at this point? And how the hell would I ever be able to trust that person?

A NURSE CAME IN, followed by Chris. I suppose it was visiting hours, not that I noticed or cared. Chris seemed shocked to see me on the floor in my zombie state. "Hey, Mooch," she said quietly. "I brought someone to see you. It's Leah. Can she come in?"

Leah was Chris's therapist, someone I'd heard about but never met. Chris always had great things to say about her. But then I'd always said great things about Javier.

Leah came in and sat gently on the bed. Even in my hypnotized state, I was aware of her presence. She had a slight build, a kind face, and long curly blond hair that made her look like a goddess. She had an aura about her that was all love and goodness. Meeting her for the first time was how I imagine it must be to meet the Dalai Lama.

"Michelle," she said, in a calm, reassuring voice. "Chris asked me to come and visit with you today. I want to be here with you, but I'll go if you want. You just let me know."

It's such a simple thing—to ask someone what he or she wants and genuinely care about the answer. Yet it's remarkably rare within the mental health system.

Still out of it, I somehow managed to nod, letting Leah know she should stay. I wanted her there. Her very presence was already calming me, making me feel safer. We didn't talk much. She just sat on the edge of the bed and smiled at me, the essence of compassion and kindness.

Eventually, I stopped rocking. My mind returned to my body and decided to join the world again. Once I could focus, Leah explained the rules of commitment. I was on a seventy-two-hour hold, and the hospital would have to go to court if they wanted to keep me longer. In the meantime, the best thing to do was to cooperate by going to group therapy and meeting with the psychiatrist. If I wanted to go home, I should let the doctor know. She made it seem as simple as that.

After about twenty minutes, Leah had to go. It was a brief encounter but very powerful. There was something healing in the way she treated me like a sane person even when I obviously was not. Unlike everyone at the hospital, and unlike Javier, Leah didn't talk down to me or seem to judge me for the way I acted. She spoke to me like I was a normal, sensible person. She treated me with respect.

I think we all have a tendency to fulfill the expectations of the people around us. When I was being treated like a crazy person, I acted like a crazy person. But when Leah treated me like a person who could take charge, that's exactly what I did. Shortly after she left, a group therapy session was announced.

Suddenly, I was gangbusters to join the milieu, and for the first time since admission, I left my room and entered the world of the psych ward.

The hallways looked pretty much like any other hospital. They were wide and clean and bright. Doctors and patients buzzed about. There was a lot of activity at the nurses' station. Group therapy was held in a little conference room where a bunch of folding chairs were arranged in a circle. I took my seat among the other patients. There were men, women, young, old. I was learning that mental illness doesn't discriminate. It affects all types.

A young woman came in right after me and sat down. I instantly recognized her face. She was my roommate, although we hadn't yet met. I'd been too busy rocking on the floor to stop for handshakes.

An older lady walked in and announced that she was a social worker. She said it was time for the group to begin. She asked everyone to introduce themselves and say why they were in the hospital. I shot my hand up right away, eager to go first. I was all go-getter energy now—a complete contrast to the basket case I'd been ten minutes before.

When I look back, it's obvious that Leah's visit triggered a switch in my personalities. For weeks, I'd been depressed, anxious, fearful, slow. Then all of a sudden, I was Little Miss Take Charge. This is a prime example of the subtle and not-so-subtle ways DID operates.

When a new personality took over, I didn't do something obvious like speak in an accent or announce myself by a different name. Still, there was a dramatic change in my mood, my attitude, and the way I interacted with the world. I was, quite literally, a different personality. Unless others are specifically looking for DID, though, they probably won't define these changes as such. Had a doctor been observing me in the hospital that day, he probably would've seen my mood swing as symptomatic of bipolar disorder—a common misdiagnosis for those suffering with DID.

Unlike the frightened mess who had been wheeled in the night before, this new personality was all brazen confidence. "Hi, I'm Michelle. I was brought in here last night 'cause I tried to kill myself."

"Why did you do that?" the moderator asked.

"I dunno. I guess I was depressed," I said, with absolutely no emotion. "And my therapist wouldn't call me back."

"Why are you depressed?" the lady probed.

"'Cause I was sexually abused by my father," I announced, as if it were a weather report.

Across the circle, my roommate started to cry, clumsily wiping away tears with the backs of her hands.

"Alma," the lady said, turning to her. "Does Michelle's story resonate for you? Would you like to share your experience?"

"I'm here because I'm depressed too," Alma whispered, never looking up from her lap. "I came to the hospital because I want help. My father molested me when I was little, and when I think about it, I just—" Alma started crying again.

Even though I'd been a zombie just an hour before, in my new state of mind, Alma struck me as a sap. All that boohooing bullshit wasn't going to get her anywhere. I was repulsed by her weakness. Depression was for sissies.

RIGHT AFTER THE SESSION, a nurse told me it was time to see my psychiatrist. This was the guy with the power to decide my fate. I was ready for a fight.

Following the nurse down the hall, I saw a tiny man driving a scooter. He was at least one hundred years old, and as fate would have it, he was also my shrink. I followed Dr. Zippy into his office. I had to stand, as the scooter made it impossible to fit a chair in the space.

He started reading over my chart.

"Oh, my, it says here you tried to commit suicide last night," he said. "Why'd you do that, dear?"

"I was pissed at my therapist," I said defiantly. "He wouldn't call me back, then he stuck me in this stupid place."

A little smirk washed over the old man's face, then he looked at me with a bit of amusement.

"It seems like you're angry," he said.

"Yes, I'm angry! I don't fucking want to be here!"

"Well, then, let's send you home," he said, as he scribbled in the file.

Wait? What? After all the drama involved in being locked up, less than twenty-four hours later—with no assessment, no med consult, nothing—they were just going to let me out?

I had to wait about an hour for Chris to return to the hospital. The minute she arrived, a nurse simply unlocked the security door and sent me on my way.

A few weeks later, I received a hefty bill from the hospital for my brief, unwanted, and apparently unnecessary stay.

HISTORICALLY, THE END of a suicide attempt triggered a period of rebirth for me. After my first, at age fourteen, I'd shaken off depression and attacked high school like Tracy Flick in *Election*. After my second, at eighteen, I'd morphed from college flunkee to straight-A student. This time around, things were different. I wasn't in school, so there were no grades to be made, no clear-cut path for how to be a winner. On the contrary, I was a loser and had been for years. I couldn't hold down a job, couldn't make a living, and despite countless opportunities, I couldn't get arrested as a writer. (This might have been easier if I ever actually *wrote* anything!)

Well versed in unemployment, I had a lot of free time on my hands, and what I did with that time was read. I read about depression. I read about anxiety. I read about psychological trauma and child abuse and suicide and psychotropic drugs. The point of all this reading was to help myself. I was desperate to understand why I had so many problems and why I couldn't get over them. Living close to UCLA, I spent my days stalking its graduate library for answers—and learning a lot about psychology in the process.

Truth be told, I'd always been interested in psychology. I was constantly in search of answers, and even in high school, self-help books were my favorite obsession. (I'm fairly certain I was the only teenager in my class clutching a copy of Gail Sheehy's *Passages*!) Fascinated by the mind and the process of psychotherapy, I nearly switched majors from writing to psychology before the Writer thwarted the effort.

Remember, in DID different identities are usually in charge of different functions. In my case, the Preppy was in charge of all things domestic, while the Writer was in charge of professional goals. Trouble is: Alters tend to remain static. As a result, the Writer never changed, never evolved, never grew up. At thirty, she was still approaching her career with the narrow mind-set of a teenager. The writing thing wasn't working; it didn't engender success or happiness. But the Writer didn't know how to see new possibilities or make new plans. She was stuck at a dead end.

Something about the suicide attempt finally shook things up. Crises have a way of doing that, of inviting change. After I got home from the hospital, I could finally see that my dogged determination to make it as a writer was making me miserable. For my own sanity, I decided to give up writing altogether and explore other interests. It was time to figure out who the hell I was.

AROUND THIS TIME, I had my first appointment with Leah, who offered to see me after obtaining Chris's blessing. Even though I'd been impressed after her visit to the hospital, I was nervous to begin therapy with someone new. I was so frightened during that first session, in fact, that I never spoke above a whisper and never made eye contact. Even with these impediments, Leah managed to work her magic. She spoke gently and exuded kindness, slowly putting me at ease.

One of the things I remember about that first session is how Leah tried to help me look to the future. She asked me what I wanted to do with my life. Before I even knew what I was saying, I blurted, "I want to do what you do. I want to be a therapist."

I couldn't even look at her when I said it. I mean, the idea was ludicrous! I'd just gotten out of a mental hospital after my third suicide attempt. I wasn't built to be the doctor. I was doomed to be the patient.

But Leah didn't see it that way. She didn't seem to think the idea was ridiculous at all. "The only difference between me and you is a lot of years of training," she said.

I didn't believe her, of course. But I sure did appreciate the way she acted like we were equals. The dynamic wasn't like doctor/patient but more like teacher/student or mentor/mentee (or Yoda/

Anakin, considering my dark side!). Leah's confidence in me—however unwarranted—filled me with a hope I hadn't known in years. Unlike other therapists, she wasn't just suggesting that I could learn to cope with mental illness or lead a satisfying life in spite of it. She was saying I could overcome my craziness so completely that I would one day be the fucking doctor! It was a revelation.

While I was initially suspicious of Leah's optimism, over time I came to learn that it was the result of her unique mind-set. When most therapists meet a patient like me—angry, impulsive, prone to wild mood swings, unable to function—they immediately see a personality disorder. I got labeled "borderline" or "avoidant" or "self-defeating" depending on my behaviors—which, unbeknownst to anyone, were dependent upon which of my personalities showed up for therapy.

The trouble with such diagnoses is that they are highly subjective and highly damning. There is no blood test for borderline personality disorder (or bipolar disorder or ADHD, for that matter). Yet once a diagnosis is in a patient's chart, she is branded for life. Forevermore, the mental health industry sees a chronic condition rather than an individual person with distinct problems and needs. As a result, patients marked with supposedly intractable disorders are often treated as if they were incapable of getting well.

Leah wasn't like that. She wasn't into diagnoses or labeling or judgment of any kind. When I walked into her office, I got the feeling she saw me—not my history of mental illness. It was refreshing to be truly seen for the first time.

As our sessions continued and I got to know Leah better, I also realized that she knew a hell of a lot about psychological trauma. Most shrinks I'd met had no knowledge of trauma and how it affects victims. It wasn't even on their radar. That's not surprising; most colleges don't offer any classes on the subject, even as electives. The few therapists I'd met who had an awareness of trauma, like Javier, seemed to be introduced to the concept through their patients. Again, that's not surprising, as a staggering percentage of mental health clients have a history of abuse or neglect in their childhoods.

Leah knew about trauma because she was a survivor herself. She'd done the long, hard work of healing through therapy. Then she'd gone off to pursue her doctorate at USC, where John Briere, one of the foremost experts on psychological trauma, ran a clinic for victims. She'd read his work and heard him lecture and incorporated all that solid research—as well as other credible research—into her practice. Working with someone who had actual knowledge—particularly firsthand knowledge—of many of my issues proved to be a godsend.

The first time I noticed how differently Leah approached things was just a few weeks into treatment. I was sitting on her couch, pontificating on all the reasons I'd never amount to anything in life. I explained to Leah how I was moody and impulsive, angry and controlling. I told her I couldn't get along with people and was jumpy all the time.

Leah listened intently as I listed off my faults. Then she smiled sweetly after I'd exhausted my last vice. "Michelle," she said. "I understand that you're down on yourself, and I understand that you feel you've got a lot of problems. But the moods, the need for control, the social problems are all effects of child abuse. They're symptoms. They're not *you*."

When I think back on this moment now, nearly twenty years later, I'm still overwhelmed with gratitude. All my life, I'd been told, implicitly and explicitly, that I was a horrible person because I was moody, manipulative, bossy, selfish, rude. My parents, my teachers, my therapists all condemned me for these traits. Now here was Leah telling me they weren't traits at all; they were merely symptoms. This was a huge distinction—the difference between being born with green skin versus a bully throwing a bucket of green paint over my head. Both made me unattractive. But paint, however thick, can be scrubbed off. Green skin, on the other hand, is in the DNA. It can't be changed; it's permanent.

I had always thought of myself as the Wicked Witch, but Leah's comment gave me hope that perhaps I could change.

This was the watershed moment when my healing finally began— a mere sixteen years, seven therapists, three suicide attempts, and one committal after my journey through the mental health system first started.

EVEN AFTER FINDING a knowledgeable, kind, and dedicated therapist, it took many more years to heal. As in the past, growth came in stages, with therapy sometimes helping me to progress in life and life sometimes pushing me to progress in therapy.

For the first few years after the committal, I saw Leah once a week. I'd drive to her tiny office in Santa Monica, sit directly across from her, and talk about God knows what. I say "God knows what" because I genuinely don't remember most of these early sessions. In hindsight, it's obvious that my alters were showing up for therapy. That's why I don't remember anything.

In the early stages therapy with a person who suffers from DID, alters often come out in therapy without the host's knowledge because the personality system doesn't feel the host is strong enough to hear what the alters have to say. Interestingly enough, I don't think my other personalities ever showed up for any session with Javier. Unlike me, my alters were smart enough to know who could be trusted.

Leah has since told me that during these early sessions I would routinely announce "I have to go" partway through appointments and walk out the door. I don't remember doing this, but I have since noticed that the phrase "I have to go" is something my alters say just before they relinquish control of the body. They are announcing their departure before they jump back into my subconscious and let another personality take control.

I know it sounds weird when I explain these things. Honestly, it felt weird at the time. I was highly dissociative during this phase of my life and often felt like I was in a hypnotic daze. While my alters were coming out more often, I still didn't realize I had them. If Leah knew, she didn't tell me because, unlike a lot of other therapists, she was careful not to challenge my denial system. "We should respect it," she'd say. "It's there for a reason."

This hands-off approach was the crux of Leah's style of therapy. While other therapists wrote treatment plans or devised confrontations or directed their clients toward certain goals, Leah just listened attentively, provided genuine empathy, and occasionally offered a nugget of knowledge if she thought it was helpful. In the biz, Leah is what we call a "nondirective" therapist—meaning she doesn't attempt to push or pull the client any which way. Instead, she works to create a warm, nonjudgmental atmosphere where the client feels safe to open up and explore. The content of sessions, the pace of progress, and the healing process are all up to the client. This approach presumes the client has an inner wisdom and, like a flower, has an innate capacity to grow strong if given proper conditions.

WITH LEAH'S NURTURANCE, I began to blossom. It started with a coup d'état. As mentioned earlier, the Writer—who'd always been my dominant personality—was forced to step down. In her absence, some of my more passive personalities finally got a chance to step forward and start changing my life for the better.

If this is hard to understand, imagine multiple personalities as a group of siblings. Each has his or her own interests, goals, and needs. But just like in families, each sibling is not going to receive equal treatment. The louder, bossier, more assertive siblings tend to dominate while the quiet, passive siblings are forced to take a backseat.

In my personality system, the Writer had always been dominant. And just like any self-centered sister, she acted like the others didn't exist. The Writer made decisions in life with no thought to how it affected the others. If they tried to intervene, the Writer bullied them into submission. How did she do this? Mostly through trash talk.

If the Preppy was feeling the urge to have a baby, for instance, the Writer—who had no interest in children—would call her a "lame, loser housewife." Then the Writer would remind the Preppy that she'd make a terrible mother because she was a "weak, crazy bitch."

These exchanges played out daily as thoughts in my head. One personality would express a thought or plan or desire ("Oh, look at that cute baby! I think I'd like to have a baby someday."), and another personality would tell her that what she wanted was stupid

("Why the fuck would you want a baby? All they do is tie you down."). Kind of sounds like the dialogue in an unhappy family, doesn't it? The kind where everyone is mean to everyone else and the bullies use abusive tactics to gain control? That's because personality systems tend to mirror the dysfunctional families in which they grew up.

After working with Leah for a while, though, some of my passive personalities grew emboldened. As a result, the domestic Preppy was able to take charge. This was an internal shift in identity, unnoticeable to anyone but me. Still, if you knew me then, you couldn't miss the effect. Everything in my life began to change.

First, I gave up writing, the only activity I had ever claimed to give a damn about. Then I started pursuing hobbies that I would've previously considered a waste of time, like sewing, knitting, and decorating. The pursuit that really grabbed me, though, was gardening. Back when I was in the throes of suicidality, Javier had once asked what brought me comfort. At first, I could think of nothing. But then I had a vision of Grammy. Even though she'd been dirt poor and deluged with childcare duties, Grammy always managed to have the most beautiful yard. As a young child, I would follow her around for hours as she pulled weeds and deadheaded flowers. The time spent with Grammy among her irises and chrysanthemums was pure joy, and the memory of it brought me peace.

Desperate for solace, I began my own garden on our rooftop patio and found that it offered serenity.

It wasn't long before the sleek, urban penthouse where Chris and I lived—and that was perfect for the Writer—was sold. It was replaced by a charming Cape Cod with a big yard, worthy of the pages of *The Official Preppy Handbook*.

I spent so many hours working on the new house—choosing paint colors, sewing curtains, planting lilacs and daffodils—that Chris started calling me Martha. As my goal in life was now to be the quintessential Connecticut housewife, I felt the nickname was a compliment.

The Writer, though, was out of sorts. I remember sitting in countless therapy sessions complaining about the "fucking Connecticut housewife" that lived inside me. I'd grouse that she was weak and dependent and lacked ambition. Other times, I'd sit on the couch and complain with equal vigor about the Writer, who made me feel like a loser for taking care of my home and always put too much pressure on me to be successful in the outer world.

Remarkably, despite these frequent conversations with Leah and Chris and Steve, I still didn't know I had dissociative identity disorder. I knew there were conflicted forces inside me; I'd known that since middle school. But multiple personalities? That was so weird, so supposedly "rare" that it wasn't even on my radar.

ENLIGHTENMENT FINALLY CAME IN 2001, when I was thirty-three years old. We'd been in the Cape Cod for more than a year and, like many homeowners, found that our little fixer was breaking the bank. I hadn't worked since the suicide attempt, a fact both Chris and our checking account seemed to notice. So I started pondering what kind of work I could do that would bring both fulfillment and a living wage.

By this time, I was taking classes in psychology at UCLA. I'd started with an intro class—fearful I wouldn't be able to hack the academic rigor. After earning an A, I took the next class and the next until I'd racked up all the undergraduate courses I could, all the while maintaining a 4.0. Despite this boost to my confidence, when it came time to choose a career, I couldn't even fathom becoming a psychologist. I felt like a crazy person, and I believe very strongly that at the very least a psychotherapist should have their own shit together before they try to help someone else.

Through a friend, I heard that Los Angeles was in the midst of a teacher shortage. This allowed me, with no training or experience, to secure a position teaching high school English to inner-city kids. While the thought of teaching high school English intrigued me, it terrified me as well. The feeling of terror is, understandably, my biggest trigger. So teaching was bound to stir up anxiety.

Ultimately, though, it wasn't fear that helped me finally acknowledge my alternate personalities.

It was love.

IT STARTED ONE AFTERNOON as I was crying in Leah's office. It was the summer before I was to start teaching, and I had just come from an upsetting meeting with the medical director of LA Unified. New teachers had to get physicals before they could start work. On the form, it asked about any "prior conditions" or medications I was taking. My doctor had revealed that I was taking psychiatric meds to treat anxiety.

Now, as a psychologist, I can tell you that more than 20 percent of Americans take at least one type of psychiatric drug. Nonetheless, the stigma of mental illness runs rampant, and seeing my history, the LA Unified doctor demanded to know more about my "mental health problems." Specifically, he requested the notes from all of my therapy sessions, which meant a total stranger with power over my employment was about to read the intimate details of my sexual abuse and suicide attempts.

I was shattered. I mean, here I was, trying to get a job, be a contributing member of society, move on with my life. It had taken me six months to pass all the necessary tests and fulfill the other requirements to become a teacher. Now all of a sudden, my history as a victim was about to victimize me again. The injustice of it was overwhelming. I cried with despair, convinced I would never be able to break free from my past and move on to a satisfying life.

Leah, though, remained calm. Despite my insistence that she fax over my therapy notes, she refused. She said it was wrong for the school district to be demanding her personal files. Then, very kindly, she said, "I know you don't understand all this stuff, but I do. And it's my job to protect you."

Right then and there, she whipped out a piece of stationery. I watched in awe as she wrote a letter to the medical director chastising him for the inappropriate request. She went on to explain that she'd been my therapist for the past four years and assured the doctor that I was perfectly capable of teaching a bunch of high school students.

In short, Leah went out on a limb for me. Not only did she protect my sensitive personal information, but she vouched for me—putting her own reputation at risk. It was a watershed moment; no therapist had ever gone out of her way for me before.

As I sat on Leah's couch watching her fax the letter, I could feel something inside my psyche shift. Suddenly, it felt as if I were floating in space while some other part of me watched Leah intensely, thinking, *Wow! We can actually trust her!*

———

IN THAT MOMENT, everything changed. All my life, I'd been searching for someone who could help me. Considering how fucked up I was, I knew I needed an extraordinarily strong and faithful person who would stand by my side no matter what. With Leah's simple act of writing the letter (after four years of unwavering kindness and reliability), I finally had proof that she cared about me and would protect me—from the world and from myself. For the first time since I was a very young child, I felt safe.

I felt loved.

When children are abused, especially by caregivers, one of the fundamental things they lose is the ability to trust. This is a devastating setback, as trust is a prerequisite for establishing normal, healthy relationships.

I hadn't trusted anyone since I was eight years old. As a result, I had lost the ability to love. I didn't realize it, of course. I thought what I felt for Chris and Steve was love, but it really wasn't. Love requires the heart to be open. My heart had been frozen by the abuse, and I'd lost the ability to feel warmth or gratitude or empathy toward anyone.

Truth be told, I'd lost the ability to feel most anything except rage and fear.

Now, suddenly, my heart melted. In an instant, I felt a rush of warm feelings for Leah as my heart expanded within my chest. It was that dramatic and that simple. I felt Leah's love for me and instantaneously felt my love for her. And just like that, my heart started working again. My ability to feel was restored.

I wish I could say, I felt nothing but unbridled joy from that point on. Unfortunately, that's not the way trauma works. When a person is hurt but doesn't feel safe to vent their emotions, those unexpressed feelings stay frozen in the body, waiting for a chance to be released.

I had twenty-five years of pain stored within me. When I began to feel again, that pain was the first thing to come out. For the first time since childhood, I started crying—for the loss of my childhood and the rape of my innocence, for a lifetime of loneliness and never feeling loved, for all the things that had been stolen from me and all the wasted years I had lost. I cried for all of it. Then I cried some more.

In order to truly heal from any kind of trauma, the victim must eventually recognize and grieve all that she has lost. Mourning is essential to moving on. Yet I find it is the thing my clients most fear. They say, "I don't want to start crying. If I start, I'll never stop." Or they say, "I don't want to cry. What's the point in that?"

I get it. For a long time, I didn't see the point in crying either. As a child, I had cried. What did it get me? A slap on the face usually, as some monster said, "Shut up, or I'll really give you something to cry about!"

Back when I was a victim, crying made me feel desperate and alone. But as a survivor, with a loving therapist to comfort me, I learned that crying could feel good! For more than twenty years, I'd been carrying around the weight of horrible feelings with no ability to release them. Now, suddenly, I was letting it all out. What exquisite catharsis. What freedom!

As I finally let out all the buried grief, I found that my dark worldview naturally lightened. Without effort, the giant chip fell off my shoulder. I became less angry, less resentful, less guarded. More open to people, I started seeing them differently. Where I'd once thought everyone was out to get me, I could now see that most people were kind and good.

For the first time, I could see and feel that I was surrounded by loving people who wanted to help me. I felt grateful and humbled by their presence in my life.

I also felt deeply grateful to God for all the blessings He'd sent to me. In the past, I'd only been able to see the ways I'd been wronged, and I blamed God for all of them! Now I could see the countless ways Spirit had intervened on my behalf over the years—the suicide attempts I'd been saved from, the epiphanies I'd experienced, the wonderful helpers I'd been sent. I began to see that God really does have a plan. Take, for instance, the time I lost my job when the Los Angeles Theatre Center closed. If not for that loss, I wouldn't have moved to Center Theatre Group, which led to meeting Chris and, eventually, Leah. Suddenly, it was obvious that God had been protecting me all along.

ALL THIS HEALING HAPPENED very quickly. In a few short weeks, I changed from an angry, resentful, suspicious victim into an open-hearted, grateful, hopeful survivor. From the outside, it might seem like Leah's letter was a magic bullet. But the truth is that there are no magic bullets in therapy. There is only showing up for the work week after week and hoping once in a while for a breakthrough.

In my case, and the cases of many other victims of trauma, the hard work I had to do was learn how to trust. My ability to attach to another person, to bond, to love had been completely destroyed by the abuse. More than anything, that's what I needed to heal in therapy.

This is true for nearly every victim of trauma, and it is especially true for victims of child abuse. More than working through bad memories or troubling symptoms, victims need to learn that it is safe to trust another human being again.

For this reason, I do not generally believe that it is possible for people to heal from trauma on their own; it must be accomplished within the context of a healthy, healing relationship. The bond that develops between a competent therapist and a client is obviously ideal for healing, but any relationship in which two human beings share mutual warmth, honesty, empathy, and trust can be therapeutic.

Medication and adjunctive therapies such as eye movement desensitization and processing (EMDR), neurofeedback, and somatic experiencing can be very helpful in relieving certain symptoms of PTSD. However, I do not believe such methods alone can sufficiently heal the wounds of trauma because they do nothing to heal a broken heart.

Only love can do that.

The Many Faces of Me

Ultimately, it was Leah's love that finally gave me the courage to face my multiple personalities. It's a basic tenet of DID therapy that alternate identities must feel safe before they will fully reveal themselves. In going out of her way to protect me, Leah had proven her mettle. Now my personalities felt free to fully come out—both in therapy and in the world!

It started that day in Leah's office as she was faxing the letter. I felt as if I were floating away as some other part took over my body for a moment. After that, it often felt as if I were watching from a distance as my body said and did things that made no sense. Sometimes I'd find myself at a toy store buying dolls and finger paints and coloring books, which I would later play with at home. Other times I would find myself singing and dancing in front of a mirror to songs I hadn't played since I was twelve. One day, as I was singing in front of the mirror, I became disturbed because I didn't think I looked like myself.

Before I knew what I was doing, I'd grabbed a pair of scissors and chopped away at my hair until I had the bangs I'd worn as a little girl.

Although I'd been in treatment with Leah for four years, my feelings for her suddenly and inexplicably grew intense. Seeing her in therapy became the highlight of my week, and I often spent hours thinking about what I would say and wear to each session. When I wasn't in her office, I thought of her constantly. I fantasized that she was in the audience for the opening night of one of my plays or at my wedding or at some party to celebrate my accomplishments. In these fantasies, Leah was proud of me, beaming—just the way a good mother should.

On some level, I understood that such fantasies were normal. I'd read enough psychology books to know that clients with attachment problems often turn their therapists into surrogate parents; it's part of the transference process. Still, that didn't explain why I would walk into Leah's office and start talking in the voice of a little girl. It didn't explain why I showed up sometimes with a McDonald's Happy Meal, plopped down on Leah's office floor, and spent the hour drawing with the crayons she provided. Hell, sometimes I would just walk in the door, curl up on her couch, and take a nap!

If I, grown-up Michelle, had been in charge of my body during these times, none of this would've happened. I tend to be rather uptight and reserved, so I found the things I was doing mortifying. Nonetheless, I was powerless to stop any of it. While I could see it going on, I had no control. It was as if I were watching my own life take place from the backseat of a movie theater.

I couldn't believe it the day I brazenly asked Leah to buy me a gift. The next week, she handed me a giant stuffed teddy bear, which I held with delight. Without understanding why, it was suddenly imperative that the teddy bear be with me at all times—on the couch, in the bed, riding shotgun in my car. The teddy, which made me feel safe and warm, was a stand-in for Leah, just like any child's beloved stuffed animal or safety blanket. Except I was thirty-three years old—a fact airport security rudely noted when I tried to take my teddy on a plane to London just a few weeks after 9/11. Imagine: grown woman clutching giant teddy bear as jumpy police try to pull it out of her arms, assuming it's a bomb.

Yeah, that's right. My insanity nearly caused an international incident!

Insanity aptly describes this period in my life, for I was constantly thinking and feeling and doing outrageous things. As my obsession with Leah grew, for instance, I found myself frequently driving to her office and sitting outside her building just to be near her. Later, through sheer psycho persistence, I managed to get her home address so I could park outside her house in the middle of the night. One time, for reasons I can't fathom, I packed a bag, grabbed a stack of cash, and went to the Greyhound bus station. My plan was to just take off, but it was thwarted when Leah unexpectedly called and somehow convinced me to return home.

Why was I doing these things? I had no idea! I just had weird compulsions that I couldn't stop or understand. I'd often find myself at different places but not quite remember how I got there. Sometimes I would find drawings and writings about the abuse I'd suffered but not remember creating them.

In therapy, which I sometimes remembered and sometimes didn't, I kept telling Leah that I felt like my psyche was trying to tell me something, like it was giving me some kind of test. "It wants me to figure something out," I told her time and time again.

But what?

What?

Then one afternoon I inexplicably found myself in the lobby of Leah's office building, but I couldn't remember how I'd gotten there. Suddenly, Leah was standing in front of me. Apparently, I'd called her, but I didn't remember that either. As I walked into her office, I felt disturbed and disoriented, like I was waking from some crazy dream. All the shenanigans of the past few months started flashing through my mind—the weird voices, the strange behaviors, the memory loss. Suddenly, it all made sense.

"Leah," I said tentatively. "I think I have multiple personalities."

She smiled knowingly, almost like she was relieved, and asked, "What makes you think that?"

"Well, I always feel like there are different people inside of me, different people controlling me . . . and I don't remember how I got here."

"So you think you have multiple personalities," she stated plainly. "Are you okay with that?"

It was a good question. The answer was no! No, I wasn't okay with that! I'd learned enough about psychology to know that multiple personality disorder was a very serious diagnosis, maybe the most serious diagnosis in the whole damned diagnostic book. The knowledge that I had a serious mental illness was devastating. As far as I knew, sick people couldn't be ambitious. They couldn't become successful writers or doctors. They couldn't become anything because they were handicapped. So having multiple personalities meant my life was over. It felt like a death sentence.

Obviously, my misgivings about mental illness are what kept me from facing my disorder for so many years. It was overwhelming to accept that I was not normal and never would be.

Diagnosis is a double-edged sword. On one hand, it can be a tremendous relief to finally have a name for all the mysterious problems and symptoms one experiences. There's a wonderful "Aha!" moment as everything finally makes sense. On the other hand, a serious diagnosis can feel like a scalding steel collar that simultaneously binds and brands a person for life.

Too often, I've watched mental health professionals dole out life-altering diagnoses with no thought to how such labeling might affect the patient. What's more, they are often all too eager to share some bleak prognosis with the patient and his family because it is based on what they know to be the "facts." While it's not always possible or prudent to avoid diagnostics, psychologists and psychiatrists need to be extremely aware of the power of their words. If an authority tells someone they are doomed to lead a lessened life, chances are that person will believe it and live down to the expectation.

I will be forever grateful to Leah for patiently allowing me to figure out my diagnosis on my own. She obviously knew I was a multiple; she was buying me teddy bears and crayons, after all. But she never imposed the diagnosis on me. She respected my denial system and allowed me to build up the strength to finally face the truth when I was ready.

AFTER I REALIZED I was a multiple, a lot of things in my life immediately made sense. I'd been dealing with the battle between the Preppy and the Writer for years, so it was a relief to finally understand that this inner conflict was the result of two distinct identities who were constantly fighting for control of my life. Right away, I also understood that I had a third identity—a little girl who was responsible for the bangs, the coloring books, and the bear. Though a child, this identity was one of my main personalities and quite persistent at getting her needs met. Her goal was always to feel safe and loved, so she was the one primarily responsible for attracting trustworthy people like Leah, Chris, and Steve into our life.

For years, I'd been aware of a destructive force inside me—an angry, hateful persecutor who constantly put me down, called me names, and told me to kill myself. This force is what always drove me to attempt suicide. It was cruel, abusive, and relentless. Once I realized I was a multiple, this inner persecutor finally made sense. It was an alternate personality who for some reason hated me and wanted me dead.

I was also aware of a benevolent force inside me. This protector had been around since I was very young and felt paternal, almost God-like. It was the force that kept me going through all the years of torture, the force that pushed me to survive and thrive. I felt this identity as a protective presence inside me. Usually, it offered silent strength. But once in a while it voiced its no-nonsense wisdom. It was the voice that told me my parents would never love me so I should stop trying to win them. It was also the voice that told me I shouldn't trust my parents long before my conscious mind knew why. This benevolent identity seemed to know my whole history—a history I couldn't remember—and it felt like it was in charge of doling out the truth to me when it thought I could handle it.

By the time I left Leah's office, less than an hour after realizing I had multiple personalities, I could already identify five of them. It took no effort to figure out the main players living inside me.

Why would it? I'd been dealing with them all my life!

Still, the knowledge that I had dissociative identity disorder, a mental illness, was hard to swallow. I felt deeply ashamed and, in my humiliation, assumed others would be equally horrified. Driving home, I wondered how the hell I was going to tell Chris. I braced myself for the end of our seven-year relationship.

When I walked in the door, she was making dinner.

I begged her to step away from the stove.

"I've got news," I said. "It's very upsetting. I really think you should sit down."

Reluctantly, she moved to the kitchen table.

I sat across from her and struggled to find the right words.

"Chris," I whispered. "I have something to tell you, and it's really serious. It's the kind of thing that might completely change our lives. I saw Leah today, and it turns out . . . I have multiple personalities."

Chris stared at me blankly, then rolled her eyes. "Really, honey? *That's* your big news?" She went back to the stove and started to chuckle. "I mean, please! Tell me something I don't know!"

Steve's response was fairly similar. He, like Chris, was not surprised. What's more, they could both instantly describe most of my identities, which made sense. They'd both been dealing with them for years.

HAD I FOLLOWED the normal course of psychotherapy, this major diagnostic breakthrough would've been followed by a period in which I got to know more about dissociative identity disorder. I would've spent a lot of time getting to know my alternate personalities—their names, ages, needs, goals, emotions. Then I would've worked to get them all communicating more effectively. Communication between identities is necessary to function efficiently as a multiple. The more the alters can get along, the less stress there is on the whole person.

After the personality system is stable, trauma therapy can usually move forward. Remember that even though I knew I was a multiple I still didn't have access to my full memory. I knew that Gary had abused me, but I still didn't remember anything about the sex ring or the pornography. That's because different identities experience different parts of the abuse and then hold on to those memories. In order to fully heal, DID therapy dictates that each alter show up for therapy and share his or her part of the life story with the other identities. As each part works through her or his individual trauma, healing and the integration of all the memories occur.

Unfortunately, I didn't follow the prescribed course of DID therapy. For one thing, Leah didn't have an expertise in that kind of treatment so she didn't suggest it. But even if she had, I doubt I would've played along. The whole multiple personality thing freaked me out. And so I did what I'd done a thousand times before when something bothered me.

I didn't deal with it.

I didn't deal with it for five more years.

I immersed myself in teaching instead, which turned out to be a wonderful thing. Whatever fears I had about inner-city teenagers, they melted away the minute I met my students. Right from the start, I loved all the lively, funny, intelligent kids and, I was surprised to realize that they loved me back. Teaching was the best medicine I could've hoped for, for it forced me to get outside my own head.

All my life, I'd been trying to heal by focusing on me, me, me. But it turns out that true joy comes from helping others. Within a few shorts months, I morphed from a dissociative mess whose full-time job was therapy into my high school's Teacher of the Year!

Buoyed by my success in the classroom, and making my own

living for the first time in years, I started to feel better about myself. As my self-confidence rose, so did my mood. Suddenly, the future seemed bright again.

I made new friends and reconnected with old ones. Most important, I reconnected with Chris. Even though we'd been together for eight years, I'd always maintained a wall between us. My buried grief and attachment issues made it difficult to give my heart.

Now that my heart was fully open, I suddenly experienced a new-found love for Chris. I'd always loved her, but my fear of abandonment kept me from admitting it to myself. In order to feel safe, I played a mental game where I always had one foot out the door. But I didn't need to do that anymore. I didn't need to protect myself from love and attachments. I was ready to commit.

In 2003, nearly nine years after our first date, Chris and I got married. It wasn't legal at the time, but we didn't care. We rented out the entire main branch of the Los Angeles Public Library, put on long white gowns, and threw one hell of a shindig! More than two hundred friends and family came to our wedding, including Steve, who was my best man. Leah was there too, beaming proudly, just like I had imagined in my daydreams.

After a few years of teaching, I noticed that my favorite part of the job was not helping the kids learn to read and write; it was helping them learn how to live. A lot of my students came from tough backgrounds—poverty, abuse, neighborhood violence. As a result, they exhibited traumatic symptoms like anxiety, depression, self-mutilation, and suicidality. Not wanting to be callous like my teachers had been, I took the time to notice and care.

I very quickly became known as the teacher kids could talk to, and I found myself often listening and giving advice. Counseling students felt rewarding and natural. I could see that helping other people cope with trauma was my real gift in life. Finally, I felt confident enough to become a psychologist, and I left teaching for grad school.

All my confidence seemed to wane, however, when the first day of classes arrived. Everywhere I turned, brainiacs were talking about "epistemological issues in the study of metacognition" and "heuristic approaches to phenomenological mindfulness." Huh? Suddenly, all of my old insecurities returned, and I was sure I'd made a huge mistake.

Why did I ever think a person like me—a perpetual loser with a mental illness—could earn a doctorate?

Meeting with my advisor, Patrick, that first day, I broke down in tears. "I don't think I can do this," I cried. "I'm a weak person. I can't handle pressure. I've got a lot of problems."

"What kind of problems?" Patrick asked, seeming nothing but kind.

"I . . . I have multiple personality disorder." There it was, my shameful secret.

I was sure he would throw me out of school.

"Wow," Patrick said, as he stared at me intensely. "You know, Michelle, that's a really serious thing. I've had a few clients who've gone through that, so I know it's hell. If you can handle multiple personality disorder, I wouldn't worry about grad school. It's going to seem like a breeze."

While I appreciated the encouragement, grad school was *not* a breeze! It was challenging and intense and required me to work harder than I ever had in my life! But despite constant stress and a ridiculous workload, I never lost focus and always kept my cool. Every time I finished a thirty-page research paper or passed a test or secured an internship, my faith in myself improved. I started to see myself as more than just some crazy person. I started to think I might, just might, be able to be the doctor.

I ALSO GOT IT in my head that I'd like to be a mom. This wasn't a new idea; I'd always wanted children. But in the past, I felt too unstable and crazy to take on that kind of responsibility. Now I had several years of drama-free living under my belt. I felt like I was finally healthy enough to raise a baby.

At the age of thirty-six, I got pregnant via IVF. The day I peed on the stick was the happiest day of my life up to that point. Although I suffered morning sickness for all nine months, I didn't care. Being pregnant was the best thing that had ever happened to me. Every time I felt the baby squiggling in my belly, I was in heaven. Although I hadn't met him yet, Baby Mikey was already the love of my life.

The first time I held him, my entire perspective on everything changed. I know most parents experience this when their first child is born. Anything that had happened to me in the past suddenly lost its meaning. All that mattered now was being a good mother to the perfect little man in my arms.

For me, that moment marked a line in the sand in terms of my mental health. All my life, depression and suicidal feelings had plagued me. Now I knew I would never, ever attempt suicide again. I felt so honored and humbled and blessed to be Mikey's mother that I knew I could never do anything to cause him pain, especially abandon him.

My first year of motherhood was the happiest of my life. I took a leave of absence from school so that I could fully focus on my son. I breast-fed and rocked him to sleep and took him for daily strolls in the park. We went to Mommy and Me groups and Kindermusik classes. I was so into being a mom that when Mikey started eating solid foods I decided to make all his baby food from scratch. Never mind that I'd never cooked so much as a baked potato for myself!

I realize I'm describing a very mundane thing—the process by which a new mother falls madly, deeply in love with her child. It's a tale as old as time. Yet for me, it was nothing short of a miracle. I'd never felt pure, unfiltered love before. I'd never allowed myself to grow wholeheartedly attached. The love I felt for Mikey was like a salve for my soul. It healed the past and brightened the future. It seemed to solve everything.

More content than I'd ever conceived, I assumed my dark days were behind me. My PTSD symptoms were long gone. My multiple personalities stayed safely hidden inside. No longer depressed or anxious, I stopped taking meds or going to therapy. My mental illness was a thing of the past. At thirty-seven years old, I didn't even think about it anymore.

THEN CHRIS LOST HER JOB, and I lost my mind. Both were long, drawn-out, awful processes. Chris's company was having money troubles, so they fired the president. Then they fired Chris's boss and laid off half the company. Chris was spared in the first round of layoffs, but the writing was on the wall. It was only a matter of time before the paychecks stopped.

While money worries are stressful for everyone, I took it particularly hard. I started obsessing about when Chris would lose her job, and how we would survive the loss of our only source of income.

Contrary to common sense, I believed she'd never find another job. As my anxiety ballooned, irrational visions of homelessness and starvation kept me awake at night. A dark cloud settled over everything, and I was sure our lives were about to be utterly and permanently ruined.

My reaction was over-the-top, no doubt about it. Losing a job is scary, but I wasn't scared; I was terrified. Lack of money made me feel unsafe. I feared for my very survival. Any time this happens to me, a whole host of symptoms gets triggered. I feel anxious and helpless and hopeless, just like I did in childhood. My terrifying past gets mixed up with the present. This is the nature of PTSD.

At the time, though, I couldn't see it. I was too scared to think straight. The fear was unbearable. After a while, I couldn't cope with it anymore. That's the trigger. When I can no longer stand to feel fear, I start to dissociate.

In the beginning, my dissociation took the form of old familiar daydreams. Much of the time, I walked around like a zombie while long-forgotten stories played in my head. I was once again an unwilling princess forced into an arranged marriage with a cruel prince or a kidnapped prisoner forced to live in a cage while a mad scientist performed horrifying experiments on me. These scripts repeated over and over, day in and day out for weeks. They kept me from thinking about my terrifying future by keeping my mind in the past.

Over time, though, my inability to be in the here and now started eroding my relationships. Lost in my head, I found it annoying to have conversations with anyone, including Chris. The more she demanded my attention, the more I pulled away. Eventually, I wanted nothing to do with her because, honestly, I felt no connection. No love. She was a total stranger to me.

Yearning to be alone, I moved into the guest room. That's when things got weird, and I started exhibiting some uncharacteristic behaviors. Chief among them was listening to country music all night while downing bottles of beer. I'd never been a fan of country music, and I'd never had a beer in my life. Yet there I was, drowning my sorrows with Reba and the Dixie Chicks.

It wasn't long before I started going out. Late at night, while Chris stayed home with Mikey, I'd hop in my car and drive, seemingly without purpose. Yet somehow I always ended up at some country-and-western bar. It was like I knew where these places were even though I'd never been to them before.

At these bars, I'd sit alone and drink. Again, this was something I'd never, ever done before. I was always far too shy and reserved to go to a bar alone. And yet there I was, knocking back drinks and checking out men like I'd been doing it all my life.

It was after one of these late-night trips that I got an idea. Walking into the house, I immediately stripped off my clothes and hopped in the shower. I grabbed a razor and methodically shaved off all of my pubic hair. I had no idea why.

Next, I went to the computer. We had only one at the time. It was in the living room, just steps away from sleeping Mikey and Chris. I went on Craigslist, signed in with a user name I didn't recognize, and clicked on a link for "casual encounters." What the hell was that? I pressed the button to write a post and started typing with no conscious knowledge of what I was about to write.

Slave with freshly shaved pussy seeks master to teach her S/M.
I am very bad. But with proper discipline, I can learn to be good.
Wanna start tonight?

The moment I posted, I started getting hits. One guy immediately stood out. He was a better speller than the others, and his photo featured a man who was young and good-looking. Within seconds, I was on the phone with him—which is when I first realized that this sexed-up identity spoke with a southern accent.

We decided to meet at the Roosevelt Hotel in Hollywood. On the drive over, I kept screaming in my thoughts, *What are you doing? We can't meet a strange man for sex! It isn't safe!*

But whoever was controlling my body didn't give a shit.

The walk from the parking lot to the hotel entrance was surreal. I was fully aware of everything that was going on because it felt like I had a box seat in my brain. But despite my best efforts to control my body, I couldn't. The whole thing was very *Being John Malkovich.*

In the lobby bar, I spotted the young man. We sat at a table and ordered drinks. He asked about my experiences with S/M. I told him I'd been a sex slave in childhood and that I *liked it!*

For the part of me that was watching the show, this sex-slave thing was news. I knew that Gary abused me, but I still didn't remember anything about S/M. Suddenly, all the dissociative fantasies I'd been playing popped into consciousness. I realized that they all involved bondage and torture. Wait! Could my fantasies actually be *memories?*

The man talked about his experience as a master. He said he liked to hurt and humiliate women, but he didn't know why.

"I'm guessing you don't like your mother," my voice was saying. "She's probably very stern and controlling."

Somehow the Student had jumped into the conversation to offer up a bit of psychology.

The man was impressed with my accurate description of his mother. He said he wanted to pursue a master/slave relationship.

Whoever was controlling my body was ready to get a room. Meanwhile, I sat in the back of the brain screaming in my thought, *No, no, no! We're going to get murdered, or at least catch a disease!*

But as fate would have it, the man was not ready to proceed. He said my training would begin via e-mail, with a series of questions that I had to answer. The person controlling my body was disappointed, but I was relieved. We had dodged a bullet!

In the following weeks, the man and the southern sex slave who lived inside me corresponded frequently. He asked her to describe her sexual history, and as she did, I started to learn about my past. This identity wrote explicitly about all the bondage, torture, and slave training Gary had subjected her to. But instead of describing these things with horror, she seemed turned on.

For me, the new knowledge was shocking. I had no idea I'd been abused so extensively, and based on the fantasies I now knew were memories, I suspected there was a lot more to learn. Overwhelmed, I was thrust into a crisis similar to when I'd had my first memories fifteen years before. A whole torrent of emotions swelled up—rage, humiliation, fear, sadness, disgust.

At some point, the man from the Roosevelt Hotel stopped writing, and the part of me that was a sex slave went on a hunt for a new master. She spoke to a guy in Santa Monica who wanted to meet at Starbucks. I went along for the ride as they talked about vile things like face sitting and penis worship. It wasn't a match, and the guy disappeared behind a display of mugs. Another bullet dodged. Thank you, God.

Right away, though, this alter was on to a new master. He was a disgusting old man who demanded she send a set of specific photographs. While Mikey napped in another room, I found myself donning a black bra and panties. Then I wrote the word SLUT in red lipstick across my chest and let the timer snap suggestive shots.

Liking the pictures, the man set up the first training session. He was quite explicit about what he planned to do to me. Right before our first meeting, though, he had to cancel. Phew! Dodged bullet number three.

By now, I was hip to the fact that I'd completely lost my marbles. I needed to do something to get myself safe immediately before the sex slave got us killed. I decided I better check myself into a hospital—and fast—as I was finding it hard to maintain any control over the things I did.

I'd heard of a mental hospital that specifically worked with DID patients. I knew I needed to get there right away. It was the middle of a weekday, Chris's last week of work. I called her and told her I was taking myself to the hospital.

Not having any idea what was going on, Chris insisted on accompanying me. She arranged for a babysitter and transportation. On the long trip, she tried to press me for an explanation. Out of my mind, I found it difficult to communicate. I told her I was acting weird and was scared for my safety. I spent the rest of the time rocking back and forth in a dissociative trance.

AT THE HOSPITAL, my zombielike appearance garnered immediate admission. But I wasn't placed in the trauma program, as I'd planned. My insurance company needed more information before it would authorize specialized care. So even though the door for DID patients was right in front of me, I was sent down the hall to the general ward.

Voluntarily admitting myself to the hospital felt different than being committed. For one thing, I knew I could sign myself out at any time. For another, I knew I needed to be there. I felt safer knowing I was locked in a place where I couldn't access perverted men. Well, theoretically. As it turned out, the hospital housed a program for sex addicts and sex offenders on the same floor. Every time I went onto the patio, they offered me smokes.

Despite this, my initial feeling upon entering the ward was relief. After weeks of watching helplessly as some other identity put me in danger, I was finally safe! I settled into a four-bed room that housed a bipolar woman and two schizophrenics. Unlike my first hospital stay, when I felt like I didn't belong in the looney bin, this time around I knew I fit right in.

My first day there, I mostly slept. I was exhausted after all those late nights spent trolling for men. The second day, I ate meals, played cards with a bunch of detoxing alcoholics, and waited for my transfer to the trauma program. I was impatient to move on because, honestly, the general wards of mental hospitals aren't set up to offer much help.

They're mostly warehouses to keep extremely unstable people off the street for a few days. The only "help" given is in the form of pills, which can work wonders on schizophrenics and bipolars. Medication alone doesn't do much for dissociation, though. The primary treatment for DID is talk therapy. I needed to be in a place that understood trauma. That's why I'd traveled a long distance to this particular hospital in the first place.

My third day, still no transfer, and I was getting frustrated. I flagged down the head nurse and demanded an explanation. She said we were waiting on the director of the trauma program to deal with the insurance company and that I should be patient. A lackadaisical attitude works if one's stay is being paid for by Medicare (true of many mental hospital patients), which pays for long stays. But I had private insurance, which only pays for a few paltry days. I didn't want to waste mine just playing blackjack. *I was in the hospital to get help.* Instead, I was getting the runaround. It made me irate.

That afternoon, I took a nap. I awoke to the sound of orderlies yelling next to my bed. As I opened my eyes, I saw one of my schizophrenic roommates rushing out the door.

"Are you okay?" asked one of the orderlies. "Do you feel any pain?"

Apparently, my roomie had grabbed some heavy object and tried to smash it across my sleeping head. Thankfully, she had bad aim.

So much for feeling safe.

I marched into the psychiatrist's office and demanded to be released. He advised against it, saying I should wait. Wait? Wait for what? For the trauma director who worked down the hall? For someone to crush my skull? No, thanks. I checked myself out against medical advice and arranged for transport home.

FILLED WITH FIGHTER ENERGY, I felt like myself again. I told Chris I thought my insanity was over, but she was not convinced. To tell the truth, she seemed really weird. More cautious and careful than usual. I assumed she was shaken by my hospital visit, so I acquiesced when she insisted I see Leah the next day.

At Leah's office, I felt totally fine. I gave her a brief rundown of my breakdown, conveniently glossing over the strange men and weird-sex parts. I thought I was putting on a good show of mental health until Leah mentioned the photos I'd been e-mailing to dirty old men. Apparently, Chris had been searching for pictures of Baby Mikey to brighten my hospital room when she came across my unglamour shots. She'd shown them to Leah. The ones with SLUT written across my chest. Oh, God.

Whatever semblance of sanity I'd managed to piece together was blown away by this humiliation. Both Chris and Leah knew about the degrading, dangerous things I'd been doing at night. I felt so mortified and guilty that I wanted to die.

At home later that day, I avoided Chris by locking myself in the guest room. I wasn't listening to country music and drinking beers anymore. Whoever that person was, she was long gone. All that was left was me—reserved and conservative—remembering the dirty, awful things I'd done. Even though I'd had no control over my body, the shame I felt was crushing. I paced back and forth like a madwoman, asking myself how, how, how I could've done such dangerous, disgusting things.

Then all of a sudden, I had an epiphany. The epiphany I'd been wanting all my life. I saw a curtain rise across my mind, and in an instant, I remembered *everything*. Gary's basement. Being trained as his sex slave. Being prostituted to other men and forced into pornography. I understood that all my so-called fantasies and daydreams were really memories. People, places, concrete details all came pouring back. Every goddamn thing in my life made sense.

Ever since I realized I had amnesia fifteen years earlier, I'd wanted to know the true story of my life. Now here it was, and it was *awful*. Worse than I ever imagined. S/M? Prostitution? Pornography? I had done heinous, filthy things. Filled with self-loathing, I wanted to erase myself from the planet. I deserved to be dead. Where the fuck could I get a gun?

Suicide, though, was no longer an answer. Even in my fevered state, I still understood that I had a responsibility to Mikey. I was his mom. I beckoned Chris and told her I had to get back to the hospital. Immediately! I was shaking and pale, sure I would pass out from shock.

As I sat on the couch in a stupor, Chris got on the phone. Next thing I knew, we were being transported back to the hospital. I silently rocked back and forth like a crazy person the whole way.

At the hospital, I was immediately sent to the DID wing. (Don't mess with Chris!) Right away, it felt very different than the other wards I'd encountered. For one thing, it was filled almost exclusively with middle-aged women. Also, unlike other wards I'd been on, where heavily medicated patients walked around like zombies, the ladies in the DID unit were loud and lively. They played games, chatted in the common areas, and raced Matchbox cars in the halls.

One of the first patients I befriended was Suzy, a woman in her midfifties. Suzy's story was similar to a lot of the ladies' stories on the ward. As a young woman, she'd been a single mother with a decent apartment and a full-time job. Life was going well for Suzy until she reached her early thirties and started having flashbacks of previously repressed child sexual abuse. Unable to cope, Suzy became emotionally unstable and eventually went bonkers in the Piggly Wiggly. Police were called, and Suzy was committed to a mental institution, where she stayed for many months while her kids lived in foster care.

At the hospital, Suzy was diagnosed with multiple personality disorder. Despite being highly functional before her breakdown, Suzy was informed that her prognosis was not good. Doctors explained that MPD was a very serious mental illness and that Suzy should expect intermittent breakdowns and hospitalizations for years to come. Social workers at the hospital signed her up for federal disability insurance, as she'd surely never be able to work again.

Having no reason to question the experts at the hospital, Suzy proceeded to live down to their expectations. When she got out of the hospital, she didn't apply for jobs or try to get her kids back. What was the point if she was just going to break down again? Instead, she collected her measly disability check each month, lived in a studio apartment, and spent her time going to outpatient therapy at low-cost clinics, where she was assigned a new student therapist every six months.

As Suzy had a lot of time on her hands, her diagnosis soon became the center of her life. She read books on DID, joined groups for survivors of childhood sexual abuse, and spent a great deal of time getting to know everything she could about her alters. In essence, having DID became Suzy's job. She was a professional patient.

Every summer, Suzy spent a month at an inpatient trauma program, which was paid for by Medicare. This wasn't because she was unstable and needed hospitalization. It was because she genuinely believed that in order to heal she had to shut out the world and focus solely on her illness. But after two decades of obsessive "healing," Suzy had made little progress. Stuck in the role of "patient," she could no longer conceive of a life beyond mental illness—one with a job and a family and a future.

After hearing Suzy's story, I could see that taking one's diagnosis too seriously is a trap. Yes, I was mentally ill. No doubt about it! But even in the midst of a breakdown, I had to believe wholeheartedly that I could heal and go on to lead a normal, successful life.

When I met with the hospital therapist (#8!), however, she had bad news. Without hesitation (or knowing much about me), she told Chris and me that dissociative identity disorder was a chronic debilitating illness that would render me unable to do much. She suggested I apply for disability insurance and even expressed concerns about my ability to raise my own son!

Chris was devastated. When Leah heard about it, she was outraged. Personally, it didn't faze me much. I knew me. So I knew this so-called therapist was full of shit.

Needless to say, I wasn't going to get much out of individual therapy at the hospital. So I decided to focus on group therapy instead. The program had a twelve-step-type women's group that met frequently. But when I tried to join, I was told it was full. Instead, I was placed in the group next door—a group for male sex addicts. As it turned out, two of the men were in the hospital under court order because they'd been convicted of owning kiddie porn. While it was wrong of the hospital to place me in a group with such men, I was amazed when my child identity emerged to tell them exactly how it felt to be forced into pornography.

There were some good things about the program. It was excellent at educating me about DID. I learned that in order to better function I had to "map my system." This meant getting to know all the identities that lived inside of me.

The Preppy (aka the Housewife or Martha) and the Writer were already well-known to me. What I didn't know was that the Writer had a name, Chelsey, and was a teenager, which explained a lot about her anger and grandiose thinking and impulsiveness.

My sweet child alter, who I already knew about, also had a name, Sarah. I was shocked to learn that my self-destructive alter—the one who called me mean names and told me to die—was also a child! He was a ten-year-old boy named Viscous. (This is one of the funny quirks of DID, for his name was pronounced like *vicious*. But when I made him up in my mind as a child, I probably didn't know how to spell it. So, frozen in time, he continued to misspell his name.)

And then there was the one who got me into all the trouble in the first place. My sexed-up southern girl didn't have a name. When I drew her, though, she revealed a naked body with huge boobs and peroxide blond hair. She looked just like a *Hee Haw* Honey, and I understood immediately how my child mind had used an image from television to create an identity that was well built for sex.

At the hospital, I learned that all of these parts had been invented for a purpose. And that purpose was always, always protection. The *Hee Haw* Honey protected an innocent child from the pain and humiliation of sexual encounters. Little Sarah, who remained unscathed by the abuse, protected my ability to love. Even Viscous's taunts to kill myself were a form of protection, however misguided. His job was to keep me from remembering the abuse.

At the hospital, I was taught techniques for communicating with my alters. I learned that in order to stop feeling torn apart I had to listen to what each and every identity wanted and try to find ways to make them all happy. This is extremely difficult because they often have conflicting needs. Still, I learned that I had to love and respect and appreciate all of them—even the ones I vehemently disagreed with.

One of the best things about my stay was getting to know other people with multiple personalities, all of whom had more knowledge of the disorder than I did. While I had always been ashamed of my parts, the other patients accepted and embraced theirs and taught me how to do the same. I learned that it was okay for my child alters to play games and color. It was okay for my teenager to get a little wild. It was okay for *Hee Haw* Honey to listen to country music. But it was also okay to put limits on their behavior—nothing illegal, nothing immoral, nothing that could ruin our life!

I ONLY STAYED at the program about ten days before my insurance company cut me off. Sadly, private insurance companies rarely allow patients to stay in mental hospitals for the length of time they truly need. When I returned home, I resumed therapy with Leah. Finally able to talk about all my memories and identities, I made tremendous progress. It was amazing how different things felt now that I remembered the true details of my life.

The biggest breakthrough came when I spoke of the prostitution. It was hard for me to accept how readily I partnered with Gary and went along with it. It took a while to understand that my lack of resistance was due to fear, brainwashing, and dissociation, not a desire to sell my body. When I finally realized I was not to blame for all the sexual things I had done in my youth, I broke down in tears. "I always thought it was my fault," I wept to Leah.

All my life, I felt ashamed and unbearably guilty for my actions during the abuse. I hated myself for the things I had done. Now for the first time, I felt freed of responsibility. None of it was my fault. Not Gary's attraction to me nor my mother's feelings of betrayal. Not the sexual acts I'd performed nor the bad behaviors I developed as a result of it. I didn't have to feel guilty for lying and stealing as a teenager. I didn't have to feel guilty for all the crazy shit I'd done as an adult. I didn't have to feel ashamed of my suicide attempts or hospitalizations or alternate identities. I didn't have to feel bad about myself because *it wasn't my fault.*

I was the *victim.*

The person to blame was *Gary Lundquist.*

When I finally understood this, my self-loathing disappeared. For the first time ever, I felt love for *myself.*

A FEW MONTHS after I got out of the hospital, I returned to grad school. I managed a full-time schedule as a student with full-time duties as a mother, while also working thirty hours a week as a counselor. Sometimes, as I was reading a textbook while stirring a pot of spaghetti with a baby on my hip, I'd think about the idiot therapist who said my debilitating illness would render me unable to do much. What a laugh!

I also got an amazing and humbling letter from Suzy! In it, she said that meeting me and spending time with Chris and Mikey had been a life-changing experience for her. Before our friendship, it had never occurred to her that someone with DID could also lead a normal life. After leaving the hospital, Suzy immediately got a job, got off disability, and returned to the world of the living. In just a few months, she'd lost thirty pounds and was dating for the first time in twenty years!

When it came time to choose a dissertation topic, I knew just what I wanted to do. I wanted to tell the story of my abuse. First, so I could record my entire history from start to finish. Second, so I could research the topic of child sexual abuse and figure out exactly how and why these terrible things had happened to me and others like Suzy. With the help of my endlessly supportive dissertation chair, Robert McAndrews, I selected a research method called auto-ethnography. It allows someone to study their own story within a cultural context like, say, a child living in a world fraught with rampant child sexual abuse.

I started my research in 2006 and didn't finish until 2012. During those years, I came to realize that while my story was extreme it certainly wasn't unusual. All over the world, millions of children are abused—sexually and otherwise. In time, these children grow up to be adults who are plagued with problems like low self-esteem, eating disorders, substance abuse, sex addiction, the inability to trust, anxiety, depression, self-harming tendencies, and dissociation.

As a therapist, I started meeting these people—my people—the moment I began to practice. They filled the inpatient facility where I worked as a counselor. They came in droves to the community clinic where I did my practicum. During my internship at a college mental health office, nearly all of my clients had some history of abuse. It's the same in my private practice.

There are so many people who struggle to overcome symptoms created by traumas in childhood. Yet sadly, a lot of them don't realize it. They struggle to get ahead in the world, to form loving relationships, to feel contentment and joy, but they can't. And they don't know why. Unable to see the connection between the abuse and neglect they suffered as children and their current problems, they blame themselves.

My job as a therapist is to help victims of trauma understand that they are not to blame. They are not responsible for the bad things that happened to them as children, nor are they responsible for the personal problems that developed as a result. What they are responsible for is fixing those problems. This can only be done by bravely facing the past, identifying the effects that the past has on the present, and working through all the painful emotional baggage that is sure to come up as a result.

IT WAS NOT EASY to work through my baggage. From start to finish, it took me fifteen years, eight therapists, and three hospitalizations to heal. It was expensive and exhausting and gut-wrenchingly painful. Still, I'm glad I did it.

My reward for all that hard work is a successful and satisfying life. I'm able to love and be loved, feel joy and contentment, and generally be free of anxiety and depression. I'm currently in the third decade of a loving, fun, and supportive marriage. I have meaningful friendships, some with people I've known for more than forty years. And did I mention? I have the world's best, brightest, most handsome son!

Now free of my demons, I find incredible fulfillment in helping other people let go of theirs. I do this by practicing as a psychotherapist, speaking to groups about my road to healing, and now writing about my life's journey. I am also the founder and director of Post-Traumatic Success (www.Post-TraumaticSuccess.com), a nonprofit organization dedicated to educating and inspiring those affected by psychological trauma.

Don't get me wrong, my life isn't perfect. Not by a long shot. I still experience down days and jags of anxiety. I still have periods of stress and self-doubt. But nowadays, these feelings are bearable and normal.

I have a normal life.

Who could ask for anything more?

ACKNOWLEDGMENTS

This may sound weird coming from someone with my past, but I lead a charmed life. Whatever bad fortune befell me in childhood has been more than made up for ever since through amazing opportunities, wonderful people, and an overabundance of laughter and love.

I started out life wanting to be a writer. But because of abuse-related symptoms, I was unable to pursue my dream. Instead, I was forced to focus on overcoming trauma. In doing so, I developed a passion for psychology and discovered that my true calling in life is helping others heal.

With the publishing of this book, everything has come full circle. What a miraculous journey life can be! I have been given the opportunity to educate others about trauma psychology and inspire them to heal—all while fulfilling my original childhood dream.

This dream was made possible, first and foremost, by my literary agent, Steve Ross. Steve heard about my story through a mutual friend and asked for a book proposal. Having no idea what that was, I proceeded to send him the worst proposal in history. Despite this, Steve took the time to learn more about my story and mentor me. (Who does that?) Since the day I met him, he has provided unwavering support, enthusiasm, protection, and guidance. He is one of the kindest and most generous, intelligent, funny, wise people I have ever met. I am blessed and honored to call him my friend.

I would never have met Steve without the generous help of Nell Scovell, my friend for twenty years. Nell, a masterly writer in every medium, was the first to suggest that my story might make a good book. She not only pitched me to an agent but offered continuous support and guidance as I learned about the publishing process.

I must admit that the whole idea of publishing a book about my life scared me at first. While I wanted to use my story to educate and inspire others who struggle, I worried that an editor might press me to produce a product that was overly sensationalized. My fears were assuaged as soon as I met Kerri Kolen. In my wildest dreams, I could not conceive of a finer editor. From the very beginning Kerri encouraged me to write my story exactly as I saw fit. She has championed and protected my cause and my voice every step of the way. She is an insightful and judicious editor, and this book is a thousand times better because of her.

The entire process of putting this book together has felt like a fairy tale. If Kerri is my fairy godmother, then everyone else at Putnam is a magical helper who has somehow managed to make me feel like the belle of the ball. Since our very first meeting, I have been in love with the staff at Putnam. I am particularly grateful to Ashley Hewlett, Sally Kim, Alexis Welby, Carrie Swetonic, Ashley McClay, and Anabel Pasarow. I owe you ladies, and everyone else at Putnam, a round of cosmos.

If I'm buying drinks, I need to send some over to Kathleen Zrelak and Lynn Goldberg of Goldberg McDuffie Communications, who have become my knights in shining PRmor.

ACKNOWLEDGMENTS

I am deeply indebted to all the angels who have championed this book, including Carol Brooks, Curt King, Wendy Luckenbill, Bela Bajaria, and Terry Wood. I thank Timea Nagy for reminding me what a great honor and privilege it is to be given a voice, Ramey Warren for teaching me how to use that voice most effectively, and Martha Westman and Sari Lietzman for helping me look pretty in the process.

I'm grateful to Saybrook University and all of the professors who encouraged me to research this topic, especially Robert McAndrews, Steve Pritzker, Tom Greening, and Patrick Faggianelli.

I would not be a writer today without the early support and encouragement I received from Gary Garrison and D. B. Gilles at NYU, Nancy Bennett at Delaware Township Schools, Stephen Sondheim, and the late Marvin Hamlisch.

I am profoundly blessed to work in a profession through which I am able to meet extraordinary people and share in their journeys. I am grateful to all of the clients and students I have known over the years who have allowed me to be a part of their lives. I am also indebted to my supervisor, Dr. Sheryn Scott.

Of course, I could never have become a psychologist—and probably wouldn't be alive today—if not for the tireless efforts of Dr. Leah Matson. For two decades, my exceptionally dedicated therapist has never failed to return my calls or offer appointments when I needed them. Working with a suicidal client who has DID can be extremely taxing and scary. God knows I put Leah through the wringer! Despite the constant crises I created in her life, Leah never, ever made me feel like I was a bother. I know I can never pay her back for all she has done for me, but I am humbly trying to pay it forward.

For three decades, Steve Ansell has also been talking me off ledges. But unlike Leah, the foolish guy does it for free! Steve is the world's most even-tempered person—the Ethel to my Lucy. I count on him to keep me steady and sane. Since Steve is a gifted film editor, he was the first person I entrusted with this manuscript. His notes on early drafts proved invaluable.

I could write a book about all the ways that my wife, Chris, has helped me. Oh, wait, I did! I wish every person in the world could enjoy the kind of selfless love I receive from Chris. She has always supported my dreams no matter how long they took, how much they cost, or how crazy they seemed. In addition, my wife is always right about everything (although I will never admit this to her). I don't know what I did to deserve such an exceptional partner, but I sure am glad that she's mine, mine, mine.

Finally, I must thank the young man who changed everything for me—my kind, loving, generous, beautiful son, Mikey. No one has ever brought me more joy than this funny guy, and I thank God every day that I get to be his mom. For his entire life, Mikey has been forced to sacrifice time with me while I worked on this book and the dissertation that came before it. He's endured the sound of my typing during piano lessons, ski races, and karate practice without complaint. I am blessed to have such a loving and supportive son who lets me know he's proud of me. I'm proud of him too.

I don't know why I'm so lucky, but I am overwhelmed every day by the beautiful life I am blessed to live. I pray that everyone gets a chance to experience this kind of happiness.

NOTES

INTRODUCTION

Page 5: "earliest years of childhood": Sigmund Freud, "The Aetiology of Hysteria," in *The Standard Edition of the Complete Psychological Works of Sigmund Freud*, vol. 3, ed. James Strachey (London: Hogarth Press, 1962), 203.

Page 6: Freud recanted: The reason Freud abandoned his seduction theory remains a debated question. Some historians believe he was forced to recant due to pressure from the medical community while others feel that Freud himself grew uncomfortable with the idea of widespread child sexual abuse.

Page 6: wishful fantasies: Sigmund Freud, *An Outline of Psycho-Analysis* (New York: W. W. Norton & Company, 1949).

Page 6: one in a million: Alfred Freedman, Harold Kaplan, and Benjamin Sadock, *Comprehensive Textbook of Psychiatry*, vol. 2, (Baltimore: The Williams & Wilkins Company, 1975).

Page 6: United States were sexually abused: Ascertaining the prevalence of child sexual abuse is difficult due to variations in definitions of abuse as well as people's unwillingness to admit they have been victims. I believe the best studies are those that survey adults about their childhood experiences (as opposed to studies relying on law enforcement and social service statistics or surveys of adolescents). These statistics are from a widely cited metanalysis that was based on surveys of adults: Rebecca Bolen and Maria Scannapieco,

"Prevalence of Child Sexual Abuse: A Corrective Metanalysis," *Social Service Review* 73, no. 3 (1999): 281–313.

Page 6: Internationally some regions: Naomi Pereda, Georgina Guilera, Maria Forns, and Juana Gomez-Benito, "The International Epidemiology of Child Sexual Abuse: A Continuation of Finkelhor (1994)," *Child Abuse and Neglect: The International Journal* 33, no. 6 (2009): 331–342.

Page 7: "meaning of the word *unspeakable*": Judith Herman, *Trauma and Recovery: The Aftermath of Violence—from Domestic Abuse to Political Terror* (New York: Basic Books, 1992), 1.

STALIN'S CHICKEN

Page 26: Yet when Stalin was done: There are several different versions of the Stalin/chicken story floating around. While they feature different settings and characters, the general story and moral remain the same. This version is the one Gary chose to repeat.

THE PIED PIPER

Page 27: most researched group of sexual deviants: Michael Seto, "Pedophilia and Sexual Offenses Against Children," *Annual Review of Sex Research* 15 (2004): 321–61.

Page 27: molesters as dumb, disordered: Gilian Tenbergen, Matthias Wittfoth, Helga Frieling, Jorge Ponseti, Martin Walter, Henrik Walter, Klaus Beier, Boris Schiffer, and Tillman Kruger, "The Neurobiology and Psychology of Pedophilia: Recent Advances and Challenges," *Frontiers in Human Neuroscience* 9 (2015): 344.

Page 28: notoriously targeted by other inmates: Dennis Stevens, *Inside the Mind of Sexual Offenders: Predatory Rapists, Pedophiles, and Criminal Profiles* (Lincoln, NE: iUniverse, 2001).

Page 28: verified by a polygraph test: Jan Hindman and James Peters, "Polygraph Testing Leads to Better Understanding Adult and Juvenile Sex Offenders," *Federal Probation* 65, no. 3 (2001): 8–15.

Page 28: 28 and 93 percent: Ryan Hall and Richard Hall, "A Profile of Pedophilia: Definition, Characteristics of Offenders, Recidivism, Treatment Outcomes, and Forensic Issues," *Mayo Clinic Proceedings* 82, no. 4 (April 2007): 457–71.

Page 28: molested as kids: Anna Salter, *Predators: Pedophiles, Rapists, & Other Sex Offenders* (New York: Basic Books, 2003).

NOTES

Page 28: look to children for love and affection: Gavin Ivey and Peta Simpson, "The Psychological Life of Paedophiles: A Phenomenological Study," *South African Journal of Psychology* 28, no. 1 (1998): 15–20; and Hall et al., "A Profile of Pedophilia," 457–71.

Page 29: almost all are male: Center for Sex Offender Management, "Female Sex Offenders" (Washington, D.C.: U.S. Department of Justice, March 2007).

Page 29: female perpetrators: Deborah Boroughs, "Female Sexual Abusers of Children," *Children and Youth Services Review* 26, no. 5 (May 2004): 481–87.

Page 29: vast majority are heterosexual: Kurt Freund and Robin Watson, "The Proportions of Heterosexual and Homosexual Pedophiles Among Sex Offenders Against Children: An Exploratory Study," *Journal of Sex & Marital Therapy* 18, no. 1 (1992): 34–43.

Page 29: all races and socioeconomic groups: Federal Bureau of Investigation, "Crime in the United States: Arrests by Race" (2009). Retrieved from https://www2.fbi.gov/ucr/cius2009/data/table_43.html.

Page 29: Acquaintances perpetrate: Julia Whealin, *Child Sexual Abuse* (National Center for Post-Traumatic Stress Disorder, U.S. Department of Veterans Affairs, 2007). Retrieved from http://www.ptsd.va.gov/public/pages/child-sexual-abuse.asp.

Page 29: victimizes 50 to 150 children: Gavin de Becker, foreword to *Predators: Pedophiles, Rapists and Other Sex Offenders* by Ann Salter (New York: Basic Books, 2003).

Page 29: chance of reoffending: Robert Prentky, Austin Lee, Raymond Knight, and David Cerce, "Recidivism Rates Among Child Molesters and Rapists: A Methodological Analysis," *Law and Human Behavior* 21, no. 6 (December 1997): 635–59; and R. Karl Hanson and Monique Bussière, "Predicting Relapse: A Meta-Analysis of Sexual Offender Recidivism Studies," *Journal of Consulting and Clinical Psychology* 66, no. 2 (1998): 348–62.

Page 29: preferential pedophiles: Kenneth Lanning, *Child Molesters: A Behavioral Analysis* (Washington, D.C.: National Center for Missing & Exploited Children, 2001).

Page 29: goal of gaining access to children: Ibid.

Page 32: thirty years of more: Ibid.

Page 33: starts abusing in his early teens: Hall et al., "A Profile of Pedophilia," 457–71; and John Murray, "Psychological Profile of Pedophiles and Child Molesters," *The Journal of Psychology Interdisciplinary and Applied* 134, no. 2 (April 2000): 211–24.

Page 34: spot a liar: Paul Ekman and Maureen O'Sullivan, "Who Can Catch a Liar?" *American Psychologist* 46, no. 9 (September 1991): 913–20.

Page 37: like a third of all pedophiles: Gene Abel, Judith Becker, Jerry Cunningham-Rathner, Mary Mittelman, and Joanne Rouleau, "Multiple Paraphilic Diagnoses Among Sex Offenders," *Journal of the American Academy of Psychiatry and the Law* 16, no. 2 (June 1988): 153–168.

TRICKS ARE FOR KIDS

Page 65: hurting a child is anathema: Abel et al., "Multiple Paraphilic Diagnoses Among Sex Offenders," 153–168.

Page 65: ultimate act of love: Ivey et al., "The Psychological Life of Paedophiles," 15–20; and Matti Virkunnen, "Victim-Precipitated Pedophilia Offences," *British Journal of Criminology* 15, no. 2 (1975): 175–180.

Page 68: how to dump the kids: Lanning, *Child Molesters.*

Page 72: mother blame is misguided: Rhonda Elliott McGee, "Controversial Maternal Roles of Intrafamilial Child Sexual Abuse Cases," *Dissertation Abstracts International* 65, no. 4:1548A; and Mary Ellen Womack, Geri Miller, and Pam Lassiter, "Helping Mothers in Incestuous Families: An Empathic Approach," *Women & Therapy* 22, no. 4 (1999): 17–34.

Page 72: protect and support their children: Kathleen Faller, "The Myth of the 'Collusive Mother,'" *Journal of Interpersonal Violence* 3, no. 2 (1988): 190–6; and Ann Elliott and Connie Carnes, "Reactions of Nonoffending Parents to the Sexual Abuse of their Child: A Review of the Literature," *Child Maltreatment* 6, no. 4 (2001): 314–31.

Page 73: Orwellian doublethink: I am borrowing the use of the Orwell term *doublethink* from Judith Herman's *Trauma and Recovery.*

Page 79: Goddess Lady D: Goddess Lady D of Wisconsin, "Kidnapping Fantasy." Retrieved in 2011 from http://myforce.org/Lady_D.html.

Page 81: $250 million a year: Myra Panache, "The 'Scarface' of Porn," *The Panache Report.* Retrieved in 2011 from http://panachereport.com/channels/more%20short%20stories/ScarfaceOfPorn.htm.

Page 82: young children performing: "The Sexes: Child's Garden of Perversity," *TIME,* April 4, 1977. Retrieved from http://www.time.com/time/magazine/article/0,9171,947868-2,00.html.

Page 82: sold over-the-counter: Charlayne Hunter, "Four Seized for Smut Involving Children," *The New York Times,* September 20, 1975, A27.

Page 82: kiddie porn festival: "The Sexes," *TIME.*

Page 82: 264 different monthly magazines: *Washington Post,* "Congress Is Urged to Join Battle on Pornography Using Children," February 15, 1977, A7.

NOTES

Page 82: typical magazine cost: Ann Burgess and Marieanne Lindeqvist Clark, *Child Pornography and Sex Rings* (Lexington, MA: Lexington Books, 1984).

SCARED SELFLESS

Page 87: more than a million: United States Department of Health and Human Services, *Administration on Children, Youth and Families: Child Maltreatment 2006* (Washington, D.C.: U.S. Government Printing Office, 2008).

Page 87: "horror will recur": Herman, *Trauma and Recovery*, 86.

Page 90: "mind tells itself a story": Jessica Ryen Doylen, "Psychiatrist on Jaycee Dugard: Bonding with Captors Is Mind's Way of Safeguarding Itself," Fox News, August 28, 2009. Retrieved from www.foxnews.com/story /0,2933,544020,00.html.

Page 94: "severe, sustained, and repetitive": Frank Putnam, *Diagnosis & Treatment of Multiple Personality Disorder* (New York: Guilford Publications, 1989), 49.

Page 94: DID can also develop: C. L. Anderson and P. C. Alexander, "The Relationship Between Attachment and Dissociation in Adult Survivors of Incest," *Psychiatry: Interpersonal & Biological Processes* 59, no. 3 (1996): 240–254; and Malcolm West, Kenneth Adam, Sheila Spreng, and Sarah Rose, "Attachment Disorganization and Dissociative Symptoms in Clinically Treated Adolescents," *Canadian Journal of Psychiatry* 46, no. 7 (2001): 627–631; and Ruth Blizard, "Disorganized Attachment, Development of Dissociated Self States, and a Relational Approach to Treatment," *Journal of Trauma and Dissociation* 4, no. 3 (2003): 27–50.

Page 95: imaginary companions: Rita Carter, *Multiplicity: The New Science of Personality* (New York: Little, Brown, 2008).

Page 96: DID affects both genders: American Psychiatric Association, *Diagnostic and Statistical Manual of Mental Disorders*, 5th ed. (Washington, D.C.; American Psychiatric Association, 2013), 294.

Page 102: twenty-two-fold: Miriam Denov, "The Myth of Innocence: Sexual Scripts and the Recognition of Child Sexual Abuse by Female Perpetrators," *The Journal of Sex Research* 40, no. 3 (September 2003): 303–14.

Page 103: fairly irrefutable evidence: Guochuan Tsai, Don Condie, M. T. Wu, and W. Chang, "Functional Magnetic Resonance Imaging of Personality Switches in a Woman with Dissociative Identity Disorder," *Harvard Review of Psychiatry* 7, no. 2 (July 1999): 119–122; and Annedore Hopper, Joseph Ciorciari, Gillian Johnson, John Spensley, Alex Sergejew, and Con Stough, "EEG Coherence and Dissociative Identity Disorder," *Journal of Trauma and Dissociation* 3, no. 1 (January 2002): 75–88.

Page 103: "dubious diagnosis": Retrieved from http://www.urbandictionary. com/author.php?author=Dr.+Fischer.

Page 103: "the victim role": Ibid.

TOMMY, CAN YOU HEAR ME?

Page 112: Suicide: Centers for Disease Control and Prevention, Web-based Injury Statistics Query and Reporting System (2013, 2011). Available from www.cdc.gov/injury/wisqars/ index.html.

REBEL WITHOUT A CORE

Page 129: proclivity for violence: David Knopf, M. Jane Park, and Tina Paul Mulye, "The Mental Health of Adolescents: A National Profile, 2008," National Adolescent Health Information Center, University of California, San Francisco (February 2008).

Page 130: borderline personality disorder: American Psychiatric Association, *Diagnostic and Statistical Manual of Mental Disorders,* 5th ed. (Washington, D.C.: American Psychiatric Association, 2013), 766.

Page 138: "selective prosecution or a witch hunt": Lanning, *Child Molesters,* 130–31.

THE VILLAGE IDIOT

Page 158: brief time in the camp: In noting the "relatively brief" time Primo Levi was imprisoned, I am referring to the length of time in proportion to the length of his life—eleven months out of sixty-seven years.

Page 158: suffering from depression: There has been some controversy regarding whether Levi's death was an accident or a suicide. It was well-known, however, that he was suffering from depression.

Page 158: "Primo Levi": This quote from Elie Wiesel is widely reproduced and is attributed to an article in the Italian newspaper *La Stampa* that was published on April 14, 1987. I could not, however, locate the actual article.

Page 158: Holocaust survivors: Yoram Barak, Dov Aizenberg, Henry Szor, Marnina Swartz, Rachel Maor, and Haim Knobler, "Increased Risk of Attempted Suicide Among Aging Holocaust Survivors," *American Journal of Geriatric Psychiatry* 13, no. 8 (2005): 701–704.

Page 158: "all the optimisms fail": As quoted in Art Spiegelman, *MetaMaus: A Look Inside a Modern Classic, Maus* (New York: Pantheon Graphic Novels, 2011).

NOTES

Page 160: severe depression: Cheryl Lanktree, John Briere, and Lisa Zaidi, "Incidence and Impacts of Sexual Abuse in a Child Outpatient Sample: The Role of Direct Inquiry," *Child Abuse & Neglect* 15, no. 4 (1991): 447–53; and Julie Lipovsky, Benjamin Saunders, and Shane Murphy, "Depression, Anxiety, and Behavior Problems Among Victims of Father-Child Sexual Assault and Nonabused Siblings," *Journal of Interpersonal Violence* 4 (1989): 452–68.

Page 160: suicidal ideation: Anne Rhodes, Michael Boyle, Lil Tonmyr, Christine Wekerle, Deborah Goodman, Bruce Leslie, Polina Mironova, Jennifer Bethell, and Ian Manion, "Sex Differences in Childhood Sexual Abuse and Suicide-Related Behaviors," *Suicide & Life-Threatening Behavior* 41, no. 3 (June 2011): 235–54.

Page 160: Bulimia: Teresa Hastings and Jeffrey Kern, "Relationships Between Bulimia, Childhood Sexual Abuse, and Family Environment," *International Journal of Eating Disorders* 15, no. 2 (1994): 103–111; and Howard Steiger and Maria Zanko, "Sexual Traumata Among Eating-Disordered, Psychiatric, and Normal Female Groups," *Journal of Interpersonal Violence* 5, no. 1 (March 1990): 74–86.

Page 161: anxiety disorder: Ronald Kessler, Wai Tat Chiu, Olga Demler, and Ellen Walters, "Prevalence, Severity, and Comorbidity of 12-Month DSM-IV Disorders in the National Comorbidity Survey Replication," *Archives of General Psychiatry* 62, no. 6 (June 2005): 617–27.

Page 163: "cognitive distortions": John Briere, *Child Abuse Trauma: Theory and Treatment of the Lasting Effects* (Newbury Park, CA: SAGE Publications, 1992), 23.

Page 164: "foreshortened future": American Psychiatric Association, *Diagnostic and Statistical Manual of Mental Disorders,* 4th ed. (Washington, D.C.: American Psychiatric Association, 2000), 468.

DAZE OF MY LIFE

Page 179: psychological decompensation: American Psychiatric Association, *Diagnostic and Statistical Manual of Mental Disorders,* 5th ed. (Washington, D.C.: American Psychiatric Association, 2013), 294.

Page 183: no memories of abuse: This information pertains to the first edition of *The Courage to Heal: A Guide for Women Survivors of Child Sexual Abuse* by Ellen Bass and Laura Davis, first published by Harper Perennial in 1988. Subsequent editions changed some of the language regarding memories of abuse.

Page 184: repress and later recover the memory: American Psychiatric Association, *Diagnostic and Statistical Manual of Mental Disorders,* 5th ed. (Washington, D.C.: American Psychiatric Association, 2013).

Page 185: Kozakiewicz: Nicole Egan, "Abducted, Enslaved—and Now Talking About It," *People*, April 16, 2007, 115.

Page 186: misdiagnosed for years: According to the American Psychiatric Association, "The average time period from first symptom presentation to diagnosis [of DID] is 6-7 years." American Psychiatric Association, *Diagnostic and Statistical Manual of Mental Disorders,* 4th ed. (Washington, D.C.: American Psychiatric Association, 2000), 528.

SEARCHING FOR JUDD HIRSCH

Page 213: unconditional positive regard: Carl Rogers, *Client-Centered Therapy: Its Current Practice, Implications and Theory* (London: Constable, 1951).

Page 213: therapists overrate their abilities: Deirdre Hiatt and George E. Hargrave, "The Characteristics of Highly Effective Therapists in Managed Behavioral Provider Networks," *Behavioral Healthcare Tomorrow* 4 (1995): 19–22; and Jeffrey Sapyta, Manuel Riemer, and Leonard Bickman, "Feedback to Clinicians: Theory, Research, and Practice," *Journal of Clinical Psychology* 61, no. 2 (2005): 145–153.

Page 221: waking a tiger: Peter Levine and Ann Frederick, *Waking the Tiger: Healing Trauma* (Berkeley, CA: North Atlantic Books, 1997).

ALL YOU NEED IS LOVE

Page 246: psychiatric drug: Medco Health Solutions, Inc., "America's State of Mind" (2011). Retrieved from http://apps.who.int/medicinedocs/documents/s19032en/s19032en.pdf.